WITHOUT FEAR AND
The Great War Letters and Diaries of Private James Herbert Gibson
WITH A MANLY HEART

L. Iris Newbold and K. Bruce Newbold, editors,
with Evelyn A. Walters and Mark G. Walters

WILFRID LAURIER
UNIVERSITY PRESS

940.4
8171
GIB

Wilfrid Laurier University Press acknowledges the support of the
Canada Council for the Arts for our publishing program. We acknowledge the
financial support of the Government of Canada through the Canada Book Fund for
our publishing activities. This work was supported by the Research Support Fund.

Library and Archives Canada Cataloguing in Publication

Gibson, James Herbert, 1889–1967, author
"Without fear and with a manly heart" the Great War letters and diaries of
Private James Herbert Gibson / L. Iris Newbold and K. Bruce Newbold, editors,
with Evelyn A. Walters and Mark G. Walters.

Includes indexes.
Issued in print and electronic formats.
ISBN 978-1-77112-345-7 (softcover). —ISBN 978-1-77112-347-1 (EPUB).—

ISBN 978-1-77112-346-4 (PDF)

1. Gibson, James Herbert, 1889–1967—Diaries. 2. Gibson, James Herbert,
1889–1967—Correspondence. 3. Soldiers—Canada—Diaries. 4. Soldiers—Canada—
Correspondence. 5. World War, 1914–1918—Personal narratives, Canadian. 6. Canada.
Canadian Army. Canadian expeditionary Force—History. I. Newbold, K. Bruce, editor
II. Newbold, L. Iris, 1935–, editor III. Walters, Evelyn A., 1931–, editor
IV. Walters, Mark G., 1962–, editor V. Title.

D640.G53 2019   940.4'8171   C2018-903119-0
C2018-903120-4

Front-cover photos: Pte. James H. Gibson in 1919 and a letter he wrote from
France a few days after being wounded in battle. Both items from the collection of
the Walters and Newbold families. Cover design by Blakeley Words+Pictures.
Interior design by Janette Thompson (Jansom).

This book is printed on FSC® certified paper and is certified Rainforest Alliance™
and ancient forest friendly™. It contains postconsumer fibre, is processed chlorine free,
and is manufactured using biogas energy.

Printed in Canada

Every reasonable effort has been made to acquire permission for copyright material used
in this text, and to acknowledge all such indebtedness accurately. Any errors and omissions
called to the publisher's attention will be corrected in future printings.

Look not mournfully into the past
It comes not back again
Wisely improve the present
It is thine
Go forth to meet the shadowy future
Without fear and with a manly heart.

—Henry Wadsworth Longfellow,
Hyperion, *Book IV, Chapter 8 (1839),*
as recorded in the 1917–18 diaries of J.H. Gibson

CONTENTS

LIST OF ILLUSTRATIONS

FOREWORD

In a hundred years, fewer than a handful of letters and diaries of soldiers who served in Toronto's 75th Battalion during the Great War have found their way into print, among them *One Soldier's Story* (1989), by Stanley Lemmex; *Silhouettes of the Great War* (2001), by John Harold Becker; and *We're Not Dead Yet* (2004), by Bert Cooke. All were exceptional reads. It is exciting to encounter the equally compelling letters of another soldier of the 75th, Private James Herbert Gibson, who took time to put pen to paper during what can only be described as a horrific four years in world history.

Gibson, like many others of his generation, felt it necessary to join the fight when the call went out for volunteers in August 1914. He was a young man of 26, but the terrible sights he would see and the wounds he received would transform the rest of his life. Being born and raised

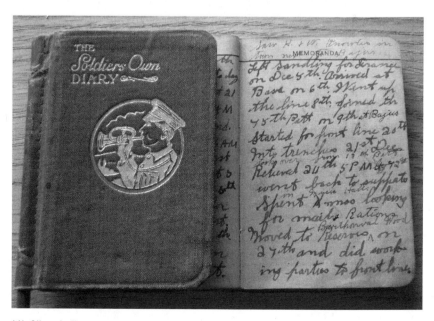

J.H. Gibson's diary.

near Perth, Ontario, he like many of his friends enlisted in the 130th (Lanark and Renfrew) Battalion, which was based there. In March 1916, he began his basic training, later specializing as a bomber. In October 1916, he sailed for England, but as happened with most battalions from Canada on arrival, the 130th was broken up to provide reinforcements to fighting battalions already on the continent. This is how Private Gibson, along with many others, found his way on a reinforcement draft to the 4th Division, specifically the 75th Battalion, following its losses at the Somme in October–November 1916.

The 75th Canadian Infantry Battalion, to which Private Gibson was "taken on strength" (British and Commonwealth military parlance for "reported for duty") in December 1916, had had a relatively short history to that point. Also referred to as the 75th (Mississauga) Battalion, it had been raised in Toronto for war service in July 1915. The secondary title of "Mississauga" came from the 9th Mississauga Horse, the militia cavalry regiment that recruited officers and men for the 75th.

On the evening of 4 August 1914, news reached Toronto from overseas that Great Britain had declared war on Germany and its allies following the German army's advance into Belgium. Even before Britain's declaration of war, Sir Robert Borden's conservative government in Ottawa had dispatched two telegrams to London assuring their counterparts in Westminster that Canadians would do their part to maintain the integrity of the Empire. Forty-eight hours after Britain's war declaration, a telegram from London was received in Ottawa accepting Canada's offer of an expeditionary force of about 22,500 men to be sent as soon as possible.

In July 1915, Lieutenant-Colonel Samuel Beckett, a 9th Mississauga Horse officer was given command of the newly formed 75th Battalion to be recruited for overseas service. His orders were to recruit a full complement of officers and soldiers—around a thousand. It took but a month for the 75th recruiters to bring the battalion up to strength. At Camp Niagara that summer, the seasoned militia officers and non-commissioned officers of the 75th began preparing their new recruits for war. The objective was to mould these volunteers into a disciplined and skilled fighting formation for overseas service. Paramount was physical training, and the men drilled from morning to night. A similar focus was placed on developing the discipline necessary to follow orders. In addition, rifle drill and maintenance, marksmanship, and bayonet fighting were crucial skills; the recruited men honed them with constant practice.

With basic training behind them, the men now focused on specialist training over the winter months in Toronto, which included signalling, scouting, orienteering, bombing, and machine gunnery. Not that physical training was forgotten—the men studied and practised the art of digging trenches, dugouts, and traverses, and building latrines. News from the front in France confirmed this to be a war of stalemate, with men eating, sleeping, and surviving in holes or trenches in the ground.

It was March 26, 1916, when the 75th Battalion entrained for Halifax. The band stood on the platform at the North Toronto station and played "Colonel Bogey"—the regimental march—as officers and men said their farewells and goodbyes to loved ones and friends. Five days later, on April 1, having boarded the troopship *Empress of Britain*, the 75th left Canadian shores. After eight days, the coast of England was sited at Liverpool. On the move again, the battalion entrained for Bramshott Camp, fifty-six kilometres southwest of London. The men detrained and marched for over an hour to the camp, arriving in the early dawn hours of April 10. This would be the 75th's home for the next several months, and much would happen here—including the possibility of the battalion being removed altogether from the order of battle.

The next several weeks brought good fortune for Lt. Col. Beckett as he learned that the 75th would form part of the 11th Brigade of the 4th Canadian Division alongside its brigade cousins: the 54th (Kootenay) Battalion, from British Columbia, the 87th (Canadian Grenadier Guards) Battalion, from Montreal; and the 102nd (Northern British Columbia) Battalion. More extensive training was carried out through the month of July and up to the second week of August, including offensive and defensive operations, constructing and maintaining wire and outposts, and, most importantly, survival in the trenches. Realistic drills included night operations against an "enemy," which usually meant Lt. Devlin's bombing section.

With a final inspection on August 7, the 4th Division was ready. In the early hours of August 11, the brigade was on the move to Southampton and a Channel crossing to the port of Le Havre, France. Hospital ships filled the harbour at Le Havre, as the 75th's ship HMTS *Mona's Queen* arrived on the morning of August 12. Thousands of wounded soldiers from the Somme battles had found refuge aboard these ships, and waited patiently for the trip to Britain, and home for many—a sobering thought for the anxious and apprehensive men of the 75th. It would be three very long years before they would leave these shores for home—more than nine hundred would not return—and they would see numerous bloody battles over that time.

On the evening of August 15, the 75th had its first indoctrination to the front lines. Over the next eight days, under the guidance and instruction of the 22nd (French Canadian) Battalion, the 75th was rotated to the front at St. Eloi Craters in Flanders, Belgium. Front-line experience was integral for any unit to become an effective fighting formation. It was the afternoon of August 24 when the 75th relieved the 22nd in the front line, to begin its first of many trench tours.

During this same period, Pte. James H. Gibson and the 130th were still in Canada, at Valcartier Camp, Quebec, going through basic drill and training. His battalion would remain there until the end of September, when it left for Halifax and overseas.

The 75th was in the front line in Belgium for three weeks, until orders were received for the 4th Division to make its way to Albert, France, the jumping-off point for the Somme battles. The first three Canadian infantry divisions had arrived at the Somme the end of August, and had already seen heavy fighting by the time the 4th arrived and entered the line at Courcelette on October 11. The 75th immediately faced a trial-by-fire, and suffered forty-eight casualties in forty-eight hours before being relieved during the night of October 13. Ten days later, on the 23rd, the 75th moved forward to a captured section of *Regina* trench, and within two days was given orders to attack the enemy in the remaining part of that trench. During the advance, it was found that the enemy's wire was again uncut, and even though the 75th inflicted heavy casualties, it suffered terribly, too. It would not be until November 11 that *Regina* trench fell to the Canadians.

But the fighting was not over at the Somme. There was still a strong German position—a trench named *Desire*, to the north of *Regina*—and it was the job of the 4th Division to take it. It was now mid-November, and cold, wet shell holes filled with freezing water and mud awaited the attackers. The soldiers of the 75th spent five agonizing days at the front in the appalling weather. The physical demands on the men in coping in such conditions pushed them to the extreme, until orders finally came down that the attack on *Desire* would go in at dawn on the 18th. The 4th took *Desire*, but at great cost: 1,250 casualties. The 75th suffered 248, 108 of them fatal. The Somme battles over, the 75th, along with other 4th Division battalions, was in desperate need of more manpower.

By November 20, the 75th was on the move back to the town of Albert, where it remained for six days. Then the movement order came in for Vimy. The first three Canadian divisions were already on the ground at Vimy, and the 4th would find its way there. In its circuitous route from the Somme, the battalion arrived in the village of Bajus on December 4. It was there where Perth, Ontario's Pte. James H. Gibson was taken on strength with the 75th, one of 124 reinforcements.

Gibson was trained as a bomber, a skill set that necessitated an individual having a good throwing arm and thorough knowledge of the grenades and bombs at his disposal—including the enemy's. Early in the war, bombers were most crucial to any patrol or attack into no man's land. They needed steady nerves as they closed with the enemy, and quick and accurate release of the bombs they carried. Any hesitation could spell disaster—not just for the bomber himself but for those he was supporting. In the later stages of the war, there was less emphasis on hand-thrown bombs and more on rifle grenadiers—soldiers who dispatched grenades from a rifle barrel. It was four days before Christmas when the 75th took over a portion of the line at Vimy and Pte. Gibson had his first taste of trench warfare.

For the next two months, the 75th got itself into the brigade routine of front-line, support, and brigade reserve, and on numerous occasions the battalion's soldiers were forward repairing front-line trenches and helping to dig new ones. There was also rest or down time, and Pte. Gibson used these opportunities to write home. The majority of his letters were addressed to May Keays, a neighbour and friend of his family, and the woman who would become his wife. Called by his middle name Herbert (Herb), that is how he signed his letters. He penned, in February 1917 (letter 36):

> Rest does not mean just eat and sleep. First comes the pay parade which is the life of a soldier, means little dainties for him. Next is clothes parade and he gets his worn clothing replaced with new. Next is bathing parade, where he comes back to civilized life again. Then there is rifle inspection, gas helmet and respirator drill, some bayonet fighting, squad drill where memories of former days come back, before you faced the guns. Then we bombers practice throwing bombs, like a baseball player would keep in trim for the match. Only bombs are not thrown like baseballs and then it would be (up) with you to catch one!!

A plan was in the works by 4th Division headquarters to mount a large-scale, four-battalion raid on the German positions atop Vimy

Ridge (Hill 145) toward the end of February. The objective was to gather intelligence, destroy the enemy's strong points, and take prisoners—but the catch was, it was to take place under cover of gas: "White Star," a combination of phosgene and chlorine. The artillery fire plan mentioned only a brief bombardment to disguise the release of the gas. This was of great concern to two seasoned commanding officers, the 75th's Lt. Col. Samuel Beckett and the 54th's Lt. Col. Arnold Kemball. The official line was that the gas would surprise and incapacitate the enemy. Not so, claimed Beckett and Kemball. Beckett shot back that his 75th had no experience with gas, and Kemball countered that the winds in that sector were too unpredictable to substitute gas for an artillery bombardment. These concerns mattered not to the 4th Division's Lt. Col. Edmund Ironside, senior British staffer to Maj. Gen. David Watson, the key planner and the man who ran the division.

On the night of February 28–March 1, 1917, the raid was on, and at 3:00 a.m. the first release of gas occurred. After a two-and-a-quarter-hour wait, the 75th raiders—481, all ranks, in seven assault parties (including Gibson)—moved into no man's land under a short, creeping barrage. On getting to the enemy front line, the raiders were met with bombs and terrific rifle and machine-gun fire. Casualties mounted. Maj. Miles Langstaff, a Toronto lawyer, was cut down on the lip of the enemy's trench. Lt. Col. Beckett, who had been watching from his own front line and saw the attack stall, immediately stood up and rushed forward, yelling as he went, until an enemy bullet struck him in his left breast, killing him instantly. Disorder ensued until Cpl. Frank Schissler leapt up and took control, steadying the men, moving them forward, and then organizing small parties to carry back the wounded.

The 4th Division suffered nearly 700 casualties that night, an enormous number; and the 75th, 221, with 71 fatal (including its commanding officer, Lt. Col. Beckett) and 31 missing. Pte. James H. Gibson was among the wounded, having sustained a bullet wound to his left arm between his wrist and elbow that slightly grazed the bone. Gibson's wound was serious enough to get him a "Blighty"—a trip to a hospital in England, where he would convalesce for the next eight months.

Once across the Channel, Pte. Gibson was moved between hospitals in Kent, in southern England. While at Chipstead, in Sevenoaks, he was told by a visiting Canadian chaplain that the 75th had suffered so dearly during the March 1 trench raid that the battalion had been broken up and the remaining men sent to other units. Thankfully the chaplain was misinformed. The heavy casualties were accurate; fortunately for the 75th, it was brought up to strength with more reinforcements before the main assault at Vimy on April 9–10.

When the main Canadian Corps attack went in at Vimy five weeks later, Gibson had been moved to Woodcote Park convalescent hospital in Epsom. It was there that he read of the big attack, and he was glad that he had been able to do his part in March. He wrote (letter 55), "Would liked to have been there for the big advance, but since I helped to hold that important position for three months and was wounded there I am satisfied that I did all I could."

The 75th fared no better in the early morning hours of April 9, as the men waited with great anxiety to go over the top. This time the 75th was to follow the 87th Battalion and push through to the crest of the ridge. Disaster awaited both battalions, however, as German machine-gun positions in an enemy trench to the immediate front had not been destroyed by earlier artillery fire. That trench had been left off the fire plan, seemingly to be used by the 11th Brigade's commander, Brig. Odlum, as his forward headquarters as the brigade moved up the ridge. It was a major miscalculation, which caused enormous loss of life in both the 87th and 75th battalions. The 4th was the only division out of four that did not meet its objectives on schedule. It would be another day before the crest—where the magnificent monument stands today— would be in Canadian hands. Casualties in the 75th were extensive: 9 officers and 96 soldiers killed, 7 officers and 159 soldiers wounded, and 2 officers and 59 soldiers missing (many of the latter would in time be presumed or verified dead). The Canadian Corps suffered over ten thousand casualties. These were staggering numbers—but the enemy was driven off the ridge.

Following the very costly Canadian victory at Vimy, the 75th, along with the rest of the 11th Brigade, went into reserve for two weeks to reorganize and train new recruits. Over the next seven months, while Pte. Gibson was recovering from his wound in England, the 75th was engaged in trench tours, small raids, and large-scale battles: a raid on the village of La Coulotte (June), a trench tour and diversionary attack, Lens (August), and Passchendaele (October–November). On returning to France from Flanders, the 75th, along with the rest of the 4th Division, took up residency at the town of Camblain Châtelain (or "Charlie Chaplin" to the soldiers, as it was easier to say) behind Vimy Ridge. It was there that reinforcements and returning casualties joined the battalion, including Pte. Gibson on December 7.

On that same day, Gibson found a moment to pen another letter (no. 111) to May Keays:

> Here we are again.... Well, I have joined the Batt. once more after an absence of 9 months. Am in C. Co. again and I find very few of the old boys still here. They all look fine though and were glad to see us, at least in one sense of the word. We are billeted in town of course and the little corner which is "Home Sweet Home" for the time being is up in a typical French garret [a tiny room in the top of a building, an attic]. Not the usual farm house buildings with the rectangular smell [sic] in the middle, but a regular town property in the residential part. On the whole this is about the best town I ever struck for billets. It is somewhat cleaner than the common run. There are any amount of Estaminets and cafes. "Cafes" after a style which I would hardly like to try to describe. The main menu is eggs, chips and coffee with chips and eggs for a change.... We all voted the other day. I wonder what the result will be.

Nearly a week would pass before Pte. Gibson's mail from home caught up to him, and at once he sat down and wrote his father. It was December 13. His father and mother had been suffering with health issues, and he was anxious to respond. He wrote in part (letter 112), "Of course, I know that years are against both of you, but I trust and pray that God will spare you until we meet again." He was sorry for not being home to help out on the farm. "I would like to be there to help you dispose of some of the fresh pork, new butter and cream now but perhaps it will not be long until we shall all be home." His father had earlier written the authorities in Ottawa asking for an exemption for his son, and if he could be returned home to help with the farm.

Sadly, his father would not receive this letter; he suffered a stroke on December 17 and died the next day. Herb carried on writing, by turns, to May, his sister Clara, and his mother two days before Christmas.

To his mother he wrote (letter 115): "I wonder how you are this morning. I hope you are much better and able to be up at least a while each day. It is my first thought in the morning and last at night, that you and Father may be restored to health again and I pray that we may all meet once more at home." His mother would not receive his letter, as she was in failing health and died on New Year's Eve.

In this same letter, Gibson articulated his most recent experience at the front. His highlight was the rations: they were getting better. Previously seven men had to live on one loaf of bread between them; this time, each man received a third, or, in some cases, a half of a loaf—but the best was "bacon and tea each morning, soup at noon and rice and tea at night, besides jam butter and cheese." He went on to say that close by was a YMCA hut staffed by volunteers who offered the troops, milk, biscuits, chocolate, fruit, and writing paper. "So you see life in the trenches is not so bad."

Sadly, Herb would find out about the death of his father in a letter (no. 121) from his sister Mary Ellen, which he received in mid-January; and about his mother's death from May's letter (no. 123) of January 3, a letter he read while in an observation post on a clear, moonlit night, January 29, 1918.

He was numb with the news. Five days later, Herb found the strength to write a letter to May (no. 124): "I thank you for your kind letters and words of encouragement at this time of sorrow. I have put off writing because I could not think to speak of it all. It seems as though there were nothing more to live for now. I am just moving about like a machine without any object in view."

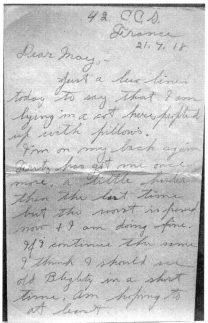

Envelope and letter home, from J.H. Gibson.

Over the next three months, the 75th carried out several front-line tours and sent out working parties, many under enemy fire, to construct strongpoints, string barbed wire, and fix and dig trenches. The weather over the winter months was always cold, with rain, wind, and snow flurries. That routine changed in late March 1918, when the Germans launched a spring offensive, their last major thrust of the war, which they hoped would bring final victory. The massive German assault did not involve the Canadians, who were dug in on Vimy Ridge. For whatever reason, the Germans attacked British formations north and south of the ridge, and left the Canadians alone.

In a letter (no. 129) to May, dated March 23, Herb made no mention of the German attack, writing, "Here we are again in our cellar. In this town we sleep in the cellars for the bedrooms are too drafty owing to numerous windows of rather large and unshapely dimensions. Am in the line again and glad to say going on not too badly. We are having fine weather, just like May days in Canada. There is not much doing here out of the ordinary, so my stock of news is small."

April found the 75th on front-line tours. Herb was in a funk hole (a dugout) on a dark, wet night at the front, when on April 5 he received a letter (no. 131) from May. He replied:

> Your letter of March 10th received and as usual welcome as the flowers in May.... Of course I did not get reading it until next morning but somehow its very presence was a shining star in the night. It has been wet this few days and of course the trenches are in bad condition. However I am well and that means everything out here. Moved out to supports last night and believe me a wash and shave was most acceptable after over a week without either. We slept until noon, had dinner, cleaned up a bit and now it is just 3:40.... This last ten days has been a rush and tumble. Going and coming, we know not where. Talk about the future and its mysteries but this is where you realize it to the fullest extent.

For several weeks in May, the 75th was several kilometres behind the front in the village of Caucourt, re-energizing, reorganizing, and carrying out further training. An army gymnastics instructor was seconded to the battalion, and physical fitness and training took precedence. The weather was cooperating, which made outdoor activities enjoyable. In addition to physical fitness, each day was taken up with musketry practice, range work, and route marches, and each afternoon sporting activities, including baseball and football (soccer). Specialist training for Lewis gunners, rifle grenadiers, and stretcher bearers continued as well, and on one afternoon the entire battalion passed through the new gas hut in a nearby village for further gas training.

Toward the end of May, the 75th left Caucourt and marched to the familiar turf at Camblain Châtelain ("Charlie Chaplin") fourteen kilometres to the northwest. Here, out of the line, began a six-week routine of exercising, training, marching, sports, and socializing that would long be remembered by all ranks. The final push was coming for the Allies, and this down time was critical to increase readiness and strengthen camaraderie.

On June 18, Herb penned a very lengthy letter (no. 142) to May wherein he mentioned battalion sports:

> Our Divisional Sports [at Pernes] are over and this Brigade carried off the spoils. Perhaps I never told you that I belong to the 11th Brigade, 4th Division. We had a splendid days outing. They were held in a rather nice town near here and we marched down in the morning, taking the field kitchens with us and had both dinner and supper on the grounds. There was everything from Lacrosse to Hand Ball. Worst part of it was, a bunch of us had to stay and go on a working party at 12 midnight. T'was rather cold hanging about until time to start work but considering the importance of the work, we did not mind. The task was digging dugouts for the staff and patients of a hospital. Tents and sheet iron afford no protection from heavy shells or bombs so one has to take to Mother earth for protection.

With the calendar change to July, the 75th was ordered back to the front, and on July 10 the battalion formed up and moved off from "Charlie Chaplin." It was late evening on the 11th when the men found themselves in the front lines once again. Forty-eight hours later, July 13, a fighting patrol of some thirty soldiers, including Pte. Gibson, left the relative safety of the front-line trench for no man's land. Under the command of Lieutenants Ibri Alkenbrack and John Leonard, the patrol was to seek out and engage German working parties. However, on this night darkness proved a liability. The 75th scouts leading the way got themselves too close to the enemy's front line. Lt. Leonard, realizing this, crawled forward to bring them back, when an enemy flare shot skyward and brought down a torrent of small arms fire on the 75th men. Three died instantly, including Leonard, and six others were wounded.

One of those six was Pte. James H. Gibson, seriously wounded by machine-gun fire. A bullet entered through his right side below his shoulder blade, smashed ribs, and exited out his chest. A second bullet caused a flesh wound in his thigh that was not as serious. Not able to walk more than a few steps, luckily he was found by another and assisted back to the start line. From there, after a ninety-minute wait, he was carried on a stretcher to a dressing station, then the field ambulance, where he was given morphine, and finally the casualty clearing station. Gibson wrote to May (letter 148) on August 1, 1918:

> Shortly after arriving here, they performed the operation. Some of my ribs were smashed so they had to remove several inches, sewed me up nicely—18 stitches and it is healed nicely. Only thing is that my lung is punctured. However, that will heal up, I hope soon. I was glad to leave the C.C.S. for Fritz visited it quite frequently at night. He dropped bombs all around us—30 one night. The nearest was 50 yards and filled our ward with dust and smoke. One poor chap was killed and several wounded. Next move was by train to Boulogne, stopped there for a few days and then across. We struck a beautiful day and I enjoyed the sail. Funny it was the same Red Cross boat as I came home in the last time. There are 2000 beds in here, so you can imagine its size.

Herb, with his second "Blighty," found himself at the King George Hospital in east London. Over the next several months, Herb moved between hospitals in Kent, Bexhill-on-Sea, and London, his preferred being the Massey-Harris Convalescent House in London. He was very descriptive of these lodgings in his letter of September 8, 1918 (no. 161):

> I may say though that the floors are polished, walls of panelled oak with deep borders of hand painting, windows coloured glass. The grounds, comprising some 30 acres, are simply grand. One of the cards shows you a glimpse of the gardens. There are bowling greens, tennis courts, in fact everything for the hearts desire. I only wish you could come and see it. We are five minutes from the famous Crystal Palace and a half hour by bus to the city. One would never know they were in London, plenty of fresh air, not a bit like smoky old King George at Waterloo. By the city I mean the Strand, Whitehall, Fleet St. etc. etc. We are allowed to go where we like between the hours of 2–9 P.M. so I went up to Westminster yesterday P.M. Yes and I must tell you about the board. You know that's what a soldier thinks of first, everything else take a second place. We get all we can

J.H. Gibson in uniform. On the right arm are three upward-pointing chevrons, which indicate that he had served over two years overseas in Europe. The first was issued when a soldier arrived in England and a further was added every year thereafter. These were blue in color. On the left arm is one large upward-pointing chevron, which was a Good Conduct stripe for four years' service without any disciplinary measures. A clean record was rather rare, as most soldiers were found to be guilty of some minor infraction. The stripe would be forfeited if the soldier got into trouble later. The two brass stripes below the Good Conduct stripe indicate that Gibson was wounded twice during the war. For these to be awarded, a soldier had to suffer an injury that was due to enemy action that required medical treatment that was recorded in a medical unit record.

put away. Not rich stuff, but real wholesome food. I thought three course
dinners were a thing of the past but got a surprise of my life when we went
to dinner here. The Major says I will be a long time in hospital yet so I am
hoping to stay here for sometime—do you blame me? The Massey-Harris
people have this property rented I believe and maintain it themselves.
Now May, I expect a letter from you soon so will close this one as it is
almost noon and I must not be late for dinner.

Even though he was far from the front, Herb kept an eye out in the
press for news of the 75th, and there was a great deal to report. It began
in August 1918, the Allies' big eastward push against the Germans,
in what became known as the last one hundred days of the war. The
Canadian Corps, the shock troops of the British Empire's army, began
a series of battles—commencing with the Battle of Amiens in early
August, and followed by the battles for the Drocourt–Quéant Line in
early September, crossing the Canal du Nord, the fight for Bourlon Wood
in late September, and the push to Cambrai, the German transportation
and supply hub, by early October—that delivered a string of decisive
blows culminating in an armistice in November. The 11th Brigade and
the 75th Battalion were heavily engaged in all of these battles. At one
point in early October, the 75th, having taken so many casualties, ceased
for a time to be a fighting formation.

Meanwhile Herb, across the Channel in London, continued to recoup
from his chest wound and regain his strength. One day in mid-October,
he dropped in to see Lt. Col. Colin Harbottle, the commanding officer of
the 75th, who was recovering in a London hospital from wounds he had
received in early September. His time away from the front also provided
Herb with more time to think about home and life after the war. In a very
touching letter to May (no. 116) of October 25, 1918, Herb penned:

I must write to you again today for since my last have got some of yours of
July and early August. You mention getting the news that I had been killed.
Well, May, why should I have been spared when others are called upon to
make the great sacrifice. Yes, indeed I do remember that summer evening
when we drove and chatted together and it makes me ask the question,
Has absence made the heart grow fonder? and do you really care so very
much that I should return? You remember we did not make any promises,
and I think it was the very best way, don't you? You have been my very
best friend. Your letters always brought cheer into billet, trench or dugout

and I have seen you in my dreams and thought of you when on outpost and patrol. I think my very first thoughts when I was hit was "what will May think?" Had I not had someone to, as it were reach out to me in "No Man's Land" that morning, I believe I should have stayed there.

Herb would not get back to France. His war was effectively over when he suffered that serious wound in July. He had recovered enough that by January 29, 1919, he boarded a troopship in Liverpool bound for Halifax and home. Herb got home to Perth, Ontario, on the morning of February 10.

Herb's last letter to his sisters (no. 186) was dated April 3, 1919. He wrote, "Here I am back home once more for good. Got my discharge on the last day of March and got home April 1st. Gee! but it is great to be home and know that you do not need to take anybody's orders."

Herb's detailed letters are a magnificent glimpse into the conditions for a front-line Canadian soldier during the Great War. But they are much more than that. They articulate a story of love for his family, of longing for home, and the despair and at times hopelessness of being so far away. These letters are truly a gem, providing an insight rarely offered by other sources on the war.

Timothy J. Stewart CD
Author, *Toronto's Fighting 75th in the Great War, 1915–1919*

ACKNOWLEDGEMENTS

We gratefully acknowledge Timothy J. Stewart and his work in writing the Foreword to this book. He has woven the experiences of Herb Gibson into the larger war and the history of the 75th Battalion, of which Herb was a part. His knowledge and expertise are greatly appreciated.

Additionally, we wish to thank team members at Wilfrid Laurier University Press, including Robert Kohlmeier, Siobhan McMenemy, and Mike Bechthold. All have helped turn this project into the book you now see.

The documents reproduced in this volume are from the collection of the Walters and Newbold families.

INTRODUCTION

Private James Herbert Gibson
No. 786167, "C" Coy, 9th Platoon
75th (Mississauga) Battalion
11th Brigade
4th Division
Canadian Expeditionary Force

The following are the personal letters and diaries of Private (Pte.) James Herbert Gibson. The letters trace Herb's service with the Canadian Expeditionary Force from 1916 to 1919. Most of these letters were written home to May Keays, a neighbour of his family's and his future wife. Herb was 26 years old at the time he enlisted. In the first letters home, Herb is thinking of enlisting, creating tension between him and his father. He had been in the 42nd Lanark and Renfrew militia for some years, and was keenly interested in the military and in history. At the time he enlisted in March 1916, his parents were 68 years old and in poor health, and they were likely counting on him to stay on the farm with them. Later letters talk about his training, his experiences at the front, being wounded (he was wounded twice in service, once seriously), his recovery, and his connections back home.

His beliefs, hopes, realizations, and tragedies are revealed in the following pages through an account of his contribution to the war. A popular slogan urged all Canadians to "do their bit" to win the war. In a war that included a large portion of the "developed" world as we know it today, a war that claimed a whole generation of young men, including sixty thousand Canadians, he felt he played a bit role (letter 45). But that role, regardless of size, was a meaningful one. In some ways, he was the archetypal volunteer. His family was descended of Scottish settlers and he viewed the war as a crusade against the evil forces of the German Empire. Therefore, he saw his contribution to the war effort as justified. Any romantic views of war that he held would surely have been quickly dashed by the reality of trench warfare—the stench, the filth, the bad food, the "livestock" (lice—see letter 30), and little sleep. In other ways, he was an atypical volunteer. His religious beliefs significantly influenced him and sustained him through his darkest hours. He was a gentle man caught up, in his own words, "on an errand the full consequences of which we did not realize" (letter 119).

Herb's great-grandparents emigrated from Scotland in 1820 and settled in Dalhousie Township, near Perth, Ontario, homesteading at Lammermoor, west of Ottawa. Herb's father, William Russell Gibson, was born there in 1848. His mother, Euphemia Nairn, was also descended from Scottish settlers and also grew up in Dalhousie Township. William and Euphemia were married on March 8, 1870. James Herbert (Herb) was born on November 11, 1889, the youngest of ten children. Their home was very likely the hub of the little community, as the post office was located in their house, the school was built on their property, and the teacher boarded with them. They had their own pioneer cemetery, and it is there that Herb's ancestors are buried. John, one of Herb's brothers, married in 1905 and left the homestead. A second brother, Willie, married in 1907 and remained on the homestead. Herb also had five sisters: Clara, Jane, Margaret, Ida, and Mary Ellen. Herb, his parents, and two of his sisters moved to a small home that was built for them, just in front of the original home. His father had by then retired from farming, and became an itinerant preacher. He covered many miles and was gone for many months over the winters. Herb's family bought a farm in April 1912 on the Eighth Line of Bathurst,[1] closer to Balderson, Ontario, and about a half-mile from May's family homestead.

Herb enlisted with the 130th Battalion in Perth, Ontario, in March 1916, and received training in Barriefield, Ontario, and then Valcartier, Quebec, before sailing to England in October 1916. Once in England, he was sent to West Sandling, where he was reassigned to the 75th Battalion, 4th Division, 11th Brigade. The 4th Division had already seen heavy fighting during the battle at Courcellette on the Somme in October 1916, and would later see action at Vimy Ridge and Passchendaele. By November 1916, Herb was in France where he joined the 4th near Vimy Ridge. Just a few weeks before the famous Battle of Vimy Ridge, the Canadian divisions were involved in a trench raid on the German lines opposite Hill 145 early on March 1, 1917. The raid was generally considered a failure, with some seven hundred casualties—including Herb, who was wounded in the left arm. After making his way back to the regimental aid post and dressing stations, he would spend the next nine months in England convalescing.

Herb returned to his battalion in the Vimy area in November of 1917. By July 1918, the Canadians were preparing for an offensive campaign "of the last 100 days." Herb was moved up to the front lines, north of the town of Arras, on July 10. While on patrol in "no man's land" on the morning of July 13, 1918, Herb was shot in the chest and leg, the bullets breaking three of his ribs and damaging a lung. With several men in the scouting party missing or dead, including his commanding officer, Lt. Leonard, Herb was fortunate to be carried back to their line given the severity of his wounds. He spent the balance of the war in England recovering, turning 29 on the day the armistice was signed: November 11, 1918. He returned to Canada in February 1919 and was discharged in March. While he was undoubtedly glad to be home, his health and ability to work on the farm had been compromised by his wounds. With his parents dead and the rest of the family out west, Herb sold the farm and moved west himself.

After returning to Canada, he rarely discussed the war and his experiences with his family. He did remember though. He was a regular participant in Remembrance Day ceremonies—his birthday—and there are pictures of reunions with other soldiers from the Great War. A few mementos around the house reflected his service. Years later, he was visiting his daughter Iris and son-in-law Eric Newbold in Burlington, Ontario, and asked them to look up John Johnston's phone number (see letter 175). After confirming Johnston was an old pal from the war, Herb and Eric headed off to Hamilton, where Herb and John spent an afternoon quietly talking. They were the lucky ones. So many of his friends from Perth and Lanark did not return home: Thomas Butler, Hugh and Willie Knowles, Jim McVeety, Melville Paul, Morton and Orville Publow, Jim Trail, Arthur Tufts, and Hubert Quackenbush. The pain of losing so many of his friends is revealed in one letter home where he writes about seeing the grave of Tom Butler: "Perhaps you can imagine my feelings May, as I looked upon the grass covered mound and wooden cross Here, standing in a foreign land, beside the grave of my chum, neighbour and finally comrade in arms, my thoughts flashed back to the quiet peaceful homes from whence we came, on an errand the full consequences of which we did not realize" (letter 119). Others, like Herb himself, returned home but were wounded. For such a small farming community, the loss of these men would have been significant.

While the compiling, editing, and transcribing of the material from Herb's original letters to notes—and, finally, to the computer—took many, many hours, our work on this book has been a rewarding experience for the both of us. We both hope that you will enjoy reading the following which allows you to get to know the man we called Dad or Grandfather.

L. Iris Newbold
K. Bruce Newbold

Note

1   A concession road constructed by the colonial government of Upper Canada when the land was still undeveloped to provide new settlers with access to surveyed lots. These roads were numbered: Sixth Line, Seventh Line, Eighth Line, etc.

1916

Pte. James Herbert Gibson,
Regimental No. 787167
4th Division
11th Brigade
75th Battalion
C Company
9th Platoon, Section Bombers

1

Depot Harbour
Feb. 15, 1916

Dear Herbert,

Your card received. It did not contain much news but was a very great satisfaction to know that you were all well. You didn't say that mother was out of bed. You said I wasn't to worry about you all. Well I know that it is no use. It is better to pray and I do a good deal of that. More I dare say than you think. It is my constant prayer that you all may be saved; more I am praying that you will turn your thoughts from war to Christ and content yourself on your nice little farm which is the best life a man can live. I see it here more than ever. These people don't own their houses and if they are laid off as they say it is all the time in their minds. A lot of men have been taken away to work at other places and the wives are here. Well how are you getting along with your wood cutting? It would be a great satisfaction to me if you tell me more of the little things about home. If you get any time to take out logs at Lammermoor you may cut those big hemlock at the upper end of the swamp that we were speaking about and I would think that this winter would be fine for taking out cedar for the floods will be frozen over now. Do what ever preparing you can without expense. It will come in good anytime. It is better to go to see how this war will turn out. Would like to see both you and John get along for you are in as good a place to live as I have ever seen in all my travels. I am getting along here so far all right but I think that they are a pretty hard people to please. I will do my best but will please my master Jesus Christ first. It is certainly easy work compared with what I have been used to. It is different working among these people from farmers. Don't expect to be here longer than the end of March. I wrote to the editor of Bracebridge paper to change the address to Depot Harbour. Why he has not done it, I don't know. Now I have an idea of coming home the Monday following the last Sunday in Feb. If you think it would suit you to meet me in Perth at 9 o'clock at night and take me back. I would be at home one Sunday. I think I could get a young man to take my services for that day. Now if it would put you to very much trouble I would not like to do that. I write to Mother and tell her what I would like to come home for.

Lovingly,
Father

2

Depot Harbour
March 21, 1916

Dear Son,

Just got your letter and read it and dropped on my knees and implored the Lord to have mercy on me and prevent you from enlisting. I cannot conceive of how a son having any natural affection for his aged parents will deliberately crush the life out of them before there is a necessity of doing so. It is, it seems to me, to gratify a desire to go because you have been advised by those recruiting officers and that others are going. You might take your mother and father's and brothers' and sisters' advice for once in your lifetime. The fact of the matter is they have no right to strip our young country of so many of you young men. It is nothing but a boast of government to get a big name. I believe that I am justified in trying to prevent you from going. You can go in spite of me but perhaps you will walk over my dead body. I suppose you have made up your mind for that. I don't think you should talk of German cruelty anymore if you go. We expect nothing better at their hands but we expect better things of our sons that we worked hard to raise. You have got more than any of them and got more of your own way than any of the others. Can't you stay till they call for you? It would be showing that you had some love and consideration for your old father and mother.[1] I believe if you go now God will be against you. What will it matter to get some glory in war if you lose your soul?

What it profit a man if he gains the whole world and lose his own soul or what shall a man give in exchange for his soul? I will continue to pray that you will change your mind to some thing better. If my prayer is not answered then I will have done what I believe to be my duty. Oh God help me is my daily cry. May God have mercy on us all.

Father

I ask you not to put your name to a paper of any kind till I come home, if you do it make the burden greater. I would of liked to have stayed longer. Some of the people here want me to stay for the summer but I may just as well leave after Sunday the 26th. If you don't hear from me again, meet me in Perth on the night of the twenty-seventh at nine o'clock. Be sure you don't sell us bare of grain. That was a big loss the pigs. We have a long time of prosperity but the scales may be turned now. Had phone call asking me if I was coming back to Muskoka again. Well surely the Lord will have work for me to do. If you would only turn your heart to Christ and his Gospel it would be a joy to me and to the rest of us as well.

March 30th: Enlisted with the 130th Battalion, Lanark and Renfrew, Headquarters Perth Ontario. Officer commanding Lt. Col. J.E. Dehertel and Major E.J. Watt. Got 12 days leave.

April 10: Reported for duty.

April 11: Started to drill in old show grounds. Felt quite at home on account of experience with the old 42nd Lanark and Renfrew. Quartered in exhibition hall and fed by Edmonds.

April 12, 14: Getting fairly well accustomed to the rifle and squad drill. Hot days.

April 15: Pay day. Off duty p.m.

April 16: Hot. Parade to English Church. Sermon by Rev. Clayton.

April 17–20: Squad and company drill. Rifle exercises. Football for physical training. Morning parade 6:30 route march around town.

April 21: Went home on my first pass. Oh happy day.

April 22: Rained so had to spend the day inside.

April 23: Went to Balderson Church.

April 24: Back to town A.M. Reported for duty 2 P.M. 130th farewell concert.

April 25–28: Usual training. On guard 1st time QMS.

April 29: Sat. Off duty in P.M.

April 30: Parade to St. Andrews in A.M. and off to Knox in P.M. So ended the first month in King's uniform.

May 1: Got my 1st inoculation and it did not hurt me much. Like a big hornet sting. Stayed indoors 24 hours.

May 2: Got pass and went out to C. McNicols and spent day.

May 3: Walked to town with Pearl in A.M. and reported for duty at 2 P.M.

May 4: On guard at No. 1 post headquarters Gore St.

J.H. Gibson's parents: Euphemia Nairn and William Russell Gibson.

May 5: Got furlough for 10 days to put in crop.

May 6: Just home in time to help take cattle to Lammermoor.

May 7: Stayed at Willie's. He drove me to McDonalds Corners. Walked until 7. Met father on Gallingers Hill.

May 8: Started to disc^2 but land very wet.

May 9, 10: Discing high parts.

May 12: Took Clara to town and got my furlough extended for 7 days on account of weather.

May 13: Nothing doing on farm so Clara and I went to Joseph Pauls, Poland.

May 14: Willies all came over to Mary Ellen's.

May 15: Got 2 fields sowed and harrowed when rain started again.

May 16-19: Raining again.

May 20: 130th mobilized in Perth. Quartered in new show grounds and boarded by Edmonds in old show hall. Clara and I went to town.

May 21: Went to Church at home.

May 22: Reported for duty 5 P.M. First night spent like soldiering, straw and blankets for bed. Battalion mobilized in Perth.

May 23: Spent getting settled and company's organized.

May 24: Big parade, sports, sham battle. Fire works at night.

May 25-26: Spent marching to and from meals and practicing march past.

May 27: Colours presented by IODE Perth on Tay Chapter. Address read by Mrs. Stewart. Speech by Lt. Col. Hemming of 3rd Div. Big crowd. Sham battle at night.

May 28: First drum head service held by Batt.

May 29: Pay day A.M. Home on pass P.M. Went for drive back to Fallbrook with May Bell Keays.

May 30: Reported for duty 8 P.M. End of 2nd month soldiering.

May 31: Up at 4 A.M. Put on full equipment and marched to breakfast. Formed mass in old exhibition grounds and paraded through Wilson, Foster, Gore, Herriot, Drummond streets to station. Led by veterans, boy scouts, firemen and citizens band with people lining either sides of streets. Address at station by Mayor Hands. 1st section pulled out at 8 A.M. with A and B company and bugle band on board. 2nd section pulled out at 8:30 A.M. with C and D company and brass band. Off to the war. Traveled by CPR to Tichborne and by K & P to Kingston arriving outside Tete Dupont barracks about 11:30 A.M. Marched through the principal streets and out to Barriefield Camp, arriving 1 P.M. Had a light lunch of bread, cheese, tea. Rested all afternoon.

3

4:15 P.M.
Barriefield Camp
May 31, 1916

Dear Mother,

You will see by this address that I have arrived at Kingston.

We left Perth at 8:30, got to Kingston at 11:30 paraded the principle streets of the town and marched out to camp before dinner. I was awful hungry. We are not doing any work this afternoon and I am in the YMCA writing this. They have four large tents here. Lots of paper, pens and ink. All you need to do is come in and sit down at a table and write. The camp is about two miles from the city on the road to Gananoque, which is a lovely stone road. It is a sight to see the cone shaped tents all laid off in rows, then a clear space with squads of men all over it, drilling, then a lot more tents. The tents are pitched on the flats and there is high rough strips covered with trees, maple, ironwood and pine. Melville Paul and Willie Andison are in the same tent with me. There are six in each tent. There was a big crowd in Perth this morning. I was looking for you and Pa.[3] We were up at four o'clock. They never said anything about me not going back at noon yesterday. All the men had a half holiday.

The board was not the best dinner to-day but will be better when we get settled. Each man has 2 heavy woolen blankets and a rubber sheet. Two men go together. Paul and I will bunk together so will be all right.

I bought a picture of the presentation of the colours, at least one of "C" Co. as it was much larger than one with all the battalion in it. There are a few men of "D" Co. in it. I am sixth man from the far end in the long row. You will get it as I had it addressed to Clara. I must have a look around for Lloyd Stewart. He is here in the 146th. You will get this Friday morning so I will be looking for an answer about Sunday. I expect we will get mail here any day.

Good bye and love to all

Address: Pte. J.H. Gibson 787167
"C" Co. 130th Batt.
Barriefield Camp
Kingston Ont.

J.H. Gibson marching through Perth, Ontario, with fellow volunteers.

June: The first two weeks here were spent in a most disagreeable manner. Rain, mud and poor food were the greatest trouble. About the 10th we got floors in our tents which helped greatly to our comforts. The YMCA was a great help to us supplying entertainment and writing material free. Many wet days were spent in their commodious tents enjoyably. Quite a number of men deserted and took French leave from here at this time. Considerable sickness owing to wet weather and poor food.

4

Barriefield
June 6, 1916

Dear Sister,

Received your letter yesterday and glad to hear from you. Hope Mother is alright again and all the rest well. I am fine. Has been very wet up here and the mud is awful. It was very damp sleeping in tents, but have suffered no ill effects as yet. We were busy all day to-day flooring our tents so we will have a dry place to sleep now. We have not done much drilling yet, have been busy getting the camp in shape. The grub is pretty good now and we have canteens (if you know what that is) and knife, fork and spoon.

(Top) J.H. Gibson (at right) with friends in Perth before leaving for training camp.
(Above) Gibson (in the same uniform) in another Perth photo from about the same time.

We had church parade Sunday. There were about 2000 men and two bands in our parade. Was down to Kingston one evening and out to the park. It is a beautiful place down on the lake shore. Mel Paul and I went over to the 146th camp and saw Lloyd Stewart. Also met a Mr. Wood from Snow Road. He knew me at once but I could not recall ever seeing him and where it was I do not know. I would not have known Lloyd at all only Melville knew him. There is a pretty good concert in the YMCA here every night. Partly religious and the rest songs and music by the men of the different Battalions. Also some lady singers from the city. Last night it was all Italian talent.

So Mervyn is to be married to-morrow. I suppose you are invited to the reception. Did they ask me? How is the crop coming along now?

There was a fellow of the 130th took a fit and died in the hospital here yesterday. He shot himself through the left breast last summer and has been taking fits ever since. One of the McVeety boys is a Captain in the Medical Corps here.

I don't know what about coming home on the 20th. It will be too early to get a furlough for haying and four days pass would not be much good. You better get prepared anyhow and will see later.

Here we are almost a week in camp. It does not seem so long. I spend most of my evening in the Y. There are about two hundred men in here writing letters now and it is a fright how much paper they waste. Some men never stop to consider what a privilege this is and take it for granted that they should get all the paper they wish to use. Were it not for the YMCA they would have to get their own writing material.

They also have a large bathing pool down in the city and anyone can go in there any time of the day and bathe, free of charge. Some of the lads have been down. Must go soon and have a wash. Well I think this is all I have to write this time so will be looking for an answer about the end of the week.

So long and love to all.

J. Herb.

That Wood fellow knows all the Watts and told me that he used to go with Ethel. Tell her so.

4A

Balderson
June 9, 1916

Pte. J.H. Gibson
Barriefield

Dear Friend,

I have been thinking of writing to you for sometime but thought I would wait till after the reception. I wish I was with you. I suppose you will have heard all about the dance from Thomas Earle. It was a swell affair—ice cream at ten o'clock and bananas after supper. I had about five or six girls to look after. Mary Taylor was there. Vera Popplewell came with us from the turn. Oscar Briggs has a new Ford mobile. Oscar wanted to take Vera for a spin but she wanted to go to the dance so he got Jimmie Cavers to go with him. We met them about Hailey's. Oscar was so mad he never looked up, but he will get over it all right. Vera said she had a letter from you.

I have got a new auto seat buggy but never had it out yet. I am going to try it tomorrow night. Wish you could get back for a few days soon. Our social is on the 20th. I don't know when the other one is. It may be muddy where you are but it can't be any worse than it is here now. It has rained almost every day since you left, all yesterday afternoon and nearly all day today. However, the papers say that this country will go dry on the 16th of Sept.

How do you like camp life? What do you think of the Germans sinking the old Kitchener? I guess the Germans got the worst of it in the North Sea fight. I heard that Major Watt was to be C.O. of another battalion to be raised in this part of the country.

I was at barn raising at Dick Hopkin's the day of the wedding. He is putting up a new barn. Wilbert Publow is working there.

I wish I could have got in to see you off but I had to draw milk that morning. Well I must close now as it is past my bedtime and I have to get up early.

Hoping to hear from you soon I am

Your sincere friend
R.E. Keays[4]

5

Barriefield
June 14, 1916

Dear Father,

I have written to them all I guess but you so will this time. It is after supper now and all work for the day is over.

I got the two parcels and card and a letter from Johnnie Mather this evening. Did not get the cake until after supper but will have a snack at bedtime and some for several meals after. I must thank Maggie and the rest of you for your trouble. Am glad to get the shoes as we have physical drill all forenoon and it was very tiresome doing it with the heavy boots on. The weather is getting warm now and a little dryer. Is the land drying yet? I suppose the hay will be growing anyhow. How are the cows milking and are the hens laying? How many pigs and chickens have you got? I expect the horses are all fat. Have they done the road labour yet? Don't forget to keep off what I worked in the winter 1 and a half days.[5] I expect to get home on the 20th for a few days. Some of the fellows are getting off this weekend. Of course I am not sure of getting off but tell John's not to stop that reception for me as I most likely will be home.[6] Was to church and bible class last Sunday and every second night they have a sing-song. We are beginning to work pretty hard now. Up at 5:30 A.M. and work until 5:00 P.M. with 2 hours off at breakfast and dinner. Will tell you the rest when I get home.

Hope you are all well.

Good Bye,
Herb

June 17: Got pass for home at 3 P.M. Arrived in Perth 8 P.M. and got home with James McNaughton. Crept in about 1 A.M. Had snack of milk, strawberries and cake, slipped upstairs but however mother heard me.

June 18: Went to church.

June 19: Helped father to do statute labour.

June 20: Took Clara and Lula to Lanark.

June 21: Johns celebrated their wedding anniversary also had baby baptised. Rev. and Mrs. Greig, all our family and a few neighbours. Had a good time and laid in a supply of cake for won't get anymore for awhile.

June 22: Willie took us to town and Clara went to Powasson and I to Kingston on noon train. E. Ferrier was my chum and we stayed in city a few hours and out to camp. Found the Batt. packing up to leave.

June 23: Advance party left for Valcartier.

June 24: Nine battalions marched through Kingston to Penitentiary and back. Very hot day and people along street gave us water when we rested. Packing up.

6

Barriefield
June 24, 1916

Dear Mother,

Back in camp again and the mud has dried up a lot since I left.
Got to the city about 2:30 and stayed there until 6:00 and came up

and had supper. There are a big bunch of the fellows over staying their passes but they will not punish them very severely.

They have most of our stores packed up and a lot of the tents taken down. The advance party leaves for Valcartier to-morrow and the rest of us go on Monday.

I do not know what to say about John coming down Monday. We are expected to leave about 2:00 in the afternoon so that he would not have much time, if any, to spend with me. But there will be five battalions left here so he would see lots at camp and see us march to the train. Would like to see him here but at the same time I would not advise him to come. There might be an excursion to Valcartier.

I suppose Clara will be in Carleton Place to-night. Hope she has a good trip. Was glad Willie's stayed until after we left. You will have time to practice writing so you can write to me.

You will not have time to answer this before we leave so I will not get word from home for a week or ten days. Will drop a card when we leave and some along the way. Hoping you all keep well and hearty.

Your loving son,
Herb

Tell John about us going Monday.

> *June 25:* Church service A.M. P.M. struck camp. On guard over kits in YMCA where we slept Sunday night.
>
> *June 26:* Reveille 4:30 got breakfast and coffee at YMCA. Fall in at 8 A.M. marched off at 9 A.M. into the city and through main streets to K & P station.[7] Pulled out at 1 P.M. over K & P to Harrowsmith, changed to CNR. Passed through Smiths Falls about 4 P.M. Mother, John and Maggie there. Ottawa 6 P.M. Stopped an hour. Delayed at Joliette 7 hours by wreck.

7

Barriefield
June 26, 1916

Dear Father,

This is Sunday afternoon but it has not seemed like Sunday at all to me. We went to Church service in the morning and then started to pack up our outfit. Then we carried it all over into the YMCA tent and piled it up. Myself and six others were left to guard it so as I am off just now thought I better write a few lines. Will have no time in the morning as we are leaving here early. It is an awful job moving. Our tents are all down and away. I do not know where we will sleep to-night. We have our full outfit now and it is quite a load when it is all on.

We are going by the CNR I expect so will be going through Smiths Falls. I suppose you got my other letter telling John not to come here Monday. How is the land now? We had heavy rain last night. Have you had any word from Clara? I got time to attend a meeting here this afternoon. The speaker was Mr. Bingham and a fine one too. His text was Matt. 26. V36–46. He made those few verses seem all different to me. I hope there is a place like this down at Valcartier. Well I have not much news now but will write just as soon as I get to the new camp. Hope you all keep well and do not work too hard.

Yours lovingly,
Herb.

7A

Barriefield at Night

It presents most interesting sight. Entertaining description[8] of tented city after dark. It is a spectacle well worth seeing.

Did you ever visit Barriefield camp after dark? It presents one of the weirdest and most interesting of sights as the long stretches of canvas tents shine out of the darkness with the glow of a light in them. The average citizen while he may occasionally visit the camp during daylight to see how the "boys are fixed" while in training for the great struggle in France, very seldom bothers to come after darkness has set in, imagining that little or nothing can be seen.

It is a lonesome sight to pass along the road from the city to the camp grounds and see the men after the sun has retired for the day. All along the bridge, up the hill and along the dusty road may be seen the men trudging home in pairs or in small crowds, while at times one fellow walks alone. They keep to the grass along the road well out of the way of automobiles with their brilliant headlights, and walk quietly and orderly to their "home." Home in this case may be the third tent of the third platoon of some battalion, but out of the masses of tents he finds the right one.

The camp grounds themselves present the same peculiar appearance of resting after a hard day's work under the broiling sun. In the dim lights of the stars the outline of the peaks of the canvas homes may be seen in straight though hazily defined rows. Occasionally the line is abruptly broken by some marquee or bigger tent which seems out of place among the lines of the usual bell variety.

Though Barriefield is a city half as big as Kingston, there is as yet few, if any, lights which would justify the name of city being given to it during the evening or night hours. There is one light at the turn of the road into headquarters, and though others will come as soon as the engineers have finished their work, the only lights at present are those from the men's tents, as they read or talk until the buglers blow that last signal of "lights out"! It is a wonderful sight for those not acquainted with the camp life to see, and people would spend their time to advantage by taking an evening visit to this camp after darkness has come.

> *June 27:* CPR through Three Rivers. Marched through the city and got lost. Had to get a civilian to direct us to station again. Quebec is a nice country to travel through and we got the view of the famous St. Lawrence occasionally. Arrived in Quebec about 4 P.M. but cannot see much of the city from train. From here we had a double header out to Valcartier. Got off train about 1 mile out and the pack got real heavy before we reached camp. Arrived in camp 7:50 P.M. Took up camp in the lines lately occupied by the 94th Batt. which left for overseas the day before we arrived. Some tired tonight so slept well. This is a fine camp.
>
> *June 28:* Getting our own kits, tents and supplies placed.

8

Valcartier Camp
Quebec, June 28, 1916

Dear Mother,

Here I am in the largest military camp in Canada, about 20,000 men here. It is a much nicer place than Barriefield was, nice and clean and dry. The soil is red and does not stick. It is almost level and is surrounded by high wooded mountains. The St. Charles River flows just behind our lines. We got here last night about 6:30. We stopped

awhile at Ottawa that night, about 9:00 we crossed the Ottawa into
Quebec, reached a place called Jolliette at midnight and were delayed
by a wrecked freight train until 7 in the morning. Then they transferred
us to the C.P.R. and brought us by Three Rivers and Quebec City. We
had a parade in Three Rivers to straighten out our legs. It is a nice city.
We did not see much of Quebec but may get out there sometime. The
country through which we travelled this side of the Ottawa is mostly
pretty good farming land and thickly settled. The buildings are all
white washed and the houses low walled, steep roofed and wide eaved,
French of course. The boys had a great time shouting and waving to
the girls along the road. I suppose you got home all right that night.
It was a pleasant surprise for me when I saw you all there, had not
expected to see anyone. I must drop Clara a card. Have you had word
from her yet? I am getting a furlough and will be home about the
12th or if I could wait until the 15th it would be after pay day then.
I want Pa to send a request for me to get home, then I will have no
trouble getting the furlough. Just state in a letter to me that he wants
me home.[9] How much visiting are you doing? I hope you keep well
and go out a lot to help pass the time. The hay will be growing well
now. It is warm here to-day. All at present and write soon. Send me
a paper if you can. My address is the same as before only Valcartier
Camp, Quebec.

Your loving son,
Herb.

9

Valcartier Camp
June 29, 1916

Dear Sister,

By the address you will see that we are in Quebec now. Arrived
here Tuesday about 6:30 P.M. Left Kingston at 10 o'clock Mon. Came
by CNR by Smiths Falls, Ottawa, across by Lachute to Jolliette, Que.
Here we were delayed by a wreck, from 12 midnight until about 7 next
morning. Then we were transferred to the CPR and came by Three
Rivers and Quebec. So we saw a lot more country than we would
have coming straight through on the CNR. We had a parade at Three

Rivers to straighten our legs. It is a fine city. We did not see much of Quebec, only lower part of the city. What kind of a trip did you have and are you having a good time? How do you like the country? This place has Barriefield beaten six city blocks. There are about three miles of cement road, electric lights and good water. The soil is sandy and the water goes away and is dry in a short time. It is surrounded by high wooded mountains and the St. Charles River flows just behind our lines. There are about 30,000 men here and more coming every day. The YMCA is not as good here as at Barriefield and we are further from it. There is an open air picture show and unless we play ball, that is all the entertainment we have. I got two surprises the day we started for here. About ten minutes before we pulled out of Kingston who came along but Johnnie Brunton and Mr. Lowry. I sent word to John not to go on the excursion as we would be away. Only a few came. Then John, Mother, and Maggie were at Smiths Falls. Oscar brought them in his car. We stopped there about ten minutes. I expect to go home about the 10th of July. I have had an awful cold ever since I was home. I guess Balderson Festival did it. It is pretty hard to get a pass here but must try and get down to the city for a day. How long are you going to stay up there?

Willie's stayed that day till late in the afternoon. Was glad they stayed so long. Well this is all for now and hope you get it for I am guessing at the address. Mine is the same only Valcartier Camp, Quebec, instead of Barriefield.

Good Bye,
Herb

June 30: Ended 3rd month.

July 1: Reviewed by Sir Sam Hughes.

10

Balderson
July 1, 1916

Dear Herbert,

Your letter came yesterday morning, one from Mary Ellen Paul and one from Lester Gibson. Mother and I were to the S.S. convention yesterday at McDonalds Corners. Had a nice time got dinner and tea at John Barr's. I got the hollow field seeded all but about 3 ridges I will leave and the other field will not try to get seeded. It is too hard work for me and the ground is so hard now, now that it is dried up. Minor Haley has quite left some of his land.

We got a letter from Clara. She got up safely and was having a good time. I wrote and told her to take the good of her visit that we were getting along all right.

We had a letter from Maggie Ashcroft. She told us that Milton Stewart was killed in action. Word has come that Bob Paul is killed in action. That is two of our boys we know are gone.

They all got home safe from Smiths Falls. Mother was tired but none the worse.

We didn't go to the festival at Balderson. I was too tired. They had a good crowd. Mr. Rev. Ferguson was here yesterday morning. John traded his mare with Bob White for a rubber tired buggy and 88 dollars in cash. The buggy is here yet. John was here helping me to seed.

I am sending you a paper. This is all the news of any importance now. So be good and take care of yourself.

Love to you from,
Father and Mother

Well Herbert I want you home for two or three weeks for haying as it is out of the question to hire a man. They can't be got. You can come about the 12th but you can please yourself any time after the 15th. If you start about the 17th you would get here about the 18th. I think I start to cut on the 17th if all is well and the weather is good. Then I will have some ready to haul in by the time you get here.

Write soon again.

11

Valcartier
July 8, 1916

Dear Sister,

Received your letter this noon and glad to know that you landed all right and was having a good time. It seemed a long time before I got word from you but yet it is only two weeks past Thurs. since we left home. I have just got one letter from home yet. Pa and Ma had been to McDonald's Corners so they must be well. I have written all together, since I came here, about seven letters and fourteen postcards and as yet have only got three letters and one card. Don't get as much mail as I used to get at Barriefield.

We have not done much drilling yet. We are busy fixing up our camp. We will have a nice place when we get it finished. Thurs. the Hon. Sam Hughes was here reviewing the troops. It was a very hot morning and lots of men fell out of the ranks and were taken off the field in the Ambulance Wagons. The 130th showed up pretty well, for when we came by Sir Sam shouted "Well done Lanark and Renfrew." But no doubt he said something similar to the other battalions. We were inoculated last Monday and will be getting another dose about next Wed. My arm was not very sore. We got two days off. To-morrow night at 6 o-clock I go on guard. Have been very lucky, have never been on guard since before I was on furlough last May. I put in my application for a furlough to-day. I intend to go home on the 16th of July so will be just a day or two ahead of you. I expect the hay will be later this year and then I want to wait until after pay day which is on the 15th. I can leave here about 6 at night and be in Perth the next day at noon.

The dancers up there must take the full benefit of the occasion and of the strangers too. I did not think you knew so many. I suppose there are lots of nice girls too eh? We see a few down here but will soon have forgotten how to address one. Was talking to a Salvation Army girl the other day and almost said "Yes Sir" to her by force of habit in addressing officers.

Will drop another line before I leave here. It will come in two days. Give my best regards to all inquiries and love to yourself.

J. Herb. G.

July 2-11: Drill.

12

Balderson
July 11, 1916

Dear Herbert,

Your card to Mother came. Would of wrote yesterday but we were up to Middleville. Had dinner at Uncle John Mather and tea with Minnie. Was up to Lammermoor last week and to Johny Closses for strawberries, got the full of a biscuit can full. We bought $1.50 worth from Sergents. I mowed the hay around the house and will rake it up to-day. John was over and cultivated the potatoes with me. It is very warm now and everything is growing good. I may cut the alfa this week. Will you be home on the 18th? It will be lots of time. Timothy is in the first flourish. Bob Nairns got word that Bob Paul is a prisoner in Germany.

Had service at Playfairville on Sunday night. We had about seventy out. Some of them was asking about you. Edgar McKerracher is very

J.H. Gibson at the Valcartier training camp.

poorly, was in bed but was able to sit up yesterday. Mother says you are not to worry about her. She is getting along all right. I am in a hurry for I have a letter to write to Clara. It seems I can't mind what to write when in a hurry. I suppose Maggie wrote to you. Perhaps you have got all the news already. We got a card from Clara. She is having a good time. I don't know whether she will be home the end of this week or not. We will not ask her to come before her ticket is out.

All for this time.

Father

July 12: L.O.L. parade at night, perhaps 100 strong.

July 13: On guard for the first time since 4th May.

July 14: 130th went to the ranges for the first time and did poor shooting.

July 15: Pay day. P.M. off.

July 16: Rain. No church parade.

July 17–21: Bayonet fighting and musketry.

13

Balderson
July 20, 1916

Dear Sister,

Just a few lines this morning for I must be out to hay. It is very hot but fine hay weather and we are trying to finish this week. I came home last Sunday at 5:00 A.M. John and Pa had one field in and part of another one cut. I was a week longer of getting home than I expected on account of trouble getting a furlough. I did not get one after all but got a six day pass. It expires on the 28th at 6 A.M. but I am going to stay until Friday of next week anyway. I was disappointed when you were not home when I came for I expect this will be my last pass before going to England.[10] So if you stay the two weeks you spoke of I will not see you at all.

Mother finds this heat pretty hard on her but I guess she is not so lonesome this week.

All for now.

Herb

I have not been anywhere yet except to Dougal Hughes funeral last Sunday afternoon. He died very suddenly and they say it was some sort of brain trouble. I may go to town tonight.

J.H.G.

July 22: Going home on pass. Left camp at 1:30 P.M. Arrived Perth 2:20 A.M. Walked home.

July 23: Arrived at 5 A.M. and gave father and mother a surprise. Father went to McDonalds Crs. I went to D. Hughes funeral with Johns.

July 24–25: Cutting hay.

July 26: Went to town at night.

July 27–31: Haying. Clara came home from Powassan. 4th month.

Aug. 1: Finished haying.

Aug. 2: Mother and I went to Willie's A.M. Saw cattle and made a few calls.

Aug. 3: Went to Paul's in A.M. Home in evening and all Keays came.

Aug. 4: W. and G. Brunton came also C. McNicols.

Aug. 5: Willie, Gracie, Clara and I went to town and out to John's for tea.

Aug. 6: Went to church A.M. Left for Valcartier 2 P.M. Pa got J. Caver's car and all went also Johns, McNicol's, Brunton's and R. Keays were at station. E. Ferrier with me.

Aug. 7: Pulled into Quebec at 6:30. Had breakfast and went to see city. Plains of Abraham, Wolfe's monument and took snap of it. Explored forts, Dufferin Terrace, Chateau Frontenac and down the chute to docks. Saw my first ocean liner and was on big river boat. Had dinner and hit for camp, arriving about 4:30 P.M. Had supper and went to bed. Bed seemed hard after being away 16 nights but slept pretty well.

Aug. 8: Went to the ranges. Scored 157 points out of 190.

Aug. 9: Drilling.

Aug. 10: On guard.

Aug. 11: Drilling.

Aug. 12: Kit inspection.

Aug. 13: Church parade.

Aug. 14: On guard.

Aug. 15: Drilling.

Aug. 16: Big march past and inspection by His Royal Highness the Duke of Connaught.

Aug. 17: Pay day.

14

Valcartier
Aug. 17, 1916

Dear Mother,

This leaves me in camp again and although the time seemed short at home, it seems far more than two weeks since I left here. I do not know yet what I will get for staying over my pass. Will not know until to-morrow.

I was lucky to have E. Ferrier to travel with. He is a good sober fellow. I hope you people got home all right. I never thought of so many friends being at the station to see me off. It certainly was nice of them and I appreciated it.[11]

We got to Montreal about 7 P.M. and left at 12 P.M. Got to Quebec about 6:30 A.M. I slept most of the way from Montreal to Quebec. We could have got a train to camp at 7:10 A.M. but thought it would perhaps be the only chance we would have to see the city. So we went to the Khaki Club and got a cup of tea to eat with our lunch, left our parcels there and took a car to the Plains of Abraham. Saw where Wolfe was killed and the place where the British Army climbed the heights. Then we explored the Fort on Cape Diamond. It is a climb to the top but we made it. Counted 250 steps and I guess we went up about 350 on an elevator. Walked along Dufferin Terrace by the Chateau Frontenac. Next was the docks and was all through the largest boat I ever saw, also saw my first ocean boat—a freighter heading for Montreal.

The Parliament buildings are beautiful and there are countless monuments in different parts of the city. I took a snap of several. A lady from South Dakota took our pictures as we stood at the foot of Wolfes' monument and she took our names and will send us some of them. I put on Balderson so they will go to you for we are so uncertain of our address and it will perhaps be two months before the lady will have them finished.[12] We spent the forenoon easily and came back to the Club for dinner, caught a 1:45 P.M. train and reached camp at 3:30. Had still a snack left for supper, so I don't think I will tackle the army grub until to-morrow. They are just going to supper now.

Did it rain up there to-day. Rained quite a while this morning and it looks like more to-night.

Well, Mother, don't worry about me. I'll be alright. I have my little Testament here and although I used to read a chapter often I am going to study more now than ever.[13]

It will be a few days before I get any word from home and that means as many long days. Letters make the days about four days shorter. Good-bye for now and lots of love to you all.

Herb.

15

Balderson
Aug 10, 1916

Dear Herbert,

Your letter came yesterday. Glad you arrived safely and that you had a chum. I would like to see those sights you speak of, but I think by your letter that you are lonesome. Well we were back home in 25

The Bible that sustained J.H. Gibson throughout the war.

minutes from when we left Perth. I gave him 2 dollars for the trip, wasn't much. First time Grace was in a car. I went to Playfairville. Had a good crowd. Well Monday I went to John's. He had Bob Ferguson and young Briggs stacking and I raked. They finished the stack about 4 o'clock just in time for a big storm came on. Rained heavy for a long time. He has two small loads of red top out yet. It rained on Tuesday and some yesterday and is quite dull this morning. Lightning struck about Harper factory some what wrecked two or three phone poles on the sixth line.[14] I tried to get central 5 or six times and failed. We are told that it struck Bob Anderson's old house but they have not told us. We were all over at John's but there was nothing disturbed here. Since Monday I have done almost nothing but the chores. Mother and I were over at Johns yesterday picking cherries. While I am writing Ligh came for the spring toothed harrow. Mother and Grace are washing dishes and Clara is washing. John was over last night and Iva. Harvey McQue has come in to fix the phone. He is done and away. Ligh wants the big wagon to go with cheese.

Well it seems as if was at the end of my news.

John and Mrs. Watt was here Tuesday night and had a fine visit.

The rain will do a lot of good.

All for this time. Love and best wishes from us all to you. Mind and be good.

Father

Mother sends her thanks for that beautiful handkerchief. God be with you till we meet again.

16

Valcartier

Aug. 15, 1916

Dear Father,

I received your card and a letter from Maggie yesterday, so although I have not much news to write I can tell you at least that I am feeling fine and glad to know you are all the same. It is very dry here and when it is windy the sand blows in clouds, our faces are like as if we had been at the threshing mill all day, but there is lots of soft water and soap. The nights are pretty cold now but to-day we are issued with another blanket. That makes three blankets and one rubber sheet to each man and two men sleep to-gether. To-morrow we are to be reviewed by His Royal Highness the Duke of Connaught. He is supposed to be the greatest soldier in the Empire. All depends on the way we show up to-morrow whether we go overseas this fall or stay in Canada until next spring. If we do well we may go in a month or so. If not will probably be back to our towns for the winter. Don't tell anyone I said so, for it is only a surmise from the way things are working out. Well, I suppose the grain will be ready to cut now. Has Gracie gone home yet? Tell Clara to write next and give me all the well young peoples news.

Good bye and love to all.

Yours lovingly,

Herb

Aug. 18: On guard at the main station entrance to camp. Some place. Halting civilians and soldiers alike.

Aug. 19: Musketry A.M. Off P.M.

Aug. 20: Church parade.

Aug. 21: Medical examination.

Aug. 22–25: Drilling on the plateau and dinnered out.

Aug. 26: Orderly at 3rd Brigade Headquarters.

Aug. 27: Missed church parade on account of orderly work. Showery.

Aug. 28: Fine. Bayonet fighting and musketry. Rapid loading with charger.

Aug. 29: Fine. Route march to Valcartier village. Stopped for dinner on shore of Nelson River below village. Played games, wrestling, swimming while band supplied music. Started back at 4 P.M. Arrived 5 P.M. and went on guard.

Aug. 30: Very tired. Batt. went to ranges and took 6 of our guards away, making it harder for the rest. Cool and showery. Serg. Dack brought in eight prisoners.

Aug. 31: Went on sick parade. Put on light duty but too sick to do anything. Lay in tent all day. Battalion inspected on the plateau by Staff. Payed in afternoon. Five months on August 30th.

Sept. 1: Rain. Parade to bank to have cheques cashed. Can hardly believe that it is September. Wrote letters and read all afternoon.

Sept. 2: Cool. Physical drill and lecture A.M. Writing letters afternoon.

Sept. 3: Very cool. Church parade A.M. Called on L. Stewart 146th Batt. P.M.

Sept 4: Drill. Went out to ranges but rain came on at 11 so did not shoot. Went to a hay barn and slept in hay until it faired up about 3 P.M. and came home. Went to illustrated lecture at Y on London England.

Sept. 5: Went for route march to Valcartier village. Dinnered up on mountain side. Grand scenery from here. Nelson River winding through the valley, village, farm houses scattered about, cattle feeding, binders going, hills and dales and the tented city in distance and battery firing from opposite slope. Return to valley and halted by river for 3 hours, then home.

Sept. 6: Cool and cloudy. Drill on plateau. In command of section for first time and got along fairly well. Went to Post Office in evening for money order. Stopped at YMCA and wrote 2 letters. Got box of apples from John's. Oh how good they tasted.

Sept. 7: Warmer. Bayonet fighting at the school jumping platform and double, leaping trench long points to sand bags and short points and jabs to dummies. Heavy rain in the evening. Q.M.S. put under arrest for drunkeness. My impression is that whisky is spoiling this battalion.

Sept. 8: Very dull. Went to the Butts to mark. Home at noon and the rain poured down. Clothes inspection in afternoon.

Sept. 9: Beautiful fall day. Drilling A.M. To Y and show in P.M. Writing.

Sept. 10: Another fine day. Church parade A.M. Service in YMCA P.M. Went on guard at water taps at 9:30 P.M. Made fire in cook house and made toast. Snug place.

17

Valcartier
Sept 10, 1916

My Dear Mother,

This is a beautiful Sunday and we have just come back from church and it is 10:30. You people will be at church just now. I can see you all sitting there and Mr. Greig in the pulpit. We do not get much good of our church service, there are so many men and some have to be so far away that they can't hear. We are mostly at the rear. I am going down to the YMCA services this afternoon and night. There are always good speakers there on Sunday and every week night they have sing-songs, hymns and popular songs.

Have you been able to go to church lately? I see Father has been taking some services in different places. Hope you all keep well and don't worry about me. There is a big bunch going home on Pass to-day. Thomas Butler has got his at last. Wish I was going too but I had my turn and others must get theirs.

We have no word of going overseas yet. Of course we will have to go somewhere out of here before very long, but where we will go it is hard to say.

There was a Batt. left this morning—a construction Batt. and they had only been here six weeks.

Well, Mother, I have had my dinner which consisted of potatoes, beef, cabbage, tea, bread and butter. What do you think of it? We had oatmeal porridge for breakfast.

We had quite a lot of rain and was pretty cold sleeping, but the days are nice now again. I was not very well for a day or two but am fine again. The apples were a great treat—just finished them last night. Have you many at home this fall? You cannot keep anything like that long here for you must share up with your tent mates. Wouldn't I like to be tackling a big lemon or pumpkin pie now. I miss the pies and cakes on Sundays, but not so much other days. I suppose they will be starting to thresh soon, not much corn cutting this year eh! John is hashing again.[15] I wrote a letter to them the other day. Did you have a reading of it? I think I described a route march we had so will not write it again. I got vaccinated last week but I don't think it is going to work. We're all getting new clothes soon. Are you going to Perth fair? I hear they are having some of the 240th there.

Now Mother this is about all the news I have to write this time. I wish you could write to me. Am expecting a letter from Clara to-day with those pictures. Have you and Pa had them taken yet? Had a letter from Maggie and Mary Ellen last week. Must write to M.E. to-day. I often think of you last at night and first in the morning and Father too.

Good bye and lots of love to all.

Your loving son
Herb

P.S. Names are on the back of snaps.

Sept. 11: Still on guard to stop all washing. Batt. went to trenches. Off guard at noon and F. Armstrong and I went off up the river and slept all P.M.

Sept. 12: Fine. Rapid loading with charger. Route march to near Lorietteville in P.M. O.C. back from pass.

Sept. 13: Fine. Parade for vaccination but I did not get it. Hair cut A.M. P.M. camp sports day. All kinds of events. 130th band played. Bonfire, concert at night. Col. de Hertel chairman. Lots of fruit and cigarettes free.

Sept. 14: A.M. pay day. P.M. did a little extended order.

Sept. 15: Raining all day. Working in Sergeants Mess. This is kind of a night that makes a fellow think of home. Wet and getting colder.

Sept. 16: Fine. P.T. and B.F. Went to show in evening. Have been looking for word from home but getting none.

Sept. 17: Lovely day. Church parade. E. Ferrier, L. Munroe, J. Walters and I went to Communion Service in the YMCA.

Sept. 18: Went to trenches. Rained and came home. Went back afternoon.

Sept. 19: Cool. Started to learn bombing at bombing school.

Sept. 20: Cool. Fired our first live bomb.

Sept. 21: Fine. Packing up. Marched out at 5 P.M. CNR to Quebec, crossed ferry to Levis and boarded Intercolonial R. Supper consisted of 1 banana, 1 orange and 2 biscuits.

Sept. 22: Misty. Slept well. Breakfast 9 A.M. Country like Ontario through Quebec. In New Brunswick high mountains, beautiful scenery. Dinner 1 P.M. Marched through Campbellton. Lumbering country. Past Dalhousie Jct. which reminded me of my old home in Ontario. Along Restigouche River. Some nice farms. Band played at NewCastle. Lots of fun with girls at towns.

Sept. 23: Fine. Pulled into Halifax at 6:30 A.M. Stayed in train till 10:30. Marched to ICR Pier No. 2 and halted. Embarked on the S.S. Lapland at 11:30. White Star line. Got berth #951 in Section M. 6 P.M. cast off and steamed up the bay. Here we lay all night protected by three British Grey hounds.

18

Halifax
Sept. 23, 1916

Dear Sister,

Arrived here at 6 A.M. Are on board the train yet, have had breakfast and am feeling fine. It is very misty and can't see anything but box cars and railway tracks.

We left Valcartier in such a hurry that I did not get time to write. Got the socks just about five minutes before we marched out. Thanks. I mailed a parcel of old letters that I want you to put away for me and also a pennant that I would like you to send to Jane and keep the cushion top for yourself. Of course I could not leave this train to post them so gave them to a civilian to post. He may and he may not post them.

I don't know whether we will be allowed to post this or not but will try. Had a nice trip down through New Brunswick yesterday. Had a march in Campbellton. I think that is Mrs. Willis's home town at least that is where Douglas Craig enlisted. You might tell her about it, also that I saw Douglas a week ago but was not speaking to him. The 182nd was ready to leave but measles broke out and they could not go.

Had a letter from M.E. Drop her a card and tell them I am away for fear I don't get writing, also Willie's, and tell Willie's I got the apples. I suppose you will be lonesome there but bear up, I have great hopes of coming home again. I am trying to live the best life I can and am prepared to take whatever comes and if we should never meet here on earth we shall surely meet in Heaven, where there is no more parting.

(Ink is done) We don't know when we leave here but this letter won't leave Halifax for three days, I expect, so you will not get it till mid week. I will have a long letter ready to mail when we land. Address a letter to

Pte. J.H. Gibson No. 787167;
C Co. 130th C.E.F.
Army Post Office
London England.

Sept. 24: Sunday. Lovely day. Slept well. Had roll call and slept and read rest of time. Food is good and plenty of it.

Sept. 25: Fine. Still in bay. Roll call 10 A.M.

Sept. 26: Fine. 100 men of C. Co. on guard in ship. Guarded bridge. Cool.

Sept. 27: Lovely day. Steamed out of Halifax Harbour at 6 A.M. with 4 other transports guarded by British Cruiser. Came off guard at 10 A.M. Had a bath and washed clothes. Watched the shores of Canada fade away in the afternoon.

Sept. 28: Slept well. Headache and sick.

Sept. 29: Fine. Good and sick.

Sept. 30: Windy and by evening a heavy sea running. Rough night. Very sick.

18A (postcard)

S.S. Lapland
Sept. 30, 1916

Miss May Keays

This is the vessel we are aboard. Some little tub it is believe me. Have got lost a couple of times already. So long.

J.H.G.

Oct. 1: (Sunday) Calmer, no better. Tried to eat but nothing doing.

Oct. 2: Fine. No better.

Oct. 3: Fine.

Oct. 4: Fine.

Oct. 5: Fine. Woke up 5:30 A.M. to behold the shores of Ireland. Through the straits fine scenery. Fleet of destroyers met us. Saw mine sweepers at work.

Postcard from the TS *Lapland*, which transported J.H. Gibson to England.

19

S.S. Lapland
Oct. 5, 1916

Dear Father, Mother, Sisters and Brothers

Hope you get the notes I mailed before sailing and the parcel, but will start at the first and describe as well as I can our trip from Valcartier. On the 20th Sept. we started packing up to leave. 21st was a very busy day, packing our kits, striking tents and generally cleaning up the grounds. At 5 P.M. the fall in sounded so we strapped on our loads and at 5:15 marched to train. Pulled out at 6:30 for Quebec, crossed the St. Lawrence by ferry to Levis and boarded I.C.R. for Halifax.[16] Our supper consisted of one banana, one orange and some biscuits. At 9 P.M. we left Levis. Next morning was misty but cleared up towards noon. We stopped at Campbellton and had a route march to supple up our legs. The country is rough and mostly lumbering industry. For a long distance the road follows a river course through the Mts. and the scenery is grand. At Newcastle the band got off and played. Big crowd at station. Lots of girls and women shook us by the hand and gave us a smile and kind word. Next morning we pulled into Halifax and at 11 A.M. packed up again and embarked the S.S. Lapland, a fine two funnelled, twin screw liner, 685 ft. long, 54 ft. broad, electric lights, in fact a regular floating hotel. There is 40 ft. of her underwater and more above it. She has 18 boilers, smoke stacks as big as Hughes' silo, and the engines something like 20,000 horse power, with a speed of 18 knots per hour. Had dinner and spent the afternoon exploring the place and got lost several times. At 6 P.M. steamed out into the bay and anchored protected by three British cruisers. Sunday morning broke lovely and clear but didn't seem like Sabbath at all, no church to go to so read most all day. Monday was fine and nothing to do. Tuesday 100 of us were put on ship guard. My post was up at the bridge. In the afternoon two other transports anchored in the bay loaded with troops. Wed. morning at 6 A.M. the engines started to throb and as we swung around and steam out to sea I realize that I am leaving home and all that is dear to me. There are five troop ships and two scouting cruisers ahead and one with us. About 4 P.M. we saw the last bit of our dear Canada fade away. 28th fine but have headache and expect am in for sea sickness. Noon sees everything going out and nothing coming in. No appetite at

all. 29th lovely and calm but very sick. Nothing to be seen but water and
sky and the other vessels ploughing along in line. 30th getting windy
and by afternoon a heavy sea is running. Life boats are lowered to first
deck and every man wears his life belt. At 3 P.M. we had our first life
boat drill. Ours is No. 5 on the port side. A very rough night and very
sick. The propellers are directly underneath my cabin and they make a
noise like huge barrel churns and the steering gear like rolls of thunder.
I never spent such a night as this.[17] Mind you I thought often of my nice
quiet bed at home and knew how you were all thinking of me. My eyes
were too sore to read so I just repeated those old hymns "Jesus Lover of
My Soul" and "Nearer my God to Thee," also the 91st Psalm gave me
great comfort. Oct. 1 calmer but am still sick. 2nd calm, stayed in bed
all day. 3rd fine. Got up determined to eat some breakfast. Five days
without eating makes a fellow pretty weak. Got down a little porridge
and a little soup at noon, small bit of supper. Stayed on deck all day
and felt better. 4th not too bad but no appetite. Raining but calm. 5th
woke up to behold the shores of Ireland off to the south east. The coast
is rough but towards noon we came by several islands and the main
land is high and rocky at the beach but away up on the slope farms lie,
like so many green checker boards, while houses and winding roads
make it a lovely scene from the deck of liner. About 10 A.M. a fleet of
destroyers meet us. They are wonderful little boats for speed and circle
about the troop ships like a lot of young ducks. Saw the mine sweepers
at work. We will dock at Liverpool some time tonight so will finish this
at our destination.[18]

Oct. 6: Rainy. Docked at Liverpool. Boarded train for West Sandling, Kent.
Arrived 8 P.M. Dark and raining. Fair supper and slept well in tents.
Oct. 7: Showery. Inspection A.M. Roll call P.M.

West Sandling Camp
England. Oct. 7, 1916

Oct. 6. Docked at Liverpool at 8 A.M. Boarded trains at 10:30 and
arrived at this place about 8. It was dark and raining a little but we
had not far to walk. Our supper consisted of all we could eat of good
thick hot soup and bread, butter, tea, and jam. Had a good sleep and
breakfast after which we were examined by doctors. It is now 11:30
and I am as hungry as a bear. This is certainly a nice country, beautiful
bridges and roads, fields as level as lawns and everything clean and neat.

The trains are funny little coaches divided into five compartments, each holding eight, and you enter from the side. We passed through London and it is some place. Aircraft is quite a common thing here. We are to be transferred to the 12th Batt. here so this is the last you will hear of the 130th. It will be some time before you get this and I hope you won't be listening to those reports that we were all sunk. Am safe and well for which I am thankful. Will be getting new clothing here and a whole six day pass so I intend to take the good of it. Hope you are all well and don't forget me in your prayers. My address will be

No. 787167
Pte. J.H. Gibson
12th Reserve Batt. C.E.F.
West Sandling England

Would like if you would send a copy of this to either M.E. or Willies so that the one writing will do. Will write in a few days when we get settled. Saw Capt. Tom Caldwell today but have not had a chance to speak to him.[19]

Lots of love to you all.

J.H.G.

Oct. 8: Fine. Church parade for first time on English soil. This is a rather nice camp. YMCA and Sir John French's club afford nice accommodations to read and write. Like the country fine and the board is good. Expect to be drill to a finish here though.

Oct. 9: Muster parade and medical inspection. Passed O.K. and put into No. 4 Co. 12th Battalion.

Oct. 10: Drill in A.M. saluting by numbers. Issuing clothing.

Oct. 11: Fine. Had our last parade as the 130th Batt. with our own band and officers. Inspected by General Steele.

Oct. 12: Payed in A.M. Issuing clothing and passes. Took train for London at 8 P.M. Arrived Charing Cross about 10:30 and started hunting for Maple Leaf Club but finally landed at Union Jack Club, Waterloo Road. Got bed for 4p.

Oct. 13: Visited St. James, and Buckingham Palace, Westminster Abbey, Admiralty and Lower London. On the Strand at night. Slept at YMCA.

Oct. 14: Went out to Kings Cross and through Regents Park to Zoological Gardens. Spent all day here and back to Salvation Army to sleep.

Oct. 15: Fine weather. Stayed around YMCA in A.M. and went to Abbey to service with E. Ferrier.

Oct. 16: Visited Wax Works. Tower Bridge and Tower National Art Gallery. Strand in evening.

Oct. 17: Visited St. Pauls Cathedral service and saw the tombs of nations great men, Nelson, Wellington, Roberts, etc. etc. United Service Museum in P.M. Theatre at night. Took train from Charing Cross at 9:45. Arrived in camp at 1 A.M. Wet and cold.

Oct. 18: Bayonet fighting and musketry.

20

West Sandling Camp
Kent, Oct. 18, 1916
No. 4 Co. 12th Reserves

Dear Father, Mother, and all the rest of you,

I wonder just how you all are tonight? I am fine only a little tired, just got back from London this morning at 1 o'clock. Went up there on pass last Thurs night. Had a fine time seeing the sights. I did not go out to see Towers people. Will go there my next pass. My purse would not stand the train fare. Most of the 130th was on pass, so had lots of company. Stopped at the YMCA "hut" they call them. They have one at all the stations and central places in the city. These huts are built for the overseas men and provide beds for 8 cents per night and good meals for from 6 pence to a shilling. Also a recreation room and writing material free of charge. It is wonderful how they look after the soldiers. The Londoners all call us by "Hello Canada" or " 'ow are you Jack." I certainly was tired at night. Travelled from about 9 in the morning till 9 or 10 at night for five days and still I did not see all the places. Friday was to service in Westminster Abbey but on account of the service did not get looking at all the tombs and monuments. The organist there is Sir Frederick Bridge, a beautiful musician although 75 years old and the choir is simply grand. Went there on Sunday also to service. Parliament House is a wonderful building. If I had known I could have gone in and heard a debate on Sat. From the Abbey we crossed St. James Park to Buckingham Palace, the London home of the King. In front of the Palace is Queen Victoria's Monument. I cannot begin to describe all

these monuments but you can get the book of Queen Victoria's life
and look up the places I mention. St. James Palace next. Here I saw
the famous Foot Guards and heard the Coldstream Guards Band play.
From here up the Mall to the Admiralty with its wireless on top. Passing
through Admiralty Arch into Trafalgar Square in the center of which is
Nelson's Monument. Across the square is the Arts building containing
the full of its walls of the most magnificent paintings. Spent most of
Saturday in the Zoological Gardens, a sight worth crossing the ocean to
see—all kinds of living things from flies and bugs to elephants. Sunday
to the Abbey. Monday morning visited the Wax Works. All the Kings,
Queens and Statesman of the 19th to 20th century are here in wax
and uncountable relics. Afternoon went to Tower Bridge and London
Tower. This bridge is a beautiful piece of engineering. The Tower of
London has seen many murders as well as executions within its walls.
I stood in the little bedroom in which the two Princes were smothered
in the bed cloths. Sir Walter Raleigh's cell and walk is in the same
tower which is called the Bloody Tower. Next we climbed the White
Tower in which is kept the Crown Jewels of England. This is a sight to
dazzle your eyes. Next is the armouries containing all the weapons of
war from the stone axe to the modern machine guns. Guy Fox's[20] cell
is below this—only four feet square. Just back of this is the dungeon
about 30'x20' and the walls are of stone 14' thick. This is where the
rebels and such like were put. Saw the execution block and axe that
was used to behead several kings and the Jacobites. St. John's Chapel is
in one part and was the place of worship of the ancient Kings. Is used
every Sunday yet. Beauchamp Tower forms the fourth side of a large
courtyard in the centre of which is the spot where stood the scaffold on
which Queen Anne was executed.[21] Tuesday morning went to service in
St. Paul's Cathedral and this is the most wonderful piece of architecture
I ever saw. After the service we saw the tombs of Wellington, Nelson,
Roberts and all the great men of England. Afternoon I went to
the United Service Museum. Here are kept all the badges, jewels,
uniforms, swords of all the great generals and admirals. The skeletons
of Napoleon's favourite horse is here also his table, chairs, saddles and
uniforms. This is just a rough sketch of what I saw. Oh yes and I saw
one of the sledges Captain Scott took to the South Pole. You remember
about it. There is a fine monument to him and his comrades in
Westminster. In Whitehall I saw the famous Horse Guards. It certainly
was a grand five days but we are back to the war again so no more play

for a month or so at least. Rained last night so lots of mud and it is stickier than the Bathurst clay.[22]

Oct. 19–20: Cold nights. Bayonet fighting. Musketry and shooting at miniature ranges. Got webb outfit.

Oct. 21: Cold and clear. Musketry in A.M. P.M. getting blankets and equipment ready to go to ranges in morning.

Oct. 22: Fine. Sunday but never the less fell in at 7 A.M. in full marching order for the ranges. As we fired our rounds the church bells were ringing in the village of Hythe, which is on a lovely hill looking out on the English Channel. Ranges are on a great bed of pebbles on beach.

Oct. 23: Fine and warm. Shooting in A.M. Dinner at 2 P.M. Moved into huts and had shower bath and clean clothes. A pleasant change to be in huts. Three letters from home.

Oct. 24: Dull. Shooting A.M. Raining P.M. Got boots. Wrote home.

21

West Sandling Kent
Oct. 24, 1916

Dear Ones at Home,

Received your welcome letter last night just 19 days on the way, so don't wait for answers before writing. I have lost track of the times I have written to someone of you. You may or may not get them all. Was glad you got the box, thought perhaps the fellow might pocket the money and keep the box but he had been honest. We are busy at target practice, will be at it all week. March about two miles to the ranges leaving at 7 A.M. getting back to dinner about 2 P.M. and do not do much the rest of the day. It is a hilly road, one hill bigger than Fiddler's Hill, and we carry our full packs, rifles and bayonets so can sleep at night all right. The country here is as hilly as Lammermoor but no stones. Roads are all paved and cemented about 18' wide, no ditches or road allowances, hedges right along the track. No land wasted here. There are villages every two or three miles and every cottage is surrounded by the most beautiful hedges. I think of Mother, each new pattern of hedge I see. She is so fond of them. Just wish she could see them. Each cottage has its own name. Some of them are Elm Lea, The Road, The Croft, Ringlinglowe, Brockland and Hillhouse.

We are in huts now and are fine and snug at night. The grub is good but not enough of it. I buy some milk and cake at night. It helps me out some. Got a letter from Willie with a $20 money order in it—4lbs in English money and that is counted a big sum here. So you were at McDonald Corners Fair. Was Willie up to the cement house. I am sure you must have had a fine time. Jack Thoma has not signed up yet? And Mary is going to write. Hope Pa and Ma had a nice trip to Prospect. And where did Mr. Ferguson go? Wouldn't I have enjoyed myself at the Harper Fair and party. Yes I hope to be home for the anniversary next year. Well this will be all for this time. Will write Sunday again. Although you may get them all in a bunch they will be different dates. My prayer is that you are all well and don't fret about me. I'm fine.

Love to all.

Herb

One of the Lorimer boys came to see us Sunday. He is in the mechanical transport here. He is Johny's brother.

Oct. 25: Rain and wind in A.M. Went out to ranges but came home too windy to shoot. Route march to Hythe in P.M. Not much to eat these days. Wrote to May and Margaret.

Oct. 26: Fine. At the ranges in A.M. Had a visit from Matthew Currie. Gas helmet drill in P.M. Slice of bread and small piece of cheese for supper. Lots of kicking but whats use. Wrote to Jane and Ida.

Oct. 27: Wind and rain. Went to ranges but too windy to shoot so came home. Lecture on gas helmets. Wrote to Tow and Maggie.

Oct. 28: Wind and rain. Shooting. Got home early. Hut orderly, washing dishes. Spent evening in Salvation Army hut.

Oct. 29: Sunday. Wind and rain. Went to ranges but did not shoot. Spent evening in Salvation Army hut. Brigadier Deans S.A. preached text John 1:1-12.

Oct. 30: Wind and rain. Went to ranges, did not shoot. Home at 7:30. Route march P.M. So ended 7 months in the King's uniform.

Oct. 31: Fine. Shooting. Payed in P.M. J. Trail and I went to Sandgate to see J. Stewart in hospital. Halloween night, nothing doing.

Nov. 1: Fine. Finished our practice on ranges. P.M. off duty. 130th boys got tobacco. Sold mine for 3'6.

Nov. 2: Fine. Bayonet fighting A.M. Trench work P.M. Got my first sight of France from hill top. Also saw two submarines in channel.

Nov. 3: Showery. Bayonet fighting. Route march in P.M. Went around the hill by Etching Hill. Concert in St. Johns Club.

Nov. 4: Fair. Bomb throwing A.M. Got mattress P.M. Writing to Mary Ellen and J. Kmgora.

Nov. 5: Sunday. Rain and wind. Church parade. Wrote to father. At Salvation Army in evening.

22

West Sandling
Nov. 5, 1916
Sunday, 2:30 P.M.

Dear Father,

I guess it is time I wrote to you now, although have just got one letter from home that was written since we sailed. Have been looking for one every day but to-morrow will see us here a month so surely will get some mail soon. I had one from Balderson that was written on the 14th Sept. and addressed to Sandling.[23] Was wondering if you had written and they went astray. Hope you are all well as this leaves me fine. Was to Church Parade this morning but it was so windy we could not hear the sermon and since noon has started to rain. We are getting used to rain now for it rains a shower every day. Some days we do not do anything, never work in the rain here unless we happen to be on a route march and get caught in a shower. Have a route march of 6 or 7 miles two days a week, usually Mon. and Fri. afternoons. See some nice country and the roads are all paved. This part is full of Canadian Camps and Hospitals. Have not seen a British soldier yet except in London. Even the civilians are scarce here, all gone to fight. Saw the shores of France the other day from a hill top near the camp. Just 26 miles across the Channel and we can see the destroyers guarding the coast and the mine sweepers dotting the surface like flies on a table with an occasional submarine skimming along the surface. They are white or greyish rather, and you can see them a long piece when they are on the surface. On fine days there are dirigibles and aeroplanes sailing about all the time and at night great searchlights shoot beams of light across the sky, in search of aircraft. I have seen some great sights since leaving home, things and places I have often read about. I guess you know more of the war than I do. Only one cent papers come to camp and there is very little news in them. I wish I had told you to send me some home papers, supposing they are old, would be news to me. I spend most of my evenings in the Salvation Army Hut. They have singing and read a chapter and a short talk every night. Brigadier Deans was there two nights last week and I enjoyed the service. Then in Sir J. French's club the Chaplain has the boys sing a hymn and repeat the Lord's Prayer to-gether. The YMCA have a little Prayer Meeting also but it is farther away and I seldom go there. There is Communion Services in the Club every Sunday at 11 A.M. and 7 P.M. Must go tonight again.

Are you still taking the services at those stations?[24] Who is in Mr. Ferguson's place and where did he go? I used to think there was a lot of wickedness in our little corner but when you get out among men for seven months, home seems like a home of saints to me. It makes me cold to hear men take God's name in vain and the awful language they use. And what puzzles me is that scarcely one denies that there is a Saviour of men and a Heaven or Hell awaiting them after death and yet they will swear and drink and do all sort of wicked things. I know I am not perfect but have been able to keep free of all these evils, in fact the more I hear it the better it makes me. I read my testament all spare time and each morning and evening I ask God to take care of you all and keep me in the right way. I pray that you may all be spared until the time when this war will be over and we are back to dear old Canada again.

Is John hashing any or is he doing the plowing at home? Has he sold the cattle yet? Is Alex Park able to do his work this fall? I suppose Bob Anderson is still talking about the war. Tell him I was asking for him and intend to write him sometime. Well it is suppertime now and I have come to the end of my supply of news so will close for this time.

Hoping you are all well and don't work too hard. Do you have family worship about 9:30 every night? I waken every morning at 3 o'clock, that is just 9:30 at home, and my thoughts go back home like a flash. Don't worry about me, I'm alright. This is a wild night of wind and rain but we are snug with a good fire, mattress, and four blankets each.

Have nothing else to say to-night.

Love to all.

Herb

Nov. 6: Cool. Rain at night. Bombing. First draft from 130th called. Kit inspection 5:30 P.M. First month in England.

Nov. 7: Wind and rain. Filling trenches on hill. Very windy did not do much.

Nov. 8: Cool. Bombing in A.M. Kit and medical inspection in P.M. for draft.

Nov. 9: Fine. Called off draft. Did some bayonet fighting in A.M. Extended order P.M.

Nov. 10: Fine. Bomb throwing A.M. Route march in P.M.

Nov. 11: Saturday. Fine. Bombing in A.M. P.M. wrote to mother. No birthday cake this year.[25]

23

West Sandling
Nov. 11, 1916

My Dear Mother,

This is my birthday as no doubt you will not have forgotten, and I have all afternoon to myself, so will write to you. I have been looking for a letter from home for two weeks, but none has come. I can't understand what is the matter, for the one Maggie and Clara wrote on Oct. 5 came in 17 days. Had another from near home that was written on Oct. 14. It came in 14 days. All the rest of the lads are getting letters and I can't see how yours have gone astray. Tom Butler had one from his sister and it said that you people were all well when she wrote, so that was some consolation. However I trust you are all fine as this leaves me A1. You must take good care of yourselves and not do anything which will cause you to get a cold. I suppose the weather will be getting pretty wintry-like in the mornings by now. It is just like Sept. here. Well Mother if I was there to-day I would likely be away hunting. Have you had any partridge dinners? We get rabbit pie about twice a week and fish on Fridays. Had kippered herring for dinner yesterday. They are feeding us good now. Is John hunting any this fall? or is he too busy? How did the grain turn out and who is doing the plowing at Gibsons? I suppose things are much the same around there, everyone busy plowing. How's Alex Park now? Tom's letter says that his picture and mine are in the Expositer. Wonder how they got a hold of mine. I suppose the next place will be the Era. I may get a few taken here just for souvenirs. They are cheap here in Folkestone. I intended going down there this

afternoon but our Batt. is on C.B.[26] now on account of drafts, which are
to leave at almost an hours notice. There are three different drafts called
out of our old Batt. All to reinforce three different batts. at the front, so
we are sure getting divided up. I was on one but they took me off Thurs.
morning, I expect on account of my teeth. My plate is cracked, and will
have to get a new one.[27] Tom Butler was taken off too, for a rash on his
body, but all my other chums will be gone in a few days. It will be rather
lonesome without them, but this is a better place than the trenches. May
be here all winter now. I have been hoping to be in England for Xmas
among the holly and mistletoe. If I am I will get another pass and will
go to see Tow's brother. Would like to go to Scotland and will if I get a
long enough pass and visit those places we used to talk about. Some of
the lads went to Glasgow on a five day pass, but they could not have had
long to stay. So you don't need to worry. I won't be in the trenches for a
long time yet. And if you do see any Gibson's in the casualty list watch
the number, 787167 belongs to me only. There are lots of other Gibsons
here.[28] We finished our musketry last week and have been taking bomb
throwing. We also have been learning Gas and the use of the Gas
helmet. Had to shoot with them on. Every man has to learn how to
put them on quickly and breath in them before going to the front, then
each man gets two in case one gets damaged. They are proof against all
gases, when used properly. We had an eight mile route march yesterday
afternoon, in full marching order, that means carrying an outfit which
weighs 60 lbs. Do four miles an hour but am used to it now and I rather
like an afternoon tramping along these English roads. The band goes
and we mostly see a few girls along the way. The Lanark boys who are
in the Queens Ambulance Corps are here now. Darou, Legary, Young,
Scott, Forbes and some others. Alex MacDonald is in the corps but did
not come in that draft. Saw a Jackson from the hill last week. Clara and
I met him at T. Scotts. A Townsend left for Canada on Tuesday and
he said he would call on you when at Bells. Almost every day I meet
someone from around home, who are in other Batts.

Sunday 3:30 P.M.

You will be getting ready to go to church at 11 there, but I am
ahead of you, have been to church twice. Parade in the morning at 9
and when we came back I went to communion in the English Chapel
with Tom. There is no Pres.[29] to go to so will have to be an Anglican
while in the army.

Our fist draft left for France this morning and a new Batt. from Ontario came in. So after dinner we all had to move to a different hut to make room for them. They came across in the same boat as we did. It is almost supper time now so will close with a fond good bye.

Your loving son,
Herb
XXX one each for you.

If you send anything at Xmas put it in a tin box if possible. Am trusting the old saying of "no news is good news" is right.

Nov. 12: Misty. First draft from 130th left at 8 A.M. 168th Batt. came in at 2 A.M. Went to church parade at 9 A.M. and Communion at 11 A.M.

Nov. 13: Warm. Route march in P.M. by Mowingreen.

Nov. 14: Fine. Second draft left for France.

Nov. 15: Cool. P.T. and B.F. Route march around by Etching Hill. Concert in canteen.[30]

Nov. 16: Cool. P.T. and B.F. and musketry.

Nov. 17: Cold. Got impression for teeth.

Nov. 18: Snow and rain. Musketry in A.M. Went to Folkestone in P.M. Had photos taken. Went to show. Battle of Somme.

Nov. 19: Snow and rain. No church parade. Writing to all the family and sending cards to R. Anderson and C. Penman. Service in Club 7 P.M.

Nov. 20: Rain. P.T. B.F. and musketry in huts.

Nov. 21: Fine. P.T. B.F. and M in A.M. Went to dentist P.M. Down to Folkestone in evening with A. Tufts.

Nov. 22: Fine. Work at the trenches but did not do much. Swinging the lead.

Nov. 23: Raining. Went bombing in A.M. Got my new plate in afternoon. Got 2 letters from home and one from Mary Ellen. Wrote to Clara and May.

24

West Sandling
Nov. 23, 1916

My Dear Sister,

This is Thurs. 1:30 P.M. and I just got your letter dated Nov. 8th about an hour ago. It was welcome indeed for whether you sent any more or not this is only the second I have got from home. I can hardly think you only wrote me one in over a month.

I have to go to the dentist at 3 P.M. so I am just going to answer this right away. Glad to know you were all well when writing and you were better of your cold. I am fine, have not been sick once since landing here. Have not been weighed since I was at London. I sure had a fine visit there and may go up again this week end. It's only two hours ride on train. A fellow needs to go somewhere to relieve the monotony of camp life. I was down to Folkestone on Sat. afternoon and got some cards which I mailed to you on Mon. Hope you get them. Folkestone is a seaport of about 10,000 inhabitants and is about 20. min ride by train. We can go there without a pass. I felt pretty anxious about you all when it was so long between letters, but one hardly gets time to be lonesome. You must cheer up. Don't get down hearted, go out all you can. I am sure you have lots of friends to visit. Have you been to see Miss Flett yet? Did you go to the Harper Dance? Who got it up? So Ma and Pa were up to Middleville. Did they go and come in one day? And Aunty got up her courage to go west. Do you ever hear from Lena? I had a nice letter from Clara Penman last week and one from May, and that is the limit of my mail although I have written goodness knows how many. It won't do for little Harper be without a Red Cross society. They are like the YMCA's here, one in every hamlet. What are they sewing? I don't know what it is like in France for clothing, but we have more stuff than we can carry and all the very best. When an article wears out we take it to the Q.M.S.[31] and get a new article for it. Socks is the one thing that we can't get too many of. Of course a lot of this clothing may come from these societies and if it were not for them we might go short often. The grub if not in great variety is good and wholesome here. But I always go to the club at night and get a snack of milk and cake. It is a change from the army rations. Yesterday we were out at the trenches all day and our dinner consisted of Sea biscuits, canned beef and water. Regulation army food and the biscuits are as hard as chips. You need to soak them about 15 min. and they swell up like peas. but you bet I did not eat them nor won't until I have to. I got some bread sandwich and cake in the morning and made out a good dinner.

Did Elsie say anything about writing to me? How long did Block stay? I heard he was down. Who is Roy rushing this fall and what are Morris' boys doing? Is Jim Cavers and Spalding home yet? Tom Butler got a *Courier* but there was not much news in it. How did Walkers' and my account of the trip over correspond?[32]

I suppose the 240th made some stir when they marched through. You fed them at Balderson. Why did they have to march from Lanark to Perth on Sunday? Those boys will think they are soldiering, but wait till they get here. This is where you soldier. The work is not any harder but you have to keep clean and walk straight. I have no trouble getting along though. If a man does what is right he never gets into trouble. Lots don't try to do the straight thing so they get anywhere from 3 to 28 days punishment. So it pays to act the part.

Well the 130th is badly divided now. About 2/3 of them have gone to France. Tom Butler, W. Andison, W. Jackson, are the only chums I have left. J. McVeety, J. Scott, and a few more are here but I never chummed with them. I expect we will be here for some time. Hope to spend Xmas here anyway. Every man gets a six day pass and free transportation. I am going to Scotland on mine. Have just been up to the dentist and got my new plate and now it feels like a whole mouthful compared with my old ones. However the boys say they look better and then they are good and tight. Won't fall out like the old ones did.

Well Clara this is all the news I can think of now. There is so little to write about you know every day is much the same. I have not done one days work in the last week though attending the dentist and loafing around. We only work 2 hours a day now. It is dark at 4:30. go to bed at 8:30 and get up at 6. I wrote to Father on the 5th and Mother on the 11th so will not put any for them this time. Will try and write you all in turn. I am trying to keep myself pure and don't forget that all good things we get comes from above. When things go hard I remember the Giver of all things and trust that all will turn out well. It is my prayer too that we will all meet again, will never give up hopes of returning to the dear ones at the old place.

Write often even if it is only a card and be sure to state the date the last one you received was written. Then I will know if you get them all and I will do the same.

Love to all.

Herb

Hello—I just had this letter sealed when the mailman came in to-night and said I was wanted at the Post Office. So went over and got a letter from Pa dated Oct. 26th. You see Jack Gibson went to Crowborough in a mining section and they sent my mail to him and kept his for me so this accounts for the delay in my mail. This one had a trip to France also. Give these cards to John's family. Will write them next. Got a nice long letter from M.E. to-night.

Dear Mother,

I am glad to know that you do not worry yourself about me so as
not to sleep a night. I was pleased to hear you were able to visit and go
to some fairs. Take good care of yourselves and I will do the same and
we will all trust God to bring us safe through. The sickness on board did
me no harm.

Good night

XXXXXXXXX

Nov. 24: Rainy. Drill in huts. Half of 4th Co. quarantined for the mumps.

Nov. 25: Rain. Sick. On light duty.

Nov. 26: Cool. Service in French Club.

Nov. 27: Cool. Entrenching on Talfords Hill. Zeppelin raid. Two captured.

Nov. 28: Cool and clear. Entrenching. Wrote to John's. Got box from I.O.D.E. Perth.

Nov. 29: Fine. Entrenching.

Nov. 30: P.T. and B.F. Route march by Westenhanger in afternoon. Eight months.

Dec. 1: (Friday) Cool. P.T. and B.F. Musketry. Gas and squad drill. Warned for draft.

25

West Sandling
Dec. 1, 1916

My Dear Mother,

To-morrow is your birthday and I got this post card to send you as it
expresses my feelings every day and more especially on Dec. 2nd.[33] The
cigarette does not fit me at all but you can imagine it is my testament
instead. I do hope you will be able to enjoy this birthday and many
more. I can hardly realize that it is Dec.—eight months almost since
I left home and over 8 since I enlisted. It certainly takes a long time
to train a man into a soldier, for just to-day I am classed as a trained
soldier. That is here, and after the troops are sent to France they get two
months more training, so I won't be in the trenches until near spring,
at least until the cold days are past.[34] I have nothing to say about camp

life. It is just the same as usual. I am well and am thankful for it and I know who is the Giver of all these gifts. Every time I see a man drunk, smoking, chewing or using profane language (and believe me that is not seldom) I can thank God for keeping me from the temptation. And these are not all. You would be surprised if I told you how many men of the Canadian Army are in the hospital today with venereal disease. Men who have come over here healthy and strong have been ruined with that loathsome thing. Yes and lots of married men with wives and families at home. I used to hear of wives in Canada not getting their separation allowance, but 9 cases out of 10 this is the cause, for when a man goes to the hospital with that disease his pay is cut down to 20 cents per day for the duration of the war. And then the wife and kiddies suffer. I am sure a man would be better to fall in battle than fall into that disgraceful condition.

My mail is coming all right now. Have heard from all but those in the west. Got one from Ethel Watt and P. McNicol today. Tom Butler and I are sending a parcel home, so you can watch for it. Did Clara get the one we sent before? This one is in John's name. Tom's articles are mentioned on a slip inside and the rest are mine. John may be able to wear the pants and either John or Pa can have the boots. I expect John will be the only one they will fit. They are no use to me and were too good to give away so Tom and I thought we would send the lot home. Clara knows what to do with the letters and put the badges with the others I sent home. The two rings are made out of German shell fired in the Great War and are for John and Willie. I would like to have got their initials put on them but had not a chance but perhaps they can get it done themselves. They are different sizes and I hope will fit them, likely their fingers are different sizes too. Anyway the rings can be worn on any finger. You will find them in one of the boots. I intended getting some souvenirs of London to send home but neglected it when there. When I come home I'll bring lots of things. You see I have never given up hope of getting back to tell my experiences and I don't want you to give up either.[35] Won't it be grand to be back there again. But Mother I'm not afraid to die, if such is my fate to be fatally wounded. I know that we shall all meet across the river, where there is no more war, or sin or parting. Trusting this finds you all well and enjoying yourselves to the best.

Your loving son,
Herb

P.S. If you send socks don't send more than two pair at once and say you might send me some pink pills and some good cough drops. Sometimes they come in handy. Oh and some OXO cubes.

Good night.

Dec. 2: Cool. Kit inspection. Cleaning equipment and writing in P.M. Mother's birthday.

Dec. 3: Fog. Service by Rev. Capt. Taylor in YMCA at 10 A.M. Three court marshals read at 11 A.M. each for desertion. Penalty 9 months imprisonment. Dinner and supper in Salvation Army hut.

Dec. 4:

Dec. 5: Fog. Left Sandling at 11 A.M. for France. Never was so sick in my life.

Dec. 6: Landed and marched to base camp. Had medical inspection and more equipment.

Dec. 7: Fine. Roll calls and more equipment.

J.H. Gibson in uniform.

26

Somewhere in France
[Base]³⁶
3:20 P.M. Dec. 7, 1916

Dear Ones at Home,

I am sitting here on a pile of blankets _____ well in France is all I can say even if I could tell you the exact spot it would not be much use to you. We left Sandling Dec. 5th and landed safely here. Am feeling good and that is everything in this country. Won't be in this place long, this is just a rest camp. Tom Butler was with me up to yesterday but had to go to the hospital last night some rash on his body. I got Pa's card dated Nov. 18 but did not get the letter or box he spoke of but it will likely be at Batt. headquarters when we get there. We are going to reinforce the 75th.

I hope Mother is better again and you are all enjoying the Xmas season. Is the sleighing good? The weather is very mild here at present. There is such a commotion around here that I can scarcely collect my thoughts to write. A bunch is putting up tents, others have just come off parade and are looking for their blankets, which I suppose some one else has taken. I often wish you could see some of the scenes and wonder what you would think of them. Say which letter of mine was in the Era and who gave it to the Editor? Send it to me if you can get another copy somewhere. Don't worry about me, everything will be not as we will be done but as God will see fit.

Love to all.
Herb

address: No. 787167
75th Batt.
Canadian Contingent
B.E.F.
Army Post Office
London England

Dec. 8: Foggy. Going up the line.

Dec. 9: Arrived and went into billets in stable. Joined the 75th Battalion at Bajus. Saw H. and W. Knowles in town next to Bajus.

Dec. 10: Inspection. Wrote to Clara.

27

France
[Bajus]
Dec. 10, 1916

Dear Sister,

This is Sunday night and we are lying in billets where the Batt. is resting. I am fine, although somewhat stiff after two or three pretty stiff marches. The weather is dull and rainy as usual and the roads are quite muddy but not deep. Our billets are comfortable enough. There are about 20 of us in a stable 15 X 30. We have three blankets to every two men and two fires going, in fire places which we built of old bricks. Jack Scott and I are lying side by side on a rubber sheet with a wax candle between us. There is only about a dozen of us from the old Batt. together. Tom Butler is at the base also W. Andison. This is a very good farming country. The farmers all seem to live in the villages which are close together. Their buildings are very old fashioned and mostly brick. Each house has its court yard and the stables are on the opposite side of the yard from the house. Just across the road is a church that seems to me to be about 4 centuries old and every mile or so along the road is a crucifix or a shrine, showing that the people at one time or another have been very religious. We walk about a mile to our meals and last night as we made our first trip down the road I noticed one in a small clump of trees at the road side. I don't think I ever had anything bring home to me more clearly and strongly how weak and helpless we are and what we would have been if that same Dear Saviour whose image hung upon that cross had not suffered and died for us. This morning when I wakened these words were in my thoughts "Saul, Saul, why persecute thou me?" and I have been thinking about it all day. Sundays are not like Sundays in the army though and more so on this side of the water. I often think of you all and wonder what you are doing. I can look almost to where you are but you can't look to me but I know you are all praying for me and that is worth more than I can tell. Don't worry about me just take it for granted that I am well. And be sure to write often and when you don't get any from me don't think that I'm not able to write but rather that I have not the time. The days are short now and we come in tired out usually and have not always got candles or paper. This is some

I brought from England with me. Will you write to Willie and Joe's when you get this and I will not need to write them. We sure have some interesting times with these French people. Last night I went out to buy a candle and I'll bet you would have laughed to see me try to make the bargain. Just now the old Madame came in and raised Hail Columbia about the fire we had, said we would burn the barn and I guess we will have to pay for the wood.[37] The wood is done up in faggots and she wants a penny each for them. They are well worth it too. I wish now I had learned more French. I think there is some mail for us here tomorrow so I may get your parcel at least I hope so.

All for now.
Love to all, Herb.

75th Batt. Canadians B.E.F.
Army Post Office
London, Eng.

Dec. 11: Fair. Changed billets. In barn. Bed on top of a threshing mill.
Dec. 12: Snow. Forming fours.
Dec. 13: Fair. Route march.
Dec. 14: Dull and cool. Got respirators. Saw Hugh and Willie Knowles.
Dec. 15: Dull. Instruction on gas at school. Wrote to father.

28

Somewhere In France
[Bajus]
Dec. 15, 1916

Dear Father,

I have just received your card dated Nov. 22 and glad to know you are all well. I am the same as usual with the exception of a slight cold. The weather is very damp here and of course there is all kinds of mud. Am in different billets from I told you of in my last letter. We are in a barn now and another fellow and me are sleeping on top of a thrashing mill.[38] Lots of fresh air and blankets but no fire to dry our socks. We do not drill a great deal. Marched about 20 miles one afternoon for a bath and change of underwear. To-day we were to the gas school. Was out for one route march this week. The roads are good in this country, something like the Town Line at home. Glad to know that you have lots of pork and wood anyway for the winter. My wouldn't I relish a nice piece of fried pork and mashed potatoes, a piece of mother's bread and Clara's ginger cakes and a piece of Maggie's layer cake or lemon pie to finish up with.[39] But I can't complain yet as I have not had to live on biscuits yet. Glad to have Mr. Greig's prayers and best wishes, but am somewhat surprised to know that my name is at the top of the honour roll.[40] What is it like? And Mr. Ferguson went west. Who is preaching there now? Do you not find the Playfairville circuit pretty heavy?

How is Charlie and Tommy looking?[41] I saw Hughie and Willie Knowles last night.[42] They are billeted quite near here. Were very much surprised to see me. I found out quite by accident where they were and looked them up. Hughie looks fine but Willie is rather thin. They have seen a lot of heavy fighting but came through without a scratch. It is a great thing to meet old neighbours in this country, all old grudges are forgotten and they seem more like brothers than neighbours.

I am sure Willie's will be proud of their son. Hope they are both well.

John is still doing a little hashing. I suppose he is as busy as ever.

Well Father I am in rather good spirits tonight after hearing from you and three other nice long letters from dear Ontario. But for want of something to write I will have to cut this short. I am going off on some bombing course in the morning so will have to get to sleep and get up early. My bedfellow is busy shaving here beside me. He is on his knees to see into the glass. I will have to do likewise for I did not shave this morning.

Good night and love to all. Hope you all keep well and take good care of yourselves. The Lord will keep us all and bring us safely through to the better world beyond.

Your loving son,
Herb

Dec. 16: Dull and cool. Bombing.
Dec. 17: Raw. Church parade. Sham battle.

29

Somewhere in France
[Bajus]
Dec. 17, 1916

Dear May,

Your two letters dated 14th and 19th Nov. reached me Dec. 14
at the same time and needless to say were most welcome. I got one
from Father and one from J. Spalding also, so got quite a news paper. I
hardly expected getting mail here so soon, but I guess they made good
connections. Rather better than the one containing the maple leaves
and a couple more which I know went astray. I must thank you now for
that parcel, although I have not received it yet. Clara sent one about the
same time so bye and bye I will be living like a King. There are tons of
parcels at Xmas time so I must be patient until mine gets through.

Well May this is what they call "Sunny France" although old Sol
does not show himself as often as I would like, about one day a week.
It is quite ready to rain at any minute of the day, and consequently the
mud is in every nook and corner and not seldom it finds its way into a
fellows mess tin, sharps ones teeth and gives flavour to bully beef and
hard tack. (Over, paper is scarce). I bet you would laugh if you saw
me now. I am rolled in my blankets, in what I call my trundle bed. It is
perched on the top of a threshing mill which is on the threshing floor of
a barn. Quite an honoured position, you see I can look down on my pals.
The first billets we struck here was what had been a cow stable, some
what more comfortable than our present place of abode, for we had two
fires going in the place, but here we cannot have a fire. Lots of fresh air
is good for a fellow though and we are getting it in large quantities. I can
hear the rumble of our guns but can hardly realize that it is the sound of
guns engaged in the world's greatest war. I have some idea when we will
be in the trenches. Carrying on with practically the same work as usual.
Marched twenty miles one afternoon, for a hot bath, some walk, but it
was worth the trouble. The roads here are something like the Town Line
at home.[43] Tom Butler and W. Andison were put in the hospital at the
base. Tom had some sort of rash and Bill a boil on his neck. Was sorry
to leave them behind, but they may join us soon. Roy Wilson came up

last week. Altogether there are only about 6 or 8 of the Perth boys in this Batt. There are several others of the 130th but from other places. It is impossible to keep track of them all here and you never know who you are going to meet. Some of the old 80th are in our Batt. and I inquired of one of them if he knew where Knowles boys were. Sure, he says, they are both in the _____ Batt. billeted in the next town. Well I just took a little walk (about 1 mile) and found them both. They got quite a surprise and not a little pleased. Hughie is fat, but Willie is rather thin. They have seen a lot of heavy fighting. You may imagine how glad I was to have a chat with old neighbours of the Eighth Line.

Now May that's all the French news for this time so I'll write some thing else. You want me to say what I think of your venture.[44] In plain English I think you are a real brick, excuse the term but it is the best I can think of just now. It may be harder on the nerves for a time than sewing but then the honour of the position is not to be forgotten. Of course I know it was not glory you were after, but other people see those things. Now I am not despising the dress maker at all, but I am sure it must have its own worries. Then dressmakers usually remain single and plod along sewing other peoples fancies. I hope to see you in the tellers box by the time I walk the streets of Perth again. My mate is ready to turn in so I will ring off. Have my boots to grease yet. Will write at the first opportunity.

Yours, Herb

Best wishes to Laura.[45] Will write later.

Monday morning

Dear May—have a few minutes to spare this morning so will try to write another page. Blue Monday we used to call it at school and it is much the same at this job. How does it affect you? At home I used to think if I did not get a good days work done on Monday, I had lost half the week, but now it seems hard to get the week started. Then it is getting so near Xmas, it makes a fellow think. I never was away from home at Xmas, but this one I expect to spend in the trenches. We may go "up the line," as they call it here, in a few days. However it will be something to say that we spent one in the trenches. I am learning to parlez-vous Francais. I may be able to make myself understood if I am here another year. These people speak very little English, in fact only what they have picked up from soldiers, not much like French Canadians. We have great fun sometimes with the kids. Dinner over so will finish this. I forgot to tell you that I am a bomber now. You know, (at least I think I told you) that I took part of a bombing course at Valcartier. Did some in England also but now am up against the real thing. Bombing has become a very important part of trench warfare. It is exciting but at the same time very dangerous. Perhaps you have read in the papers about it. I sure would be very grateful to you for sending some stories. There is not much time to read here but I expect there will be many hours of long, weary waiting in the front line. Some note paper also, it is almost impossible to get here. I brought this from England but it is almost done.

Now May, I hope you like your new job better each day. I am sure you will make good at it. And stop thinking of not enjoying yourselves on account of us, would be doing the same if I were there, so some one must have my share of the sport. True enough, there is no milk at the front except condensed stuff all the time.

Herb

Dec. 18: Cool and snow. Carry on.

Dec. 19: Cool. Kit inspection.

Dec. 20: Fine. Going up the line. Saw first battle in the air.

Dec. 21: Fine. Left last billets for front line. Into trenches. Took over from 13th Battalion.

Dec. 22: First day in the trenches. Very quiet. Took over from 13th Battalion. Move to Artois Sector.

Dec. 23: Second day. Some shelling.

Dec. 24: In trenches. Relieved at 5 P.M. by 12th Battalion. Back to supports in Music Hall.[46]

Dec. 25: Spent Christmas looking mail and rations. Got lost. Arrived home at 3 P.M. and had first meal for last 24 hours.

Dec. 26: Working party. Went with officers but got lost again. Major gave us Xmas cake and a box.

Dec. 27: Fine. Back to Reserves Berthonaval Woods. Working party got to front line in at 5 A.M.

Dec. 28: Fair. Nothing much doing. Working party at night.

Dec. 29: Slept forenoon. Rain at night. Flooded our dugout.

Dec. 30: Fine. Built new dugout. Working party at night.

Dec. 31: Rainy.

Notes

1   Herb had been in the 42nd Lanark and Renfrew militia for some years and was keenly interested in the military and in history. This must have been a terribly hard letter for him. His parents were only 68 years old, but their health was poor and they were counting on him to stay with them. His mother suffered from chronic bronchitis. It is interesting to note that the first letter is signed "lovingly, Father," but the second is not.

2   "Discing" refers to the breaking-up of the soil and sod following plowing.

3   His family did not go to Barriefield, Ontario, to see Herb off. Melville Paul was a soldier friend from Lanark who was killed in action in April 1918. Willie Andison, from Carleton Place, survived the war and married an English war bride.

4   R.E. Keays is Roy, brother of May Keays.

5   Farmers had to allocate a certain number of days toward road labour. Here, Herb is reminding his father to count the one-and-a-half days he had put in during the previous winter.

6   May was not at this reception for Herb because that same evening she and Tom Butler were at a reception for Jim McVeety. Jim was very young (17 years) and a band member, and didn't expect to see action. Both McVeety and Butler were killed in action.

7   The initials in "K & P Railway" referred to Kingston and Pembroke.

8   Herb likely clipped this description from a Kingston newspaper and included it in his letter.

9   Here, Herb is asking that his father write him so that he can request a furlough.

10   Clara did come home before Herb left. Herb left Valcartier camp at 1:30 p.m., arrived in Perth at 2:20 a.m., and then walked to Harper, arriving at home at 5:00 a.m.

11   His father did see him off this time.

12   The lady did, in fact, send the pictures from Quebec City.

13   Herb carried this little Testament throughout the war.

14   "Red top" is clover. The Harper factory was a cheese factory.

15   John, Herb's brother, had a small store in Harper, Ontario, where he did "hashing" for the farmers. They would bring their grain to his mill, with which he would turn the grain into hash for cattle.

16   I.C.R. stands for Intercolonial Railway.

17   The trip across would not have been very pleasant in October, as the North Atlantic would have been very stormy.

18   There were two very interesting letters about the crossing in the *Perth Courier*. One, by Garnet King, dated November 10, 1916, was titled "Valcartier to Sandling." The other, by Murray Walker, dated October 27, 1916, was titled "130th Trip Overseas." A later, likewise interesting letter by Pte. Walker was published September 13, 1918. Like Jim McVeety, Walker was very young and

a band member. They were together in England until April 1918, and were then sent to France. In the letter, he says he saw J. McVeety shortly before he was killed in August 1918. Pte. Walker came home.

19 Tom Caldwell's family owned Caldwell Mills in Lanark, Ontario. He came home from France.

20 By "Guy Fox," Herb means Guy Fawkes, one of a group of English Catholic conspirators who planned the failed Gunpowder Plot of 1605.

21 The Queen Anne beheaded in the Tower was Anne Boleyn, second wife of Henry VIII.

22 This letter seems incomplete, as it is not signed off.

23 The "letter from Balderson" was likely from May, who wrote at least every two weeks and sent a parcel each month.

24 "Services at those stations": Herb's father was an itinerant preacher during the winter months and preached at a number of small villages across the province.

25 This (November 11) would have been his 27th birthday.

26 C.B. = confined to barracks.

27 Herb had a bridge (plate) made to replace his front teeth, which he'd lost while still in his teens when he was kicked by a horse at Lammermoor. He drew logs from the bush for his brother Willie after he left high school.

28 The tone in the letters is getting more serious, as he knows he will leave soon.

29 "Pres." is short for Presbyterian.

30 "P.T." = physical training. "B.F." = bayonet fighting.

31 Q.M.S. = quartermaster stores.

32 Walker's "account of the trip" refers to Walker's October 27, 1916 letter, which was published in the *Perth Courier* (see n. 18).

33 The card he speaks of has this verse:
    To my Mother
    To-day more than ever I'm thinking of you
    With all my heart's yearnings sincere
    Just patiently waiting the time to return
    Just longing again to be near.

34 He knows he will be going to France soon.

35 He speaks of "getting back to tell my experiences." In actual fact, however, Herb spoke very little of the war after his return. See letter 122.

36 Herb arrived at "Base" on December 6, 1916.
    Letters from France were censored, but by using his diaries we were able to determine his location at various points, and have added these to the letterheads in square brackets.

37 Another soldier in the barn was Craig Greer. They would have been in the same platoon.

38 His partner above the threshing mill was Craig Greer (see n. 37, above).

39 Ginger cakes or cookies were one of his favourites. See letter 68a.

40   The honour roll must be in the Balderson United Church. At the time, however, it was Presbyterian.

41   Charlie and Tommy were Herb's horses.

42   Hughie and Willie Knowles were both killed in action. They lived opposite Herb on the Eighth Line.

43   May had been living with her Aunt Charlotte Paul, in Perth, and was learning to be a dressmaker at Shaw's store when she applied to the Bank of Ottawa (which later became the Bank of Nova Scotia).

44   Laura was one of May's sisters. Iris (Laura Iris) was named after her.

45   The "Town Line" would be the Lanark-to-Perth road.

46   *Music Hall* was the name of a particular trench.

1917

Jan. 1: Fine. Working party in A.M. and at night. Hard tack for New Year's dinner.

Jan. 2: Fine. Up to front line again. Relieved 102th Battalion. Working at night. No dugout to sleep or eat in.

Jan. 3: Fine. Went for water. Heavy artillery fire. Hit by piece of shell in back. Went into tunnel until Fritz stopped shelling.

Jan. 4: Rainy. On sentry at corner of Snargate and Central Ave.

Jan. 5: Fine. Heavy bombardment of artillery trench mortars. Still on sentry.

Jan. 6: Fine. Went to tunnel to sleep and stayed until next morning. The mud is terrible. Eat and sleep in this open trench.

Jan. 7: Snow and rain. Listening post.

Jan. 8: Relieved by 87th. Came out to billets and Camblain L'Abbe.

Jan. 9: Dull and cold. Resting and cleaning up. Everything covered with mud.

30

France
[Camblain-l'Abbé]
Jan. 9, 1917

Dear Ones at Home,

I expect you will have been looking for this for some time. Dec. the 21st was the last time I wrote you. We have been in the trenches ever since and had no opportunity or paper to write. We came out yesterday for a rest, and once more I am sitting in a YMCA at a table writing. I am feeling fine and can eat anything they put before me and can sleep anywhere. You should have seen me when I reached here last night. Tired, hungry, mud from head to foot, had not been washed or shaved but twice in three weeks. Spent today cleaning up and I am not half through yet. Tomorrow we get a hot bath and clean underwear. And we sure need it. I can feel the sand almost in my bones. I have not been troubled with catarrh at all, wonderful isn't it, considering the place I have slept in. My feet do not trouble me either. The livestock are more trouble than enough though.[1]

I got Clara's letter and one from Maggie with Xmas card about the 3rd but I have not got the box yet. I hardly expect to get it now. There are so many go astray and if they get broken that is generally as far as they go.[2] I have been very lucky though in the way of Xmas cake. Was sent to help carry our Chaplain's kit, the day after Xmas and he gave us two boxes between five also two nice pieces of cake. Then we had our ration of plum pudding which was about 2 inches square and 1/2 inch thick. Tonight every man got a little parcel from Toronto. Each contained a pipe, tobacco, cigarettes, chocolate, gum and a handkerchief. Xmas day they started a bunch of us for mail before breakfast and we got lost. The result was we did not get back until 3 P.M. Some Xmas, eh! On New Years Day I worked from 8 A.M. till 2 P.M. and from 6 P.M. to 1 the next morning. Some New Year too and the regular army ration for dinner. How did you all spend yours? In the same way as we used to I hope. What kind of weather had you? It was fair here and the heavy guns just boomed enough to let us know that the war was still going on. This is what they call a quiet front. In day time there is little else than artillery fire, but night brings snipers and machine gun fire. The machine guns ripping off about 100 or 200 shots at once, reminds me of a bunch of wood peckers on a hollow tree. Artillery fire is like thunder without any lightning.

I have been in a couple of pretty heavy bombardments, lasting about two hours. Got hit on the back with a piece of stone once.[3] Some dugouts are twenty feet deep so when you get in there you are safe. But take it all around, the front line is not nearly as bad as it is pictured in the papers. This is all now. Will write in a few days again. Hope you are all well and be sure to write often. I have not seen Tom Butler for a month.

Good bye. Love to all.

Herb

Jan. 10: Cold. Bath. Presentation of medals. Wrote home.

31

Somewhere in France
[Camblain-l'Abbé]
Jan. 10, 1917

Dear May,

Here we are again, but where are we? Sitting in a little French kitchen waiting on Madame to cook me some eggs and potato chips. This is the 2nd time I have seen that sort of food since I hit the foreign soil. Potatoes and eggs are sure a luxury here. I expect you have received a note from me since I came across the channel, at least I hope so. I got yours of the 15th Dec. tonight and I concluded that you are not getting all mine. I am quite sure that I do not get all my mail and have not got any parcels yet. We went into the trenches on the 21st Dec. and came out on Jan. 8th. So you see we spent our Merry Xmas and Happy New Year in the front line. Some Xmas. I had my first meal of the day at 3 P.M. and it was soup and hard tack with a little square of plum pudding. 1st Jan. I worked from 8 A.M. to 2 P.M. and from 5 P.M. to 1 next morning so it was not quite the same as New Years used to be. We are out now for eight days and are in a very nice little town. It is a welcome change to get a wash and a nights sleep. Fancy, I had only washed and shaved twice since the 21st Dec. Did I need a wash?! Mud from head to foot but of course it is clean dirt. There are other little things that trouble a fellow also. Can't you guess?

This is a quiet front here but enough doing for a fresh guy. The Huns put over a pretty heavy bombardment two days. We lost a few killed and several wounded. I got a bruise on the back with a stone, thrown by a bursting shell.[4] The heavy guns are about the only ones going in the day time. The night brings on machine gun and snipers fire and bombing raids. But on the whole, May, the front line is not so bad as the papers picture it to be. Of course I have not seen much yet. The trenches are hard to keep in repair at this time of the year on account of the rain.

I have not seen T. Earl since the 8th Dec. but I expect he will join us in a few days, also R. Wilson and W. Andison.[5] All the other 130 boys who are in France are billeted quite near us, but have not seen any of them since we were in the front line, when I happened on some of them quite unexpectedly.

Well how did you spend Xmas? Gee but this does not seem like Jan. 11. It snowed a little today, but the weather is more like our Octobers. Lots of concerts and dances this year I hear. Won't you go to a few extra for me? I suppose you go to the theatre quite often. I hear that there are a lot of the boys home from the west this winter. Times will surely be lively, but just wait until we get home from the war. We will raise some stir. Military operations are still going on in old Perth eh! I am glad you like a bugle call. Well perhaps if you had heard one blow reveille every morning for 9 or 10 months you would get tired of it. Of course we do not hear them in the front line.

Well May, I wonder if you are all alone tonight? I can't help wishing I could keep you company some of those evenings. But then I always had a habit of staying late, so perhaps it is just as well I am not there. Could tell you some yarns now though. Some funny, some sad and perhaps some interesting.

Have been in a couple of hot corners already but I don't mind as much as I expected.

I am glad you like your job and getting along well. No cows to milk or dishes to wash eh! And Sat. afternoon and evening downtown. Gee! Wouldn't I like a Sat. afternoon and Sunday off. All days are alike in this country. You would never know it was Sunday.

Hope you will be able to read this.

Ever your friend,
Herb

P.S. I expect the long time between letters was due to us crossing to France.

Jan. 11: Cold. Bombing. Payed. Writing some.

Jan. 12: Cold and dull. Firing live bombs. Got 8 letters.

Jan. 13: Cold and some snow. At gas school. Eight more letters and a Christmas box from Perth.

Jan. 14: Fair. Cleaning streets.

Jan. 15: Fine. Came up to reserves. Working party at night.

Jan. 16: Cold. Washed, shaved and had a haircut. Working party at night.

Jan. 17: About 3 inches of snow. Writing letters. Working party at night.

32

Dugout, France
Jan. 17, 1917

My Dear Father and Mother,

I intended writing again last week but we were moved quite suddenly and I did not get time. I expect you will be weary waiting on the letters, yes, I know just how you will watch for the mailman coming up past Hughes, stopping at Minors and coming up to Gibsons and no letter. Of course you know my intentions are good, but as I told you before, there would be times when it would be impossible to write. Even now I am not sure when this will be mailed. We are up in the reserve trenches again. My company was to have stayed in rest billets five days longer but orders were changed. We work at night and sleep through the day. Well, I need not say sleep for yesterday I spent the day washing, shaving and getting my hair cut, and this morning I am writing to you. I hope you are all well and that Mothers' shoulder is better now. Do take care of yourselves. It will soon be time for the La Grippe again. I am fine, think I have gained since I left England. I suppose there will be sleighing and lots of frost there now. We are having a cold spell here. Was very cold last night when we came in from work and this morning there is about three inches of snow. But we have a good dugout, with a fireplace in it, so we can make it snug. It is about 12ft x 15ft and there are 11 of us in it. Most of them are from Brantford, Ont.

Father's letter of Dec. 5 just came on the 10th of Jan. At least I just got it when I came out of the trenches. I just got 20 letters in three days, but I suppose the rush is over until I go out again. I also got one box from Perth, but yours has not arrived yet. Did you pack it well? The one I got was burst and had to be repacked at the Home Depot.[6] Boxes are a great thing in a soldiers life. I am just eating a piece of cake out of a chaps box now. Xmas cake is usually shared among the occupants of the dugout. Well, I think your grain turned out pretty good. Elma said in her letter that Charlie was kicking up his heels like a 2 year old. Tommy will be fat too. Would not mind if I could have a drive with him now. Are the hen's laying? Things are a great price. Willie gave me some prices. When in the village I had eggs a few times to change off the army rations. Three eggs, bread, butter, and coffee cost 1 1/2 franc or 30 cents. I bought a half lb. butter to bring up the line and it cost 34 cents or 68 cents per lb. Bread is not so dear. You can get a fair sized loaf for 1/2 franc or 10 cents. So Clara is sewing shirts for soldiers. Wouldn't mind if I had one of them. We had a bath and got our underwear changed. The suit I got is pretty light. I have not got the paper you sent yet. Have you been up to see that new Gibson yet? I am sure they are proud of him. Had a long letter from Willie. They spoke of sending a box. Hope they do. Had one letter from M.E. too, after she had been down to see you. I guess John is over often isn't he? Is he as busy as ever. Must write to them this week if I get a chance. Will send the next one to them. That was a fine addition to the roll of members at Balderson. How I long for to sit in the church there and listen to Mr. Greig. You know there is no Sabbath here that is visible, you know. The war goes on outside but one can keep the Lord's day inside. I hate to do things on Sunday but orders are orders and must be obeyed. I keep my testament in my breast pocket all the time. It is a great thing to know that the same God is watching over us all though many miles apart. And He will bring this war to serve His own great purpose although it is hard to see it in that way, for a great many.

I think this is all this time, my envelopes are rather small.

Keep on praying for me and we will hope together and pray that we may all meet again in this world. If not here we will meet in the next, where there is no war or sorrow.

Good bye and God bless and keep you till we meet again.

Yours lovingly,
Herb

I got a nice card to send you but these envelopes are too small.

XXXXXX

Jan. 18: Cold. Working party A.M. and P.M. Not much grub these days.

33

Dugout, France
Jan 18, 1917

Dear May,

I have a few minutes to myself just now so will write a short note. I hope you received the one I wrote while out in billets. I am back in the reserves again and work at night. It is now 2 P.M. and I have to get a lunch and be ready for 3:30. We usually go out at _____ and get in at _____ but I think there is something special tonight.[7] A trip up to the front line I expect. I do not mind working nights if we get the day off but sometimes we do not. I enjoyed the six days in the village. I bought everything to eat that I thought I'd like and then to crown all I received your handsome box. Many thanks, May. It was so thoughtful of you. The shortbread was broken up but good never the less. The candy, socks and cake all excellent. I brought a part of the cake up the line and just finished it last night when I came in off the working party. You bet it tasted good. The box had been broken and repacked at the

Home Depot so I would advise you, if you have occasion to send any more boxes, to soldiers across the sea, to pack in a tin box, wrap with paper and then sew a cloth cover on. This is the way most are sent and they stand the trip good. A towel is a good thing to sew around, then the chap has a towel to dry his windows with. I also received some more letters from you dated Nov. They come in bunches of eight and then none for some time. I got a bunch of papers today from home, *Era*, *Courier*, and *Expositor*.[8] Lots of news, have read most of the day. The weather is quite winter, have about 3 inches of snow. There are 11 of us in a dugout 12'x15'. Have a fire and are real snug. Rations have been rather short this week though. One loaf bread for 7 men for 24 hours, isn't much is it? Of course there are lots of hard tack and bully beef.

Hope you are getting on well and enjoying life to the fullest. Say thanks to Laura for me and tell her not to study too hard.

All for this time.

Yours,
Herb

75th Canadians B.E.F. France

Jan. 19: Cold. Moved out to reserves. Berthonaval Wood. Ration party P.M.
Jan. 20: Cold. Working party A.M. on Snargate. Ground is hard frozen and has to be picked consequently the amount of work done is small.
Jan. 21: Cold. Working in Maistro line.
Jan. 22: Cold. Sick, excused duty. Sore back and chest
Jan. 23: Cold. Excused duty but A.M. feeling better. Writing letters.

34

France
[Reserve Line Dugout]
Jan. 23, 1917

Dear May,

Had a letter started to you in answer to yours of the 21st Dec, but did not get it finished, when last night I got one dated Jan. 2nd.[9] Both nice newsy letters. Don't worry about them being too long for me to read and as for the censor he never looks at letters coming in. Perhaps you don't know that we are not allowed to seal ours and do not need to put any stamps on either. Yes, May, two weeks is a long time between letters but you can rest assured that I will write just as often as ever I can. I thought Dec. 21 was your birthday but was not sure but will always remember the day now. I entered the trenches at 1:15 P.M. that day. You were wondering where I was and what I was doing. Well, that's what. But I'll not spend time on that now. I think I told you all particulars. I did expect to be in Blighty for Xmas but got disappointed, however we came here to fight not to play.

It is some experience alright to travel abroad, but not the pleasure it would contain if it were not wartime. Everywhere you see signs of war, war. I have made some resolutions for the New Year but you did not say what yours were. The old year is gone and there has been a great many changes as usual but for me one big one. From being my own boss with a good bed and lots to eat, to being under orders and fed on Army rations in a foreign land. I don't see many of the old 130th men. There are only a few of us in the 75th. Most of the men in "C" company are from Toronto and Brantford.

This morning was like a morning at home—about 2" snow and hard white frost. Have been on the sick list these two days. Grippe I think. Went to the M.O. and got a few pills and excused from duty, so I am lying in my dugout rolled up in overcoat, sheepskin coat and blankets. Am feeling better this P.M., so think I'll be ready for the front line in a day or two. We have six days to put in front line and then we go out to billets for another rest. The time seems to slide by quickly changing around in this way. To tell the truth I have done more shoveling than anything else over here. Putting France into sand bags and building them up for protection against Fritz's bullets. Have only seen one German behind his lines and have never fired one shot yet. It is like the old game of hide and seek that we used to play at school. I'm glad your concert came off O.K. and that Santa remembered you. Wouldn't I like to be there for some of those entertainments. I had not heard a song since I left England until the other night, while on ration party. You see a party goes to meet the mule trains every night and carry the rations to where the Batt. is. Well the train was late this night about 2 hours so a bunch got started to sing. They started comic, then popular, then patriotic, then sentimental and ended up with "Mother."[10] Did you ever hear it?

I'll write the words for you:

M is for the million things she gave me
O is only that she's growing old
T is for the tears she shed to save me
H is for her heart as pure as gold
E is for her eyes with love light shining
R is for right and right she'll always be.
Put them all together they spell Mother.
A word that means the world to me.

A few batteries near us were firing and the sky being clouded and the ground covered with snow, the flash of the guns lit up the men's faces and you could see that each one was thinking of their own dear ones far across the sea.

You want to know about the French girls. Well, there are not many around the towns that I have seen and the few there are OK. Well, I would rather have our own Canadian girls. Anything and everything Canadian for me. You can tell the world that Canada is "the" country. Now perhaps this is enough hot stuff for this time. Will write as soon as I come out of the line if I don't get a blighty.[11] This is a somewhat disjointed letter isn't it? There are likely things you would like to know that I don't write, so don't be afraid to ask questions and I'll try to answer them.

Good bye and good luck.

Herb

P.S. The Expositor would be very acceptable if it is not too much trouble for you to send it. Tell Jennie K. that I saw Willie last week and both of them were well.[12]

35

Reserves, France
Jan. 23, 1917

Dear Father,

Your welcome letter of the 28th reached me last night and is the first answer I have had to those written in France. Hope Mother is well again and that you all miss that old La Grippe. I have had a touch of it this two days, but went to the M.O. and got some pills and excused duty, so I am feeling pretty good tonight. We are still in the reserves yet. The weather is cold and some snow on the ground. I got a new pair of boots today, No. 9's, so I can put two pairs of socks in them.

Glad to hear that you and Ma were out to tea on Xmas, and that you have lots to eat this winter and lots of wood. Dear me the winter will be half over by the time you get this. I wish you would send me those papers every week. I got one bunch and had a great time reading them. Lots of things you don't write that I like to know. If I had known you people were going to put my letters in the paper, I would have taken more pains with them. I just scribbled off a lot of things as they came to my mind. Yes indeed there will be changes before I get home. I have never given up hope of reaching home myself, but who will be gone in the mean time worries me. I got Maggie's letter and must answer it now. Sorry they have lost another crop. I don't hear from Dakota at all since I left Canada. Had one from M.E. this week. But I am sorry to say that I have not got your box yet. There are tons of parcels of course and no doubt some are lost. I wish you would send me some good writing material and a couple of indelible pencils, they are so hard to get here, also some stuff to make hot drinks, such as condensed cocoa, chocolate or ginger.

I have read the tracts[13] and they are nice and I passed them around. Send more. I suppose there is lots of snow in Ont. now and frost. I think this is all the news for tonight. Hope you all keep well.

Yours lovingly,

Herb

P.S. Clara might write oftener.

Jan. 24: Cold. Feeling pretty good. Working party at night to Snargate.

Jan. 25: Clear and cold. Working party on Wortley Line.

Jan. 26: Clear and cold. Left reserves and went into front line. Relieved 102nd Battalion.

Jan. 27: Clear and cold. All is quiet. Doing listening post every night and sleeping in daytime in tunnel.

Jan. 28: Listening post.

Jan. 29: Clear and cold. Listening post.

Jan. 30: Quiet. Listening post. Lieut. Clarke wounded by sniper.

Jan. 31: Clear and cold. Had to roll our feet in sandbags to keep from freezing. Relieved by 87th.

Feb. 1: Clear and cold. Out to Coupigny. Rest. Billets.

Feb. 2: Clear and cold. Rest to-day and got payed. Nice town.

36

France
[Coupigny]
Feb. 2, 1917

Dear May,

Here I am once more, this time from rest billets in another town behind the lines. Came here from the front line yesterday and will rest for a week. Rest does not mean just eat and sleep. First comes the pay parade which is the life of a soldier, means little dainties for him. Next is clothes parade and he gets his worn clothing replaced with new. Next is bathing parade, where he comes back to civilized life again. Then there is rifle inspection, gas helmet and respirator drill, some bayonet fighting, squad drill where memories of former days come back, before you faced the guns. Then we bombers practice throwing bombs, like a baseball player would keep in trim for the match. Only bombs are not thrown like baseballs and then it would be (up) with you to catch one!! Had a good turn in the lines this time. The weather being clear and cold the mud frozen up we could keep clean. I was on listening post all the time while in the front line. At dusk you creep away out as near to Fritz's lines as possible and watch any movement of his and signal it. There was clear moonlight which caused you to see things that had no life, move. At day break you crawl back home and go sleep all day. You sure need it for the strain is so great. I used to wonder what No Mans Land was like and how it would feel to be there but now I know all about it.[14] Well May I have four letters here from you dated Nov. 8, Dec. 11, and 26 and Jan. 8. Strange I got the last first and first last. Two of them have been all over Europe in search of me. However there is news and cheery words in them all. My mail is still mixed up with John Gibson's. I hope you get all I write. I am sorry I can't write oftener but you will bear with me I know. I saw the same pictures of the Somme as you saw. So you saw the Battle of the Somme and want to know if it is like what I see. No I was not at the Somme and this front is not like that for there is no drive at present. Have not seen any mines nor many casualties, nor continuous artillery fire, but the rest of it is the same. I suppose all the concerts are passed now and things will be quiet. Lots of diamonds this year eh! I hope they save a few good times for me.

Well May I hope there is something in this which will interest you. It is so hard to write letters here but some day I hope to tell you all about my experiences. We go through things here that the people at home have no idea of.

Give Laura my heartiest congratulations for her good success.

All for now. All the time.

Herb

P.S. I am sending you a little remembrance in same mail. Hope you get it OK.

Feb. 3: Clear and cold. A.M. Physical jerks and squad drill. Downtown and had some eggs and pie. Some good stores here and YMCA.
Feb. 4: Church parade.

37

Somewhere in France
[Coupigny]
Feb. 4, 1917

Dear Mother,

You will think this is a strange way to start a letter, but it is three lines of a favourite song the boys sing here. It is very nice and you hear it in the trenches and out.

I am wondering how you are today and hoping that you are well again. It is almost a month since the date of my last letter and it seems a long time. My letters take about 20 days to come direct to France. I ought to have them in less time. Maggie's letter said that you had a sore ear and that is such a painful thing. But I know you will be taken care of and have lots of good neighbours. I hope Father is quite well again. I think he should give up those services until the warm weather comes anyway. It is quite a drive for him in the cold.

How is Clara? I think by her letters that she is lonesome. I guess she misses me badly enough. But now I would not care to be a civilian in Canada and stand all the jibes they get. This is a rough life but one can be true inside for all. I am glad I have 10 months of it in. It has meant more to me than most people at home know. However, we must all bear up. All will work out for good in the end. We will just leave our future in

God's hands and let Him shape it for us. He who sees the sparrow fall, sees us also and will lead us if we will but follow.

This is a clear crisp Sunday afternoon. The first real Sunday I have enjoyed since coming to France. We had Church service in the YMCA at 9 A.M. by our Batt. Chaplain and after they had communion for those who wished to stay. About 40 stayed for it. This is the 3rd time I have taken sacrament in English form. It is the only way in the army and means the same as our own so I just be as one of them. So this afternoon there are no parades and I am doing some writing. The Y is quite large here but the prices are high. We only get $6 a month here and it doesn't go far. When a fellow comes out of the trenches he is just crazy for something different to eat. Three eggs, 2 slices bread and butter and 2 cups of coffee cost 40 cents, a tin of pineapple 20 cents, peaches 45 cents so that is the way it goes! Almost every man goes back to the trenches broke, which I believe is the best way.

My I wish those boxes would come. Some get them registered but I think it must cost too much.

Has John got the bag that Tom Butler and I sent. There are a lot of things that I would like to tell you about this place but dare not. So all I can say is that I am well and hope and pray that you are better again. Don't worry about me Mother. I am alright. It will be a happy time when this war is over and the boys go back to Canada. No more European tours for me.

Cheer up, it may soon come.

Your loving Herb

Feb. 5: Clear and cold. A.M. Squad drill. Bombing P.M. Practicing attack.

Feb. 6: Clear and cold A.M. Got boots fixed P.M. Bombing.

38

France
[Coupigny]
Feb. 6, 1917

My Dear Mother,

A line today to say that I am fine, hoping you are well again. Had a letter from near home last night but it did not mention anything about you so I concluded that you are no worse or they would have known.[15]

It is clear and cold today. The kids are out sliding on the ice but I do not see any skates. I have had my dinner at the cookery and then went over to the Y and got a cup of cocoa and some gingerbread. The cocoa is free and is much appreciated by the boys. There is a concert in the Y every night. Our band is playing tonight. But our time here is short now, then we take our turn in the lines again. However our next rest will be a month. Yes a whole month and by then the weather will be warm.

We heard here today that the Americans had declared war on Germany. Wonder if it is true. If so I do not think the war will last long. Germany cannot fight the world. It is just two months today since we landed in France, seems longer.

Well Mother I think this is all today. Will send a postcard in a few days. Trusting you are able to be up and praying that we may be spared to meet again.

Your loving son,
Herb

Feb. 7: Frosty. Left billets at 7:30 A.M. for supports, arriving 3:00 P.M. Relieved 102nd Battalion. Roads very slippery.

Feb. 8: Frosty. Working party 8:00 A.M. to 2:00 P.M. Music Hall. Ration party at night.

Feb. 8

Dear Mother,

I did not get this away when written. We are up in the support trenches again, back to the dugouts and working parties. Weather is still cold. I wish I had told you to send mitts. We have lots of socks but are very shy of mitts. I am wearing a pair of socks on my hands. Have struck a good dugout this time again. There is 14 in it. I am bunking with a chap from Carleton Place. Gorman is his name. Don't worry about me Mother. There are only about six days out of 24 that I am in any real danger.

We have not got our mail today yet. Am looking for a letter and hoping it brings good news from you.

One of John Gibson's parcels came here yesterday for me so I am expecting that he is getting mine. They may turn up yet for one of our fellows got a parcel the other night dated Nov. 29th. It takes them a long time to come, so register the next.

Your loving son,
Herb

Feb. 9: Clear and frosty. Carry on. Good rations these days. Go to rugby dump every night.[16]

Feb. 10: Fine. Carry on. Tom Butler came up. Very good dug outs here but very crowded.

Feb. 11: Fine. Working

Feb. 12: Clear and cold. Working party A.M. Stand to at 11 P.M. 2nd division going over.

Feb. 13: Fine. Relieved by 87th. Moved to reserves. Working party to Music Hall P.M.

Feb. 14: Clear and cold. Tired so slept until noon. Artillery drill and lots of aircraft about.

Feb. 15: Cool. Working party every night and four mile walk.

Feb. 16: Milder. Working party at night. Drill P.M.

Feb. 17: Fair. Drill P.M. and working party at night. Practicing to make an attack on Fritz.

Feb. 18: Fair.

Feb. 19: Fine. Went out to gas school. Saw some old 130th chums. Battalion went to front line.

Feb. 19, 1917

Dear Mother,

When we came out to rest there was one of these packages awaiting each man.

I traded my tobacco for chocolate. I think I told you of the other box I got from a Church in Toronto so I have fared pretty well with these and others. Yours will surely come soon.

Yours,
Herb

39

Reserves, France
[Dugout]
2/16/17

Dear May,

Here we are again, on a rather cold, raw morning. We have no wood this morning for our dugout, so no fire, therefore I am rolled up in my blankets. My fingers are numb so if I make mistakes, why, next time I'll do better. Your welcome letter came last night, with all its news. No you don't tell me anything twice. Each letter contains a budget of somethingness. Every item is of interest and you always wrote nice letters but I believe you are getting better.

I just expected that you would not be Junior long. Step by step and you will reach that place where you step inside an iron cage and pull the door shut and with nimble fingers and quick eye, count over the green backs. Then there are higher places that may be reached by those who have the energy.[17] And I know you have grit enough for anything even though you are a Conservative! Ha Ha! Any how be sure and lead Mr. Butler in the straight and narrow way. I bet the bank is a fine warm place on the stormy mornings. Have you got the roads beaten down yet? Gee but I would enjoy a sleigh drive now.

Well May by now you must have got a letter or two. At least I sent them. Yes it will soon be March. The days do not drag very heavily here, we are changed about so much that there is always something to look ahead to. I must thank you again in advance for your parcel. I will likely get it next week. Anything from Canada is all right.

Yes I know all those people you speak of. I did not know that Mrs. Arthur had been home. Well, well, and Mack could not get across the line eh! He ought to try eastward. Ha! Nothing to stop him until he reaches the front line and then fight the rest of the way.[18]

What happened that Bush is leaving Perth? Pro-German is that it. Who is going to occupy his stand.

Lots of diamonds flashing around Perth, eh? Perhaps that is the best thing for Mary and Albert, he might settle down then. I suppose it was hard driving that killed his driver.

Now May there is not much to write about. Artillery duels are quite common around here now. They sure kick up a dust some times. Our 18 pds. have a vicious bark and the big guns in the rear a duller boom. Then you can hear the shells coming through the air like a train. They hit with a ripping explosion that shatters everything in their vicinity. Some raids have been pulled off lately but only of minor importance.

Yes May I will do my best to get you a good souvenir, perhaps not gold or silver but it will be a real article anyway. I hope you get my letters and the handkerchief I sent from the last billets.[19]

Good bye for now and every success.

Herb

Feb. 20: Rain. Working party A.M. and P.M. Repairing front line trench.

Feb. 21: Working party in front line P.M. but Fritz drove us out with whiz bangs.[20]

Feb. 22: Rainy. Battalion moved back to reserves Berthonaval Wood. Awful mud and dark nights. Ration party.

Feb. 23: Dull and misty. Gas drill in A.M. Working party to frontline. Fritz shelled us. Mud.

Feb. 24: Dull and raw. Gas drill in A.M. Ration party at night and had a good long sleep.

40

France
[Front Line Dugout]
2/24/17

My Dear Mother,

I wonder how you all are tonight. I do hope you are able to be up. Have not had a letter from you for some time. The last was written Jan. 14th. It takes so long to get any news from home and no doubt you find the same. They don't tell me much either about how you are. Did the doctor give you any thing to help you this time? Can you eat well? Clara does not write as often as she might. I think at least once a week would be nice. I have no news to tell you. This is the same old war. I got a nice box and letter from Ashcrofts in England last night. Wasn't it kind of them to send me a box. Hope to get one from home soon. Tom Butler is here now and I saw a lot of our old 130th men this week. Had a long talk with Lett. Simpson one day. He is a corporal now.

I am fine although I have failed some I guess.[21] The work, especially at night, gets monotonous but otherwise I don't mind the rough life. I do miss a quiet Sunday though and that is the only time I get lonesome is when we start out on a working party on a Sunday morning or evening. But duty calls and then one can read and pray just as well no matter what is going on. I hope Father is well again. Is he still taking those services?

Now Mother don't worry about me too much. I am all right here or where ever I may be and we shall all meet in the sweet bye and bye either a home on earth or in a better land.

Lots of love to you all.

Herb

P.S. You will have to keep Jane and Ida informed about me. I can't write to U.S.A. Anyhow, they never write to me.

Feb. 25: Back to front line.

Feb. 26: Beautiful day. Carrying ammunition and writing letters. Sleeping.

26/2/17

Dear Father,

I did not get this letter off to mother when written so will add a piece to you and it will go out tonight. This is a lovely morning and I am feeling fine. Am writing this in the front line. I don't get a chance to write many up here. I am lying in my bunk in dugout about 300 yds from Fritz. He can't get at me here even with his heavy guns. He never pays us a visit personally, but likes to send over his high explosive. The thaw has brought lots of mud again but we will be going out of the line for a months rest, soon. I am looking for a letter every day, last one was dated Jan. 14. I know you look and long for letters from me, but I am doing the same. I know how you used to feel when away and I did not write nearly often enough. I am (like thousands of other Canadian boys) learning a good many lessons out here. We will appreciate home when we get back. I hope and pray that you are all well and that mother has recovered.

Lovingly,
Herb

41

Somewhere in France
Feb. 1917[22]

Dear May,

Here comes some of your writing material, received it a few days ago while in the front line. Thanks May, you know how much I appreciate it. The other things were excellent. We can't get that kind of chocolate here and the gum we get is inferior to Canadian goods. The tooth paste is best of all for I have not had a thing but water to clean my teeth with for a month. The maple leaves were in good condition. I'll put some in my pay book and testament. Yes, anything from Canada is all right. So you are having a pretty cold and stormy winter. We had it cold here but has turned milder and the snow is all gone and the frost nearly all out, result is that there is lots of mud. I did dread the thaw coming, the cold weather was much nicer, one could keep clean and dry but now everything is plastered. Dugouts can't be kept clean and rifles, equipment and clothing take some work to keep a little decent. Went on a working party last night and some of the chaps got mired completely. Just after we got started out Fritz got nasty and started shelling part of the road we were to travel, so we had to wait until he got his demonstration over. Yes, I am a bombardier but have not thrown one at Fritz yet, nor fired a shot. Those are the kind we use, but there are others also much larger which I guess is not in that collection.

You must be pretty good on the skates now, eh. I am afraid I'll be done for that when I get home. I'd be wanting all to go in file. BATT. fires in town, too much fuel. Well I wish I had a fire now I would make some Oxo.

Glad to know that you and the Junior pull all right. It is best to keep on the good side of the lads. Ha Ha.

I was out of the line one day last week and saw a lot of our old 130th boys who are with the 3rd Batt. Had a long talk with Lett Simpson. He is corporal at present but has applied for a commission as machine gun officer. I also saw F. Armstrong and L. Affleck of the 38th in the line one day. They said all of the 130th boys were O.K. Pte. Penny is the first 130th man to get wounded, got a bullet through the right shoulder. A good blighty. This is a dull raw day and the artillery is firing its usual days ration of steel and explosive over to the foe.[23]

There is little else going on here but artillery duals, but we have the supremacy. If Fritz puts over 10 shells, we put over 20 and a size larger caliber. Does this stuff interest you May? It seems to me that I tell you the same thing in every letter. Everything is about the same routine and outside of that there is nothing else to say, at least that we can say.

Lindsay is the same old sport eh. But I prefer one at a time. What do you think? Everyone seems to think that Spalding has found some one he thinks more of than Georgina. It is almost dinner time now and my chum (Orville Gorman from near Ottawa) is warming water to make some tea. We don't get tea at noon just Irish stew. I got a nice box from my brother-in-laws people in England last night and there are some tea and cocoa cubes in it. Wasn't it good of them to send me a box. I was to visit them but did not get time before I was called away.

They live in Huntingdonshire. It is awful to think that I have never gotten one of the parcels sent from home yet.

Hundreds of parcels go astray so I suppose I must put up with it. Well May I think this is all for today. Wishing you every success in your work and thanking you again for the good things you sent. Perhaps I will have a chance to get a little souvenir for you soon.

Good bye for now,
Your true friend,
Herb

Feb. 27: Fair. Working party in afternoon but not much work done. Too hot to sleep in caves.

Feb. 28: Dull. On ration and water all day. Fritz putting a few shells over. Large piece just missed my leg. In Tottenham caves.

Mar. 1: Fine. Went over top. Wounded in left arm. Walked to ambulance station. Ambulance to Villers au Bois and to CCS at Bruay. Bath. Clean clothes. Good bed.

Mar. 2: Fair. Slept well. Porridge for breakfast and pudding dinner. Enjoyed it. Left by Red Cross train for base arrived 4 A.M. Cold morning.

Mar. 3: In ward C. These comforts are sure worth the pain. Four meals a day and nice bed. No. 20 General Hospital Camiers, France. Large tented hospital.

41A (Telegram)

Night Letter
Great North Western Telegram Company of Canada

Ottawa Ont.
March 3, 1917

William R. Gibson
Balderson, Ont.

Sincerely regret inform you 787167 Private James Herbert Gibson, infantry, officially reported admitted, Twenty General Hospital, Camiers, March third, nineteen seventeen, gunshot wound left arm, slight.

Will send further particulars when received.

Officer in Charge,
Record Office

41B (Telegram)

Wounded in arm.

A telegram from the Record Office Wed. A.M. stated that Pte. Gibson, son of Mr. Wm. Gibson 8th Line Bathurst, had been wounded slightly in the arm. He went overseas with the 130th.

41C (Telegram)

Ottawa
April 9, 1917

Department of Militia and Defence

From: The Adjutant General
Canadian Militia

To: William R. Gibson, Esq.
Balderson, Ont.

787167 Pt. James Herbert Gibson
Canadian Expeditionary Force

Sir,

I have the honour to state that information has been received by mail from England, to the effect that the above noted soldier was admitted to the Military Hospital, Fort Pitt, Chatham England on March 11th 1917 suffering from a gunshot wound in the left arm.

Any further information received will be communicated to you without delay.

Mar. 4: Fine.

41D (Telegram)

Ottawa
May 9, 1917

I have the honour to state that information has been received by mail from England to the effect that the above noted soldier was transferred from the Military Hospital, Fort Pitt Chatham to the

Canadian Convalescent Hospital, Woodcote Park, Epsom England on April 4th 1917 suffering from a gunshot wound in the left arm.

Mar. 5: Snowed 2 inches in night. Feeling fine and good appetite. Arm dressed once a day.

Mar. 6: More snow and wind. Sleeping most of time. Time seems to go slow doing nothing.

Mar. 7: Windy and cold. Stayed in bed all day. A Glasgow Highlander on one side and a Warwickshire on other. Marked for blighty.

Mar. 8: Fine. Up all day. Went to recreation room in afternoon.

Mar. 9: Snow. Wrote some letters. Up all day.

42

No. 20 General Hospital
[Camiers]
France, March 9, 1917

Dear Father and Mother,

I expect by now the Militia Department at Ottawa will have notified you of my being wounded. I don't know what particulars they would give you but am expecting you will be thinking of the worst possibility. I got a bullet through my left arm between the wrist and elbow. The bone is slightly injured but not serious. It was quite painful but is doing fine and I have a famous appetite. We get lots to eat here so I shall soon gain up. Porridge for breakfast and pudding at dinner, four meals a day. I am booked to go to England but the Red Cross boat has not come for us yet. Quite a change here than in the trenches.[24] The weather is cold and snows a little every day. It will be a long time before I hear from you. My Batt. will not know until I get settled in England where to send my mail. And you need not write until you hear from me again. Hope you are all well.

Lovingly,
Herb

F. Adams said he would write.[25] Did you get it and the card I sent?

J.H.G.

43

No. 20 General Hospital
[Camiers]
France, March 9, 1917

Dear May,

Well. What do you think of my doings now? Those flying things
you spoke of were rather quick for me, so a bullet caught me in the left
arm, midway between wrist and elbow. The bone is injured but nothing
serious I think. It was quite painful but is doing nicely and I expect to
go to Blighty any day. Have been here a week almost (1st March I got
it) and it is sure a pleasant place to be compared with trenches. Lots
of good food and I have lost my appetite and found a horse's, I think!
Don't write until you hear from me again as I don't know where I will
be sent yet. Was in the C.C.S.[26] for two days before coming here. Hope
this finds you O.K. All for now.

Yours as B.4,

Herb

Got a letter from you the night before I got wounded.

Herb

> **Mar. 10:** Dull and foggy. Left Camiers at 4 A.M. Arrived Calais and crossed
> on King Albert boat Stad Antwerpan to Dover. Train to the auxiliary hospital
> at Gravesend England. Arrived 4 P.M.
> **Mar. 11:** Dull. Some visitors

44

The Auxiliary Hospital
Ward A1
Gravesend England
March 11, 1917

Dear Sister,

Sunday morning finds me here in "Blighty" as the English soldiers
call it. My arm is not very painful, and lucky enough I have the <u>right</u>
one to <u>write</u> and eat with. I'll begin at the morning of March 1st and
relate my experiences to you. On that morning (5 A.M.) my Batt. and

three others made an attack on the German trenches. They were ready for us and our losses were quite heavy. Our Col. was killed, also a Lieut. and three other officers wounded. I got mine about 20 yards off Fritz wire, so started back to our own trenches in a hail of bullets and shrapnel. It was a hot place but a higher hand lead me through it and I soon found myself safe in one of our underground tunnels. Here I got first aid and being able to walk started out to the ambulance sta. It was a walk of about 4 miles. Here we had all the bread, butter, jam and hot cocoa we could eat. From here we went in horse ambulances to field clearing sta.[27] Had wounds dressed properly, got inoculated, had more to eat and drink. Motor ambulances took us from there to Canadian Clearing Station[28] where they bathed us, put on clean clothes, had a supper in bed and directly fell asleep. Woke for breakfast of porridge, bread and tea. I was so tired I slept again until they woke me for dinner (beef steak and pudding). Slept afternoon also. About 5 P.M. I left on Red Cross train, got separated into different wards from all the fellows I knew, so was all alone on train. About 4 A.M. landed in No. 20 General Hospital at Camiers, France. Got another bath and clean cloths and went to bed. Mostly Imperials here, good nurses and lots to eat. Two days after I was marked for England, but did not leave until 4 A.M. on 10th. Came by train to Calais and across to Dover, thence by train to here, arrived at 4 P.M. This is a military hospital out and out, but I think we shall be treated well. Mostly English here also. I wish I had got to a Canadian hospital but had not the luck. Quite a town this and they tell us they give the wounded a fine tea once a week and we can go to any entertainment free of charge. They give 10 days leave after you are better so I am going to Scotland and to Ashcrofts. I will perhaps be better before I get an answer to this but the hospital will forward them. I'll be getting a bunch returned from France soon. I am so anxious about mother, almost two months since I heard how she was, but I trust she is better now. Writing material is scarce, but will soon get some. Don't send any more parcels. The worth of them in Canadian bills would be better, registered of course. I will write often.

Love to all,
Herb

Mar. 12: Rainy. Went downtown to picture show. Free.

Mar. 13: Fair. Downtown A.M. and P.M. Wrote some letters.

45

Auxiliary Military Hospital
Ward A1, Gravesend, England
March 13, 1917 5 P.M.

Dear May,

Here I am in Blighty and it is sure great to be back in civilization once more, with a clean bite to eat and a bed to go to every night. Don't write and say that you are sorry I am wounded, for its really a dandy little blighty, as the soldiers call them, I have got. It has not pained much and has got me out of the trenches for at least two months, I expect. Ten days leave after we are better is given to all the wounded. So Hurrah for a good time. I am counting on going up to Edinburgh. This is a rather nice town but we are only allowed out 4 hours a day 10 to 12 A.M. and 2 to 4 P.M. It is on the Thames and is about 20 miles from London. Being a military hospital they put on some restrictions. Would like to have struck a Canadian Hosp. but I think we will be sent to Can. Con. Hosp. soon. I have none of my old chums here although there were about 12 of us started out together. Mostly all Imperials here but they are a nice lot of "Blokes." Did you get the note I sent from France? In case you did not I will start at the first and tell you my experiences.[29] At 5 A.M. on March 1st we climbed over the front line trench accompanied by 3 other Batts. to make an attack on Fritz's trenches. They were ready for us and turned rifles, machine guns, bombs and shrapnel on us, just as we reached their wire. It was a hot place and a lot of our fellows fell. I got mine close to his wire, so started back, sprinting from shell hole to shell hole. I'll tell you straight May, I never expected to get back but I finally rolled into our own trench, just a few yards from one of our tunnels, in which was our 1st aid station. Here I got dressed and being able to walk started out to the ambulance station. It was about 4 miles out so I reached there about 10 A.M. Got bread, jam and hot cocoa here, then went by horse ambulance to Field Ambulance Station. Had my wound properly dressed, got more to eat and then by motor ambulance to the Can. Clearing Station. Had a bath and clean clothes and put to bed. This was about 6 P.M. and I slept most of the time until next night about 5 P.M. boarded train for the base hospital. Stayed there a week, then by train to Calais. Crossed the channel on King of the Belgium private steamer which is a Red Cross boat now. Landed at Dover thence by train to here. So passed two weeks like a couple of days. It will be a month yet before my arm is better, then 10 days leave and back to France again. It will be warm and dry by that time so I consider myself extremely lucky—1st to be here at all and 2nd to have such a slight wound. Quite a number of the 130th men were wounded and some killed. I don't know how Tom Butler came out, did not see him after.

What kind of weather are you having? Any signs of spring yet? It is mild here, no snow at all nor frost. Went to the picture show yesterday and must go tomorrow again. It is quite a job to put in the time here, rather a lazy life, walking around with arm in a sling, dressed in blue.

There are two other Canadians in my ward. One is from B.C. and the other is from Tasmania but has been all over the globe. Fought in the Boer war, has been in Australia, Japan, and finally New York when he crossed to Canada and joined the 13th Montreal Highlanders.

When I talk to men who have seen as much as he has it makes me think I have not seen anything. And when I talk with British soldiers who have fought in Egypt, Dardenelles and then spent 18 or 20 months in France it makes me think I have not done anything in this war. A fellow in a cot next to mine in hospital in France had been in the trenches 22 months and that was his first wound. Wonderful it seems. Then I have seen fellows get wounded before they have been in the line half a day. It will be some time before I get my mail back from France but it can't be helped.

Write to this address and if I am transferred to another hospital they will forward them.

> Good bye and good luck,
> Herb

Mar. 14: Fine. Went to play in P.M. "Sherlock Holmes" in Palace Theatre. Booked out.

46

Aux. Hospital, Ward A1
Gravesend, England
March 14, 1917

Dear Mother,

I am wondering how you are this morning. It is about six weeks since I had a letter from home and it will be a couple more, before my mail gets back from France. They won't know where to send it for a week. But if no news is good news, as I trust it is, you must be better. I hope you all keep well and don't work too hard this spring. I am fine and my arm is healing nicely. I go up town every afternoon for a walk and sometimes go to the picture show. It is a lazy job and the time drags a little, hanging around, arm in sling and dressed in blue clothes. But I am thankful to be out of the trenches at this time of the year. The spring flood was just starting when I left. It will be two months before I get back to France so it will be dry and warm by that time. It is great to have a clean bite off a table and a bed to go to every night, instead of meals at any old time and a bed of sand bags, one blanket and overcoat to lie on, that is if you were not out all night on a working party. I have not heard how many men my Bat. lost in the attack but I know several 130th boys were wounded and some killed. No doubt you will see an account of it in the papers. We lost our Col., 1 Lieut killed and several officers wounded. I did not see Tom Butler after, so I don't know how he came out of it.

I wrote a letter and postcard but had no stamps for them, so I do not know whether they will get through or not. A lady visitor took the letter on Sun. and by what she said I think she stamps a few for soldiers newly home from France. I have not got any money since Jan., and will not get any until I get out of hospital. Up town yesterday I met a Congregational Minister and he gave me 6 penny stamps, then I got paper at the Wesleyan Church Soldier's home. So I'll make out while here, then I am going up to Ashcroft's. I may take a trip up to Scotland too. We get ten days leave when better but I suppose those ten will go like two. Last letter I had from Mr. Ashcroft he said to be sure to visit them so this is my chance.

Well Mother I often wonder what you are all doing. I can see the old place in my dreams. Have dreamt alot about home since being in

Hospital. I guess it is because I have nothing else to do. It is dull this morning and all the boys are going out but I'll not go until afternoon. The doctor here is a civilian and comes in around 10 A.M. Rather nice fellow seems to be. I think this is all for now.

Hoping and praying that we shall be spared to meet again at home.

Your loving son,
Herb

47 (postcard)

Aux. Hospital
Gravesend, England
March 13, 1917

Dear Father,

I am feeling fine today. My arm is doing nicely and am out every afternoon to Wounded Soldiers Club in the town. Hope you are all well and don't work too hard.

None of my chums are in this hospital.

Love to all.

Mar. 15: Raw. Left for Seven Oaks and 2 P.M. Arrived at Dunsdale hospital at Westerham at 5:30 P.M. Fine place this.

Mar. 16: Fine. Went down street for a walk in afternoon. Saw Wolfe birth place and monument.

Mar. 17: Lovely day. Reading and writing in A.M. This is a lovely spot. Lots of good things to eat and the best of care. My ward is a nice roomy one with a cosy fireplace. Seven cots in it, one Canadian beside myself.

48

Dunsdale Hospital
Westerham, Kent
17/3/17

Dear Sister,

This is a beautiful morning. The birds are singing in the trees and the squirrels and rabbits are frisking about merrily. This is certainly a beautiful place and I count myself lucky to be here. It is a fine residence

and has been given over to the Red Cross for a hospital. The house
is large and half between ancient and modern in design and is built
half way up a hillside. The grounds are beautiful, hedges, flowers (just
coming up) shrubs, walks, drives, huge oak, ash and beech. Fir and
other small ornamental evergreens make it look something like home.
The hill rises steep behind the house and a little stream runs down
through artificial falls and pools to a large basin-like pool in the garden.
The grounds are large and everywhere you go there are different
designs of flower plots and ornamental shrubs galore. I wish you could
see some of these English residences. Kent is full of them. This is a very
poor description of one.

The village of Westerham where Wolfe was born is about 5 mins
walk from here. It is a nice little village about the size of Lanark,
only it has a railway. I am enclosing some postcards of the place.
The gentleman in the shop where I got them said he would get me
permission to visit Quebec House where Wolfe spent most of his time.
They have all his relics. Of course I said I would be delighted to see
them. Real descendants of Wolfe live here.

Well, I have had my dinner and a better one you could not wish for.
Beef steak and gravy, beans and carrots, potatoes and bread. Then rice
pudding and you know how I like rice.[30] For breakfast we got porridge
and sugar with lots of milk. Sometimes there is ham for breakfast and
fish for dinner. Yesterday there was currant pie for dinner. And if you
don't get enough first time there is always a second helping.

There are seven cots in my ward. It is a nice cheery room, with a
cosy fire place, large bay window and four others. Even cushioned arm
chairs to sit in. Can you imagine me dressed in grey flannel and slippers
sitting in a huge chair drawn up to the fire with a book or paper? There
is a library at our disposal, all good sound literature so I am taking
advantage of it.

I must try and go to church tomorrow. We are allowed out from 1
P.M. to six so have lots of time. Oh, I forgot to tell you about the nurses
(sisters we call them). They are all genuine ladies and we get the very
best of care. I am afraid I will be better too soon, I know I will be sorry
to leave here. One sister is a Canadian and takes special interest in me,
for they don't have many Canucks come here. She is married to an
officer who is at the front.

I had a letter from Mr. Ashcroft[31] today and he wants me to get
transferred to the hospital in his town, but I think I'll stop here. Well

Clara, it will soon be a year since I left home and I would not mind if this war was over and it was "all aboard" for Halifax.

We must all hope and pray that all will come out for good. It will be spring there by the time you get this, so eat an extra bit of taffy for me.

Remember me to all the folks and be sure and write often.

Will close now hoping you are all well.

Your loving brother,

Herb

J.H. Gibson (second from left) convalescing at Dunsdale Hospital in England.

49

Dunsdale Hospital
Westerham Kent
17/3/17

Dear May,

You will see by the heading that I have changed my place of abode once more and a pleasant change it is. This is all the heart could desire, a regular soldier's paradise. I came here a couple of days ago by train to Seven Oaks and from there a distance of five miles in a limousine. Some class to me eh! This is a private residence and the owners gave it over to the Red Cross for a hospital. There are about 35 patients and we get the very best care. The nurses are genuine ladies and one is a Canadian from Toronto. She takes special interest in me of course for not many Canucks come here. She is married to an Officer who is at the front. The food is the very best and all you want of it, which is a great change to having your rations served out to you—so much and no more, often less.

The house is between an ancient and modern design. Large airy halls and winding stair cases. My ward has an old fashioned fireplace, large bay windows and is in the South West corner so the sun shines in all day. There are 7 cots and we have a writing table and fine cushioned chairs. Can you imagine me dressed in grey flannels and slippers, sitting in a huge arm chair drawn up to the fire, with a book. Perfect peace. Oh it is such a rest to get away from those guns. There is an amusement hall and library full of good books. I am reading "The Deerslayer" by Cooper. Of course it all happened in Canada and the New England States, that's why I picked on it. Have you ever read it? We can go out from 1 P.M. to 6. The doctor comes around in the morning. The grounds are lovely. Huge oak, ash, beech and fir and smaller evergreens shrubs and bushes. Gravel walks and drives, smooth lawns all around. A hill rises at the back and a little stream comes rippling down the rocks into a large pool in the centre of the garden. I wish you could see it May for this is a very poor description. I'll get a picture postcard and send it to you. The village of Westerham is about 5 mins. walk from here and is a nice place. This was Wolfe's home, as you know. I saw the house he was born in and his monument on the village green. I am going to visit Quebec House where his descendants live. They have all his relics. Wolfe was always one of my heros.

This is a lovely day and the trees are beginning to bud. The grass is quite green for there is no frost. Farmers and gardeners are all busy.

Well how is old Perth? Just the same I suppose. No matter where you go and what you see May, there is still no place like home. It will be a glad day when it is all over and we set sail for Canada. I think we will cheer ourselves hoarse.

I have not heard from my chums at the front since coming across and am anxious to hear how they came out.

I think this is all for this time, so Goodbye and don't forget.

Yours truly,
Herb

P.S. My arm is doing fine.

Mar. 18: Lovely day. Walked to Limpsfield and back—8 miles.

Mar. 19: Cool and a little rain. Went down street for walk. Had tea with Mr. Askew, jeweller in Westerham.

Mar. 20: Colder. Walked downtown in afternoon and left my razor to be honed.

Mar. 21: Snowy. Reading "The Deer Slayer." Concert at night by hospital talent.

Mar. 22: Fair in morning but snow flurries P.M. Went down street for razor.

Mar. 23: Cold. Canadian and I went for walk and had tea. Concert in evening by Hearts Yeomanry.

50

Dunsdale Hospital
Westerham, Kent
23/3/17 5P.M.

Dear May,

I am just in from my afternoon walk and I am feeling rather lonely in spite of the kind people and pleasant surroundings. Our Canadian sister here handed me a Canadian paper today and the first name on the Casualty list was that of our late Col. Becket. as I read down the list I found several 130 boys in the wounded list, my own included, but I got a shock when I came to those killed. T. Butler's name was near the top followed by several others I knew. I am hoping it is a mistake, but the odds are against me for it is a revised list and bears his exact number. They have my number wrong but I know it is me they mean. They have 787617 instead of 167. Poor Tom, we being in different platoons at Sandling, caused us to be apart most of the time but when we left for France I remember him saying to me "Well surely we will stick together now." Reached the base in France (we marched side by side from the coast into camp 12 miles) and here the doctors held him back. I marched out at 4 A.M. the next morning and he went to hospital leaving me without a real home chum. Next I heard of him was about the middle of Jan. He was up the line but in our reserve company. Still I did not see him until he joined us on the 10th of Feb. while in supports. As luck would have it he got in my company as O.C.'s orderly. He did not know me first glance, until I hailed him. I says "Surely we will be together now." Then we spent our time in reserves and then into the front line. This was his first time in and being an orderly, had no duties except attend to his officer, until we went over the top. The last time I saw him was about 2 A.M. March 1st when I passed him on my way out of the caves where we were living. He was in a party which was detailed to help any other party in need of reinforcements and help to storm strong points, such as machine gun positions while I was in a bombing section. Here again we were separated, he being on the extreme left and I on the extreme right of the line. This was the first time he did any fighting and the first bombardment he was in. I had been under several artillery fires and had some idea of what it was like but it must have been terrible for a man in his first time. It is beyond description, May. I enquired about Tom after I came through the dressing station but no one had seen him but as many of the unwounded were still busy bringing in the wounded, I concluded that he was with them. I was told that Roy Wilson was killed but his name is not in this list. Lett Simpson (I saw he and Harold Edwards at the Ambulance station) told me that E. Ferrier had lost a leg. Did you hear that? I was glad to meet those faces there and they were much more interested in our welfare. Fred Adams offered to write home to Father that night and I gladly accepted the offer. I always said, May, that the people of our neighbourhood, would never realize that we were at war until some of their own fell in battle. I consider that Roy and Jack Spalding have done their part by offering their services, but there are those who have not. This is my view of the matter. What is yours?

I am so anxious about Mother. The last letter I had from home was written Jan. 14 so it is over two months since I heard how she was and hearing of my being wounded and not knowing how seriously would be very trying for her. My dear parents and Clara are my only worries. The others of the family have all got their families to take up their attention, but I know those in the home I left spend many hours none too joyful. I sometimes think it was cruel for to leave my aged Father and Mother but some one must go and I felt that having no one depending on me for a living I was duty bound. I always believed too that God has every man's career planned out for him and to turn aside from it is impossible no matter what else he may dream of doing. Do you think so? His will be done is all we can say.

This is a beautiful Saturday morning, clear and cool. I read and write in the morning and go for a walk in the afternoon. I have finished "The Deerslayer" and am busy at "The Man From Glengarry."[32] Have you ever read it? It recalls bygone days and brings me back to Canada's hills and dales and I can see the old sugar camp as it was when I used to carry sap in a four quart pail. Those were the happy days when we used to play at war with snow forts and snow ball missiles. What a change the passing years make. May the boys who play at war now never see the real thing.

We had a fine concert last night here. A number of the soldiers stationed in the town came up and sang, recited and played the violin and piano for us. It was a splendid little entertainment. Almost every evening we have music and singing by boys of our own bunch. The sisters help us out too, some of them are fine singers.

But somehow I could not go to sleep and the night nurse found me awake every time she came into the ward. She must have told the day nurse for she asked me first thing when she came on duty why I did not sleep. I did not tell her yet. You may guess the reason.

I feel sorry for Mr. Butler. He is a pretty good age and needed his only son.

I have not got any word from my Batt. yet and it is likely to be some time before I get any letters returned. In the meantime I am hoping that all is usual around home.

Good bye for now, May

Yours sincerely,
Herb

Mar. 24: Fair. Down street for afternoon tea. I am reading "The Man From Glengarry" and it reminds me of the happy days gone by, school days and sugar making especially.

Mar. 25: Went to Congregational Church P.M.

Mar. 26: Cool and snow squalls. Went for daily stroll and had tea.

Mar. 27: Fair. Reading "The Magnetic North."

Mar. 28: Fine. Stayed in all day reading. Quiet talks about the crowned Christ, S.D. Gordan.

Mar. 29: Fine. Invited to Mrs. Webster for tea. Had a nice time and a "bon" tea.

Mar. 30: Fine. Got six letters this A.M. Got telegram from home at 7 P.M. All well.

50A (postcard)

Dunsdale[33]

March 30, 1917

Dear May,

Yours dated Feb. 9th reached me this morning after chasing me around for three weeks. I have waited patiently for them to return from France and have been rewarded by getting six. This is a "bon" morning and I am feeling fine. Just one year today since I signed up. Wonder what another year will bring. You have had a rough winter there, but it will be almost over now. The buds are coming here and people are busy in their gardens and on the farms, but they tell me it is a late spring. Was out to tea yesterday at an old English mansion. Had a fine time and a swell tea. Will write a letter soon. Eat an extra bit of taffy for me eh!

Au revoir,

Herb

51

Dunsdale Hospital
Westerham Kent
30/3/17

My Dear Sister,

I have waited patiently for my letters to return from France and was rewarded this morning with five letters and a postcard. I was certainly glad to hear from you. It was dated Feb. 2nd and said that Mother was improving for which I am thankful and I hope she is better now. The cold weather is past and she will soon be able to get out. I am fine and will soon be out of hospital and away on my ten days sick leave. I have sure put in an easy time. Just one year today since I enlisted. Wonder what another year will bring. This is a beautiful day and the buds are coming out and people are busy in the gardens and on the fields. I was out to tea yesterday at Mrs. Websters, a fashionable lady near here. Had a fine time and a swell tea. Tarts and jelly rolls and blanc mange etc. I could hardly walk home. But this hospital is closing for a couple of weeks and we are all sorry to leave. I don't know where they will send us next. I see in this week "Canada" a lot more of my chums either killed or missing. Roy Wilson is killed and several others more. Also a whole string of wounded. I believe my company lost half of its men.

I got a card from Shorncliffe Depot saying that I am attached to the First Central Ontario Regiment, so I will be going back to West Sandling again. Perhaps some of the old 130th will be there yet. Had a letter from G. Penman and said that Rex was in England but did not say where. One from May, L. Cavers and Ray Paul saying that the Hopetown Div. are sending me a box. But I'll never see it nor yours. All parcels arriving for casualties are divided among his platoon so they will do some one good.

Yes it will be a glad day when it is all over and the troops set sail for Canada. Things are looking good in France now the British and French have driven the Germans back a long way. It is to be hoped that this summer finishes it. One winter in the trenches is all I want, although it was not a bad place where we were. Never was above the knees in mud.

I don't hear of any of the Balderson boys enlisting, perhaps they will have to come yet. I am not sorry I came but it is you at home that worries me. Try and bear up, perhaps the time is near when we shall return. But we will leave all in His hands and all will be well.

Give my best regards to all enquiring friends. I wrote to John's a few days ago, also to Spalding. I never hear from the west, at least Dakota, at all. Had one from Maggie in Jan. I will answer Arthur's postcard when I get settled again where ever we go.[34]

Love to all,
Herb

51A

The Bank of Ottawa
Perth, Ontario
March 30, 1917

Pte. J. Herb Gibson
Somewhere in France

Dear Herb,

Here we are, Eva and I, at the office all alone finishing up some
work. At least that is what Eva is at while I hold the revolver in readiness
for an attack, should anyone try to hold us up. But until now only the
janitor has disturbed us. Just for a moment the lights have threatened
to go out, and the clock ticks so much louder than in office hours, but
we're not creepy, not very. It is nine-fifteen now so I guess we will soon
go home. I got your letter yesterday but you said not to answer until I
got further "permission" so alright.

Good night for now, more later.

Sincerely,
May

Mar. 31: Dull. Dunsdale Hospital closed. Sent to Chipstead Seven Oaks.
Not so nice a place. Went to Seven Oaks in afternoon and to the theatre.

Apr. 1: Stormy. Service in evening.

52

Chipstead V.A.D. Hosp.
Sevenoaks Kent
1/4/17

Dear Father,

Sunday morning and I think it is going to be a nice day although
it snowed a little this morning. I am happy now for I got your telegram
O.K. on March 30th at 7 P.M. Those two words "All well" certainly
raised my spirits, and now I know, that you know, that I am not badly
wounded. I suppose you got the letter I wrote in France also, for the
one from Gravesend did not take long to go. The telegram did not state

the time sent but I guess it would not take more than two days to come through. I am going to send it home for a souvenir. I have changed my home again as you will see by address. Dunsdale Hosp. closed yesterday for a couple of weeks and we were all sent out. Sorry too, for it was a No. 1 place and the sisters were all so nice. This is just 3 miles from Dunsdale. It is not nearly so nice a place but quite all right. I don't expect to be here long for as soon as the wound is healed I will be sent to a Canadian Convalescent Hosp. Then when I am all right, will get my sick furlough from there. We had a Canadian Chaplain come to visit us the other day. He gave me a card with the Lord's Prayer and took my name and address. He told me that the 75th had lost so many men that the survivors had been put into another unit. So there is no more 75th Batt.[35] I knew that we had lost heavily but had no idea they were that bad. It certainly makes one think when he sees the names of his chums in the casualty lists. Men whom you shared rations and dugouts with for three months and marched beside in and out of the line. But God's will be done and I have great reason to thank Him for this great mercy to us all. There is no news to write so I will close now. Will likely get some more letters back from France soon. But I am awfully glad that you sent the telegram instead of waiting to write.

> Good bye for now.
> Love to all,
>
> Herb

Apr. 2: Fair. Motored to Chatham hospital. Went for a walk around town. Held up by a Major for not saluting.

Apr. 3: Cool. Left Chatham at 2 P.M. Stopped in London 1.5 hours and landed in Epsom Convalescent camp at 6:30 P.M. In hut 20, F division.

53

Military Hospital
Chatham
3/4/17

Dear May,

Good Morning! and how is your health? Fine I hope, as this leaves me O.K. Have started to ramble again though, as you will see by the heading. Dunsdale Hosp. has closed for a couple of weeks and we had to get out and sorry we were too. But perhaps it was just as well, another three weeks there and we would have been completely spoiled. So I came here yesterday on my way to the Canadian Convalescent Camp at Epsom. Expect to go there today but it is now 10:30 and no sign of moving yet. You never know, we might be here for days. There are about fifty Canucks but have not met anyone I know, except one lad from Smiths Falls and I just knew of him. Wallington is the name. But I should worry. It is not so nice here as at Dunsdale but somewhat better than the front line.

I had a letter from Sgt. Lett Simpson the other day and by the way the letter runs it is pretty bad over there. Have not heard from any of my pals yet but a Canadian Chaplain who came to visit us, told me that the 75th had lost so heavily that the remainder were put into another unit. So there is no more 75th Canadians. I knew we lost heavily that morning but had no idea we were cut up so badly. No doubt by now you will have more particulars than me.

I got a bunch of mail returned from France last week. Clara's of Feb. 2nd, yours 9th and L. Cavers 2nd and some others. And the same night I got a telegram from home saying that they had received my first letter written from Gravesend and that they were "All well." Believe me those two words made me happy if ever anything did. It was over two months since I heard how Mother was. Will soon be getting mail again from France and in another 10 days will look for some direct from Canada. I am informed that I am attached to the 1st Central Ontario Regimental Depot and will be going back to West Sandling again. I don't expect to be at Epsom long as my wound is almost healed. Then for ten days glorious liberty. I mean to take the very best out of that time and then back to, Form Fours, Right, Left, Wheel, Quick March, for France.

Say! May don't you get tired of my never ending talk about myself? It seems to be all I can write about.

Well it must be near sugar time again isn't it. Any taffy pulls at all? I think I could eat about a pail full of maple sugar now. You must eat some for me.

So you think Georgina has lost control over Jack. I believe it was a one-sided affair anyhow. What is Jimmie up to this spring? Do tell me all about who is rushing everybody else. This is all I can think of now. Don't answer to this address. I will write again. I have written quite a few here to pass the time away.

So long.

Yours as ever,

Herb

P.S. Did you get the cards I sent you?

53A (postcard)

Woodcote Park
Convalescent Camp

Hello May,

I wonder what you are doing this lovely Easter Sunday. Weather has been very disagreeable lately but has cleared up now I think. Am down in Epsom now as you see. There are about 4000 men here in blue. It is rather regimental but I think I can stick it for a while. Have done nothing yet, but have to start special physical training on Tuesday.[36]

Apr. 4: Fair. Into blues again and examined by Doctor. Went to dentist and had one tooth filled. Met some of the 130th boys. Went to concert at night in camp theatre. Had free pass for first night.

Apr. 5: Fair. Nothing doing. Cinema at night.

Apr. 6: Snowing. Service at 10 A.M. (Good Friday) Concert in cinema at night.

Apr. 7: Fair. R.L. Borden in camp. Presentation of medals.

Apr. 8: Fine. Church parade 10 A.M.

Apr. 9: Fair. At dentist forenoon and special exercises P.M.

Apr. 10: Snowy. Special exercises forenoon and afternoon.

Apr. 11: Snowy. At dentist in morning. Did nothing afternoon.

Apr. 12: Summer, spring and winter combined. Clothing parade. Getting fitted up again.

54

Military Con. Hospital
Woodcote Park, Epsom, Eng.
Apr. 12/17

Dear Sister,

Must write you a note today, for I know you are looking for one.
I am fine, hoping you are the same. How did you spend Easter and
what kind of weather had you? We have had awful weather here, snow,
rain and hail turn about. I hope it clears up before I go on my furlough
for I want nice days.[37] I expect to be here for a couple of weeks yet,
perhaps more. I am taking special exercise for my arm now, 1/2 hr. fore
and afternoon. Not much eh! It is a machine consisting of two uprights
four ft. high, a roller across and a rope attached with a weight on it,
two cog wheels and ratchet. You turn the roller and roll up the weight.
They have all sorts of machines for developing the muscles in limbs
and body. This is all I do but some men are on light duty and are busy
a few hours each day (weather permitting) fixing up gardens in front of
the huts. The spring is very backward, there does not seem to be much
improvement in the last month. Had quite a fall of snow last night.
    I met another 130th man the other day, Warrington from Fallbrook.
He was in the 3rd Batt. and came across with blood poison last Jan.
There are five 130th here that I know of. It is all chance meeting them
in a large camp like this. I met my company Sergeant Major (75th) last
night. We were wounded the same morning. He has word from the
Batt. and they are not broken up, but had been in the line since we left.
I wonder if they were in this last big fight. I expect you have read in the
papers of the Famous Canadian Victory, Vimy Ridge. The Canadian
papers would be full of it. Good for them. I know what they were up
against. No harm to tell you now that I spent the winter on that famous
old hill and it is where I was hit. We held the most important positions
there and although it was quiet at first it gradually got hotter and hotter.
Artillery fire almost continuously and when we were not attacking
Fritz, he was making a counterattack. It was strongly entrenched and
honeycombed with tunnels. Ours were fitted with bunks and some of
them had electric lights. Fritz could not reach us, even with 9pd. but he
had the same kind of places himself and to drive him out was no child's

play. I think the war will finish this summer. I don't see how they can hold out for another winter. And now that America has declared war, it means a lot for the Allies. I should get some mail soon now. If you wrote on the 30th this will be 13 days. I have written a lot of letters since coming back so should get a shower. But news is scarce, at least I can't think of anything to write after I have described the place I sent a lot of views. Did you get them? If there is anything you want to know, ask me. I think you better address in care of W. Ashcroft. Summer is coming over here and Mother will be able to get out. I hope you drive out a lot and try and enjoy yourselves. How is Tommy. Tell me all those things.

Love to all,

Herb

Apr. 13: Rain, hail and snow. Special exercises P.M. Got 13 letters back from France.

Apr. 14: Cloudy. At dentist in morning. Wrote some letters and went to the pictures at night.

55

Military Con. Hospital
Div. F 20, Woodcote Park
Epsom
14/4/17

Dear May,

Yours of 16 and 26 Feb. reached me yesterday with 11 others, some bunch eh! I expect another bunch yet but should soon get some direct from Canada.

I had a most enjoyable day yesterday reading them all and today I re-read them and have started to answer some. Of course I have written to most of the senders since coming back so there is not much use answering them, although I like to answer all I get. A cousin of mine up Muskoka way, whom I have never seen, wrote me on the very day I was wounded so I knew some one was thinking of me on the eventful day. I suppose you have been reading of the great victory won by the Canucks at Vimy Ridge. I may tell you now that I spent the winter on that famous hill. Some important place it was. Old Fritz thought no troops on earth could ever take it from him. But give the men from the North a job and he will do it. Would liked to have been there for the big advance, but since I helped to hold that important position for three months, and was wounded there I am satisfied that I did all I could. I can look back there and see it all and see our men advancing across that same ground where some of Perth's boys fell.

I hope you got what you were waiting for at time of writing. I sent one home at the same time and they got it sometime before the 26th so yours must have gone by Toronto perhaps.

Yes, I got three or four different accounts of the doings at Harper so I think I got it all. Too bad you did not get out to some of them. I hope your cold did not get any worse and your Mother did not scold you too seriously. I know what it is like. After being out nights and getting a cold, Mother would say "Yes, I told you to wrap up." Still you know a good scolding does one good sometimes.

I hope you are having better weather than we are. We have had spring, winter, summer and fall combined this while.

Oh, say, what was I going to ask you. Oh, yes. How big is the moon over there? Ha Ha, I wish you could come over here for 7 cents, let me see that would be 3 1/2 pence wouldn't it. Say what does a nickel look like?

I would love to have a nice drive with you now and a little chat afterwards, but I suppose if this war continues I will be too old for such exertions.

Yes and the stay-at-homes will have picked up all the nice girls. Ho! well I don't care do I?

Nonsense this is but I am trying to fill this page. Did I tell you that I am going to Huntingdon on furlough so address your answer in care of Wm. Ashcroft, Wild Goose Leys, Abbots Ripton, Huntingdon.

Sincerely,

Herb

P.S. Hurrah for the U.S. eh.

Apr. 15: Fine. Went to church and downtown.

Apr. 16: Fair. Got teeth in.

Apr. 17: Fine. Special exercises. Met a couple of 130th boys.

Apr. 18: Fair. On fire picket so had to stay in hut. Wrote some letters home.

56

Convalescent Hosp. Div. F 20
Woodcote Park, Epsom
April 18, 1917

My Dear Father,

I will now answer your letter of Feb. 18th which came in a bunch of
others from France. I am looking for some addressed to Gravesend now.
If you got my letter on March 29th that is 20 days ago so that should
be time for one to cross. This changing around hampers a fellow's mail
but I think most of my letters reach me by and by. But I have had awful
luck with parcels. This bunch of letters told of three being sent and
would arrive after I left France. I am thankful to be here though and the
parcels will be divided among my platoon mates over yonder behind the
guns and will be appreciated by them. I have not heard from my Batt.
since leaving and I do not know whether they were in this last big push.
What do you think of the war now? You never say.[38] The Allies have
made great progress this last week. Lens was a strongly fortified place
and the British captured a lot of guns and ammunition. The Americans
sending food over here will be a great help even if they do not send an
army. I don't think the Germans will be able to hold out for another
winter. Perhaps we will be home for Xmas this year. It will be a glad day
when all is settled. The more I see of it the more useless it seems. There
was plenty of room for us all to live without having to fight over land.
At the same time I am more convinced that we must defend our homes
from the ravages of a tyrant. I hope Canada never sees its land and
homes ruined by war. The small piece of battle ground I have seen may
never be farmed again. It will take an awful work to fill in trenches and
shell holes, if they do.

Well you had a cold winter there. I am glad there was lots of wood
handy. Will there be enough for next winter? I suppose you had lots
of hay too. How is your seed grain? I hope it is not so wet in seed time
this year. Are your cows all strippers[39] that you were milking them in
Feb? Only two more weeks and the factory will be going again.[40] Isn't
it wonderful how the time passes. About that Citizen.[41] I sent them all
arrears in Feb. 1916, but they could not find my name in their books.
But I think if you look among my receipts you will find one from them.

I hope your colt will make a nice driver.[42] It seems a long time since I had a drive in a buggy, over eight months ago. How is John getting along? Is he as busy as ever? What are all the neighbours doing? I hear from J. Spalding and J. Cavers occasionally but do not hear from any of the other boys. Oh yes, and Roy Keays.[43] I believe it is my turn to write to Rob. Anderson. Really I can hardly keep track of all my letters.

Have just returned from doing my exercises. I go at 10:30 am and 2:30 P.M. for 1/2 hour each time. It is almost dinner time now. My hut is on fire picket today so we all have to stay inside. Three huts are on picket each day and are ready should fire break out anywhere.

I have lots of time to read but am tired of papers and books.

My Testament is always at hand and every time I take it up find something new in it. The Old Story is always new.

How is Alex Park this spring?

Well I think this is all this time and I hope and pray you all may have good health and try to enjoy yourselves until we shall all meet again. I am sending Maggie some papers today. Don't work too hard this spring.

Love to all,
Herb

Apr. 19: Fine. Special exercises. Putting in a soft time here.

Apr. 20: Fine. Medical inspection in A.M. Continue special exercises. Play at night "Confusion."

Apr. 21: Fine. Nothing doing. Went to the cinema at night. Got bunch of letters from France.

Apr. 22: Fair. Church service 10:30.

Apr. 23: Fine. Everything as usual.

Apr. 24: Fine. Medical exam. Told to carry on. W. Maw and I went to concert.

Apr. 25: Fine. Special exercises. W. Maw and I went downtown.

Apr. 26: Fine. As usual. One hour exercises and putting in the time. Moved to another hut.

Apr. 27: Carry on. Got first letter from Perth direct to hospital.

57

Convalescent Hospital, Div. F29
Woodcote Park, Epsom
27/4/17

Dear May,

Yours of April 4th reached me today and is the first direct to
hospital and you may be sure I was pleased to get it. Last one was
written March 4th so there must be some more went to France. I don't
believe I answered that one so will make this do for both. Have not got
any letters from home yet which were written since they heard I was
wounded. The last one was March 7th and evidently they did not know
then. I am kind of impatient to hear how they got the news. It worried
me for I thought if they got no particulars that Mother especially would
think of the wound as being serious. However their telegram relieved
me greatly and there must be a great bunch of mail not far away now.

So my hopes that Tom had been taken prisoner or that there was
some mistake, have been shattered. Poor fellow, he was so short a time
in the line. I think I gave you all the particulars that I could regarding
the last time I saw him and our relative positions in the line. I told
John all about it and asked him to tell Mr. Butler. The little I could tell
might relieve him a little. It was awfully nice I think for them to have a
memorial service for the boys. Well May, one thing I can say was that
he was a good living boy. Yes it makes me lonesome when I look back to
shell torn Vimy Ridge and although I cannot see the exact spot I know
of a burying ground where it is altogether likely that those two graves
are. It lies in a hollow under the shadow of Vimy Ridge and lads have
buried their "Pals" there, carefully erecting wooden cross and inscriptions
to mark the spot but many a shell lights there as elsewhere, plowing up
the mounds and shattering the crosses. But I must stop now although I
could write a good many pages on this particular spot in France.

I am feeling a little down hearted tonight as no doubt you see by
the run of the writing. But May! I have no one here to confide in so I
am writing as though I were talking to you. Must cheer up and write of
other things, trusting that He who created all things will bring about His
own good purposes. So Elsie is going off this summer. Do you know I
always thought that Jimmie would win there. Who is he rushing now?

Yes, I remembered 1st April. It was very stormy, we tried to get the sisters to believe a story of a zeppelin raid but nothing doing.

You are sure some typist now and perhaps when I get home I shall see how you look behind the iron bars. Oh not prison bars no no.

Perhaps you won't know a common rear rank soldier then eh! Bankers come in with a higher class than that.

I was all tickled with that description of your dream. It must have been pleasant. What kind did you have when you had the measles? Did you see any "German" fairies? I am afraid not, Sorry to hear you had that nasty trouble. Were you sick long? Spring time is with you again. It is the best time of the year isn't it.

I don't see much change here for the last month, spring seems to be backward in coming forward. We had snow just last week.

Well May, I am sure putting in a soft time here, it is almost a shame to take the money. Won't be here much longer though, I expect, for I am as well as ever I was. Think I will go to Glasgow first. You see our furlough tickets are free but have got to go straight to farthest point but can stop off on the way back. So I will go to Glasgow for a day or two and then work back.

I hardly know what address to give you. Hard to say where I shall be when you get this. I think you better put on Abbots Ripton, Huntingdon, care of Wm. Ashcroft. Well good bye May and good luck from one who does not forget you.

JHG.

58

Convalescent Hospital
Woodcote Park, Epsom
April 2, 1917[44]

Dear Father,

Yours of April 2nd reached me yesterday also one from Willies. Glad to hear you were all well. Mother will soon be able to get out. I am as well as I ever was now and expect to be discharged soon. Two months rest is pretty good and 10 days sick furlough. I went to the English Church service this morning. The sermon was splendid. Text Philippians 2.14 13.16. He endeavoured to answer the question "Has Christianity been a failure." Spoke of the writing of Blackford who said that all the great cities of the world were not centers of truth and light and that from San Francisco to Baghdad and Cape Colony to Iceland was ruled by earthly kings. And on top of all this the great war of the 20th century, started by professed Protestant nations with a Roman Catholic nation in harmony with them. This is the argument I have heard plenty of comrades in arms put up. But the Chaplain reasoned in this way, although the great cities were not centers of light, how much greater would be the darkness but for the influence of Christianity, which has brought about all the great reformations. Our part in the war, he claims, is the greatest proof that Christianity is not a failure and that men are still willing to give up their lives for the protection of what he knows is right. I am thankful for the blessing of having a Christian home and a Saviour who is always with me. I confess that I do not live a perfect life, but I am trying. I can't see any reason why that I should have been spared through danger any more than my comrades, except that my time had not come.

You will have my letters by now, telling all that I know about Tom Butler. Poor fellow he was not long in the line. However I can say that he was a good living boy. We used to go to Communion Service at Sandling every week, and I never heard him complain about anything.

Well surely everyone in that part will know me by now. I would sooner they had not got my photo, but since they have I hope they print it half decent.[45] Really I have not done much yet although 13 months in the army, only about 3 in France and I never fired a shot or threw a bomb. Therefore I have not taken any lives for the simple reason that the enemy got me first. I had only seen one German (except prisoners) before that morning. And I am not sorry that I did not kill any for I used to wonder how I ever could do it. Now this is confidential, a stranger might infer that I was a coward.

I am glad your cattle did well. I suppose you will be sending to the factory again in a few days. It is getting more like summer here this last few days and is quite warm today. The grass is growing and I see the farmers on the fields. The boys here are busy week days making gardens around the huts, those who are fit to work a few hours each day.

I had a letter from Mr. Ashcroft and he thinks I will like that part of the country. So I expect to have a good time. Have decided to take a trip to Scotland first, for a day or two. We get free passage so I may as well see all I can.

I will have to go to the farthest point direct, but can stop off on the way back. I would like to go to Ireland but will not this time. I may get another chance to visit the land of the Shamrock.

Well I hope you get the crop in all right and don't work too hard. Surely there will not be so much rain this spring. I had a letter from Ashcrofts which was written in Feb. They certainly paid a big price for seed wheat. Surely they will have a good crop this year. Maggie hoped I would be home to go out, help them harvest it but I guess not this year. Supposing it stopped now, it would take several months to get us all back home. I think this is all for now.

So write often and take care of yourselves.

Your loving son,
Herb

58A

LITTLE BRASS MAPLE LEAF

Oh, little brass Maple Leaf[46]
You bring a message to me
A call to loving service
In no uncertain way.
A call that women are needed
In these awful days of war
To sacrifice, work, and be ready
As they never were before.

On the uniform of our boys
You flash—very splendid and bright.
They have yielded pleasures and joys
As they train to defend the right.
You were known and loved in England
By many training days
When they learned to know our Johnny Canuck
And love his happy ways.

And by brave deeds they have done
You are known across in France
When on that April morning
Came the call "Advance"!
They did so without flinching
As Canadian boys always must.
But many Maple Leaves were left
Lying in the dust.

And in the year that followed
You added to your fame
Now when we call ourselves Canadian
We glory in the name.

And many a sister and sweetheart
Prays for a soldier there
And guards the Maple Leaf he wore
With tender loving care
And many a young wife presses you
Cold, to her aching brow,
You grow hot with her tears and kisses
For one is gone from her now.
But when her first grief is over
She can say of him with pride
"He gave his life for his country
T'was for all that is highest he died"

And a Mother watches daily
And will not give way to grief
And beside that Mother's Bible
Is laid—a Maple Leaf.

—May Bell Keays, 1917[47]

Apr. 28: Warm. Pte. Lamb and I went down to Epsom. Got a letter from home and from Janet.
Apr. 29: Fine.
Apr. 30: Warm. Still on special exercises.

May 1: Warm. Working in gardens in A.M. Gave in my name and address for furlough.

May 2: Warm. Medical inspection. Had long talk with J. Trail who just arrived.

59

Woodcote Park Hosp.
Epsom, Surrey
2/5/17

Dear May,

Just a line this evening to say that I am getting my discharge from here this week and am going up to Perth Scotland also Lanark. I will not have more than one day to spend in each place as I want to be four or five with my brother-in-law's people and a couple of days in London. The weather is lovely and warm here now and I hope it stays nice for a couple of weeks any how.

I am sending you a snap, not much good but I never take a nice picture anyway. This is Pte. Lamb of 52nd Canadian from Hespeler, Ont.[48] We have chummed for a month and a half. Nice name eh! Pretty decent chap too. He came from France with debility, but has gone on furlough now. Can't tell you positively where I shall go after leave, as that depends on what category the M.O. puts me in. I got a glimpse of my papers today and I think they were marked D.I. If so that means six months training in England. Of course I am not sure, in fact one is never sure of anything in the army (except lots of C.B. if you do wrong).

I had a very pathetic letter today from Mr. Tufts of Tweed Ont. He wished to know if I could give him any particulars regarding his son Arthur's death. He was killed March 1st but I can not tell him anything about it. In an engagement like that one just sees what is going on in his immediate vicinity. Besides it was just gray dawn when I started back.

Now May dear I shall be expecting a photo of yours right away. I won't coax you awe'do.

Here wishing you the best of luck.

Sincerely,
Herb

May 3: Warm. Went for special exercise to pass the time. Downtown with J. Trail.

May 4: Warm. Got letter from Clara and three dollars enclosed from Mother. Downtown in evening.

May 5: Fine. J. Trail, O. Noonan, R. Morton and I went to Epsom in P.M. Meet bon belfe.[49]

May 6: Fine. Went for walk in Ostead Park.

May 7: Left Epsom on Furlough at noon. Stopped in London at Gaiety Theatre.

May 8: Cool. Went to Zoological gardens. Met friend at five. Started to Scotland at 8:50 P.M.

60

London
May 8, 1917

Dear Sister,

At the present moment I am sitting in a railway coach, bound for Perth, Scotland and as the train doesn't leave until 8:50 I will pass the time in this way.

I received your letter last week but was rather busy getting ready for furlough and besides several 130th boys came into camp last weekend and we spent all the time we could together. Down to Epsom town mostly. J. Trail, O. Noonan of Christie Lake and R. Norton and I were the bunch.

We sure had a good time while it lasted. I left hospital yesterday the 7th, at noon, and have been in London since. Missed the train last night but it doesn't matter for my ticket is good any time. Will get to Perth about 9 A.M. tomorrow and intend staying there a day and come back to Lanark. Gee, if it were only our little Lanark Ontario, couldn't I spend a great week. I have to report back to Hastings. Don't know what kind of a place that will be. Supposed to do six months physical jerks there. Perhaps the war will be over by then, so cheer up. It makes me lonesome when I know you are so lonely. Do try and keep up your spirits. All will come out right. Go out all you can and have a good time and when you come home, prepare to go somewhere else. I know you must have spent a lonely winter but now since Mother is better and can get out, surely you will be alright.

About your proposed marriage I can say nothing. You will have to judge for yourself. If you think he is worthy of you and give you a good home that is all that is necessary I think. You must not worry about not having a home though, for if I get home, you can always make my home your home. If I don't then my property will be yours. About leaving Father and Mother, I know they would be terribly bad off without you but perhaps could get a nice girl to stay with them until I return.[50] But I would like to be there to give you a good wedding for you deserve it and we could make it a grand event.

Wed. morning 11 A.M. Laidlaws Temperance Hotel, Perth Scot.

Arrived here about 9 and am staying at a Temperance Hotel. Seems to be a fair place. Have just had a wash and brush up and awaiting dinner to be served.

I can scarcely realize that I am in Perth Scot. Had a nice trip up. It was just daylight when we entered Scotland and I met in with a Perth soldier going home on leave so he told me all the places etc, etc. Passed through some lovely country. He is going to take me around town this afternoon. I took notes along the way so when I get time I will write you an account of it.

Write and tell me more about your new beau. You never even mentioned his name.

All for today.

Love to all,
Herb

May 9: Cool. Landed in Perth at 9 A.M. Stopped at Laidlaws Temperance Hall. Lovely country and town. Bought a few souvenirs. Show at night. Slept well.

May 10: Cool and misty. Left for Glasgow at 9:00 A.M., arrived 11:00. Walked around to Queen Street Station and took 1:00 P.M. train for Edinburgh. Arrived 2:30 P.M.

May 11: Misty. Slept in B.B. Hut. Met an —— and we went out to Forth Bridge. Got a taxi and went all over town.

May 12: Foggy. Went to Royal Scottish Museum and to theatre. Left for Huntingdon at 7 P.M. and got layed off at Peterboro from 4:00 A.M. to 5:00 P.M. on Sunday.

60B (postcard)

May 12, 1917
Edinburgh, Scot.

Dear May,

Just a line today to say that I am in the most beautiful city I ever
saw. Was around the principal parts yesterday. This bridge is worth
going miles to see.[51] The grand fleet lies just below the bridge. Leaving
tonight for Huntingdon.

> *May 13*: Fine. Arrived at Mr. Ashcroft at 6:00 P.M.
> *May 14*: Fine. Had a walk around farm and to Huntingdon in evening.

61

Abbots Ripton
Huntingdon
14/5/17

Dear May,

Here we are again and another new abode. Yes and this is so much
like home I shall be sorry to leave it. I arrived here yesterday just at
tea time and they saw me turn in the gate so Mr. Ashcroft came out
to meet me and they sure gave me a Royal welcome. I have just to
make myself at home and if you saw me now you would say that I
was living up to their request. Have my coat off and sleeves rolled up
for they say I seem more like one of them. I enjoyed a tramp through
the fields this morning and made a trip with the cultivator across a
20 acre field and back. Mr. Ashcroft is quite like my brother-in-law
and manages a large farm. He takes the milk to Huntingdon so I am
going with him this evening. This is a lovely farming country, almost
level and large fields. Gee! but it is great to be back on the land again.
I applied for an extension of furlough today but ten to one I don't get
it. Two letters from you reached here before me as I had directed them
to be sent here from Dunsdale. Have been on pass since last Monday.
Spent a day in London and then hit for Perth Scotland arriving there

Wed. morning. Nice town this but saw it all in one day so I set my face
for Glasgow. The weather was disagreeable cold and misty. Glasgow
had no charms for me, nothing to see but dockyards, factories, saloons
and theatres through a curtain of smoke and fog so the same evening
found me in Edinburgh. Here is the most beautiful city I ever saw. The
buildings are of stone, showing excellent workmanship, streets well
paved and wide and clean. Prince's Street, which is the main street, is
said to be the prettiest in the world. I visited Holy Rood Palace, which
was the home of Mary Queen of Scots and is now the home of the
King when he visits Edinburgh. Was through Knox's house which is the
oldest occupied house in the city. You have heard of John Knox haven't
you? Edinburgh Castle is a grand structure on top of a steep hill and
overlooking the city. The Royal Scottish Museum is the best I ever saw.
They have some fine universities and homes for boys and girls, churches
and halls. The bridge across the Forth River is worth going miles to see.
I forget if I sent you a postcard of it or not. Dear me, that memory of
mine is getting awful. Now I sent several postcards from Edinburgh and
blest if I can remember to whom. I am going to write a full account
of my trip later on as I took several notes on the way. I am going to
Huntingdon this evening with Mr. Ashcroft so I will have to say good
afternoon May.

More later.

Herb

May 15: Fine. Wrote some letters. Went for a wheel to Huntingdon in
evening and saw place where Tow worked.[52]

May 16: Fine. Went to the fields and worked cultivator some. Miss V.
Ashcroft came to see me. Left Huntingdon at 7:30 in London 9:15. Slept
in YMCA Hut. King's Cross.

May 17: Rainy. Left London Bridge for Hastings at 6:30 arrived 9:00 A.M.
Reported at 1st C.C.D.

May 18: Warm. Medical inspection in A.M. and moved to E. Company in
afternoon, 47 Chapel Park Road, Hastings.

62

E. Co. 1st C.C. Depot
Hastings, Sussex
May 18, 1917

Dear Sister,

I am settled here now and as I have the afternoon to myself will try and tell you about my ten days leave.

You may have it published if you wish, perhaps some may care to read it.[53]

"Ten Days Leave"

Every man who has been overseas is given a "sick furlough" when he is discharged from hospital and he looks forward to those days with something like the impatience of a school boy for his Easter holidays.

Ten whole days and nights, without Corporals or Sgt. Majors, in which to forget that there is a war on. By and by the day comes when he is called to state where he wishes to proceed and is given his pass and free travelling warrant.

I took mine to Perth Scotland, for I had always been curious to see what the original Perth-on-Tay was like.

Two hours by train took us into London Bridge Station where we changed to the Underground Electric Railway for Euston Station, the terminus of the Caladonian Railway. Boarding the train at 8:50 P.M. we travelled up the West Coast of England and reached Gretna Green, which is on the border of Scotland, shortly after day break. The "Land of the Heather" is more beautiful than anything I had ever pictured. The hills and valleys and streams seemed all so home-like and peaceful. The little white washed houses surrounded by trees and flowers seems more comfortable than the biggest mansion in London.

Running north through Carstairs you enter the coal mining country, not so pretty but rich nevertheless. Motherwell, Lanarkshire, is a large manufacturing town of steel and iron. Huge smelters working day and night turning out tons of war material.

The next town of importance is Glenboig Junction, also a busy place and here the farming land starts. Rolling land but very rich as the new grain showed. Sheep seem to be the principal stock raised.

Passing near Falkirk, the railroad enters the Allan River Valley, which lies between the Sedlaw and Orchid hills. Bending towards the hills, you come to the historic old town of Stirling, the headquarters of the Argyle and Sutherland Highlanders. Stirling Castle looks down upon the town from the highest hill and just across the valley stands the Wallace Monument. A few miles winding through the hills and you come to the Cars of Stirling, a beautiful tract of land, watered by the River Earn and sheltered on the north-west by the Denning Hills. Most of this is owned by John Dewar (guess everyone has heard of him) and the castle and estate is called Dupplin. Half an hours run from here you enter a long tunnel and just on the other side is Perth. I spent one day here, for although a city, most of the places of interest can be seen in that time. The Tay is much larger than "our Tay" and as the tide comes in here the bridges are very high. It was low water when I saw it and could easily have waded across, the river bed being pure gravel. Some fine pearls are found here.

From here, I turned towards Glasgow, but as the weather was dull and misty, together with the smoke from the huge docks, I could see very little of the city, so the same night I walked along what is said to be the prettiest street in the world, namely Princes Street, Edinburgh. Spent a comfortable night in the YMCA rest hut, which is always open to Soldiers and Sailors, at the very lowest prices. I might say here that this Association has done and is doing a great work for the boys in Khaki and blue.

Early next morning I started out to see the Forth Bridge, which spans the Firth of Forth at Queen's Ferry. It cost $3,500,000 pounds and the labour of 5000 men day and night for seven years. Total length is one and a half miles, height 381 feet above high water, deepest foundation 91 feet below high water. 51,000 tons of steel and 5,000,000 rivets were used. It was past noon when I got back so having met a friend we hired a taxi for the afternoon and started out to see the city.

Edinburgh is a much nicer city than London. The streets are wide and there seems to be an abundance of fresh air for everyone and very little smoke. Of course, it is a city of learning rather than manufacturing, everyone knows of the Universities and colleges of Edinburgh. Its buildings are built chiefly of stone and show fine workmanship. Well we started from the National Arts Building on Princes Street, past Scott's Monument, Post and Record Offices and the Old Prison. Nelson's monument stands on a high hill at the foot of Princes Street and each day at noon a cannon is fired from it. Now we come to Old Edinburgh and from the top of Jacob's Ladder which winds up the hill, we look down on Waverly Station, the largest station in Great Britain and also upon Tolbooth's church and burying ground. The graves are all enclosed by stone walls which was to prevent body snatching, common in the time of Burke and Howe. Next is Robert Burns Monument opposite the Royal College. Turning down into the valley we view Holy Rood Palace, home of Mary, Queen of Scots and the home of the present King when he visits the city. Passing along the Royal Road we enter Canon Gate, a street lined with buildings dating back to the thirteenth century. Some of them are Tolbooth's Prison 1591, John Knox's house 1549, which is the oldest inhabited house in Edinburgh. The owner was kind enough to show us through it and we saw all John Knox's furniture, study and papers, also the first Bible which was printed in Scotland 1575. On the outside, above the door, these words are inscribed "Lofe God abofe al and ye nychtbour as yi sely." We also saw Knox's church, St. Giles Cathedral. Next is the old Scottish Parliament. Soldiers, especially Canadians are privileged, so we were conducted into the High Court, first court I ever was in and a criminal case was hearing. Prince Charles Mont. is near here, also the Heart of Midlothian, just a rough heart, shaped with stones in the pavement but marks the spot where in olden times all executions took place in public. From here we climbed up to Edinburgh Castle which stands sentinel over the city. I was sorry we had not time to look through the castle but if one explored every one of these historic old places, he would need six months leave, so we passed on to see the house where Sir Walter Scott was born Aug. 15, 1771, Edinburgh Infirmary the finest place of its kind in the world, surgeons hall, University Usher hall for which a well known brewer gave 100,000 pounds and the committee took 25 years to find a site for it, St. Mary's Church; Donaldson Hospital for Orphans beside the Water of Leith, across which is a very high bridge, known as suicide bridge on account of the number of persons who have thrown themselves over it, Fettes College, Dr. Stewarts college and Craig Leith Hospital are also fine buildings.

Next morning we visited the Royal Scottish Museum, but one would need a week to look through it so we just ran through it as I had to catch the afternoon train for the south. Leaving Edinburgh the railway runs along the coast through Berwick-on-Sea and across the Tweed River into England. Night came on again, preventing a view of the country and at 4:30 next morning we reached Peterboro, a city about 16 miles from my destination. Owing to so many trains being cancelled, I had to stop here 13 hours, so went and got a bed and had a good sleep. Reached Abbots Ripton and walked out to Mr. Ashcrofts, a distance of 2 miles and was just in time for tea. Here I spent the remainder of my time, which seemed to just fly and Wednesday evening started for Hastings, where I arrived Thurs 9 A.M. This is a splendid sea side resort, having a fine beach. We are billeted in dwelling houses and do Physical Training 4 or 5 hours per day.[54]

Perhaps you better not put in this page. I guess the first ten will be enough. I just wish you could see all these places. I am sure you would enjoy it although I found it very tiresome travelling. I wish Mother was here in Hastings though, beside the sea, it is just grand.

I am sending you some views of the beach. This is Monday 21st and as I have been inoculated have the day off so am finishing this. They put it in my breast this time and it is pretty sore.

I got 10 letters returned from France the day after I came here. The ones which were written about 15 of March, and I got yours of April 25th about an hour before I left Ashcrofts. He will forward all that come.

I guess I better stop now.

Love to all,
Herb

Am sending a little parcel soon.

May 19: Fine. Sea bath in A.M. Went to see "Seven Days Leave" played, had tea downtown and spent evening on the beach. Met J. Stewart of 130th.

May 20: Fine. Inoculation A.M.

May 21: Fine. Had day off and wrote some letters. Hastings in the evening.

May 22: Warm. Started doing P.T. Bath parade.

63

75th Batt.
E. Co. 1st C.C.D.
Hastings, Sussex
22/5/17

Dear Sister,

Here are a few little remembrances from various places which I visited. The little testament is for Father, I got it in John Knox's house in Edinburgh and is the smallest book ever printed and bound. The heart and heather broach is for Mother purchased in the same place and is pure silver, designed in a style about the year 1830. The other broach is for Willie's Margaret, am sending it in the bunch, please send it to her, bought it in Perth Scot. The silver bangle is for Elma also from Perth-on-Tay and the broach in same box is for John's Maggie. I bought it at St. Leonards. Lastly a ring for yourself and I hope it fits. It is from Perth also and they are pure pearls out of the River Tay. One is a little chipped you will notice. The Canadian button is one I wore on famous Vimy Ridge and the others are off Imperial uniforms. I am sending you my badge too, so now you have all three I have worn. Isn't the old 130th the nicest yet?

I will register this so you will surely get it O.K. Maggie's letter of 25th reached me today but I have not got the money she spoke of. Got Mother's three dollars alright. Well will answer Maggie's letter in a few days.

Love to all,
Herb

Posting both box and letter at same time. Likely you will get the letter first.[55] I mean to send each one a little keepsake.

May 23: Warm. P.T. Downtown in evening with J. Stewart.

May 24: Cooler. Light duty at Q.M. stores.

May 25: Warm. P.T. and Bath parade. Air raid on the South East Coast.

May 26: Hot P.T. Drill in A.M. Down on the back in afternoon.

May 27: Hot. Church parade in A.M.

May 28: Hot. P.T. in A.M. Military sports in the afternoon. On Fire Picket.

May 29: Cool and foggy. P.T. as usual. Poor grub to-day. On fire picket.

May 30: Fine. Pay day. Bath in afternoon.

May 31: Warm. P.T. all day. One year since the 130th left Perth for Barriefield camp.

June 1: Fine. Bath in A.M. and P.T. in P.M.

64

75th Batt.
E. Co. 1st C.C.D.
Hastings Sussex
June 1/17

Dear May,

Yours of May 13 reached me today and was glad to hear from you as I always am. Had been looking for one for a few days and knew there was one somewhere near.

So you thought that a funny address eh! Well this one is also quite lengthy. It means, Canadian Command Depot, and formerly was called the C.A.C.C. or Canadian Army Casualty Corp or as the boys nick-named it Charlie Chaplins Army Corp. There are about 4000 of us here at present, most of whom have been wounded, of course there are always a few taken sick before going to France. The wounded are termed as Overseas's and the others as local casualties.

I like the place alright and am contented although 4 hours per day of physical jerks get rather monotonous. Have been on fire picket all week so cannot leave the billets after retreat. Can't go downtown but can always fill up the time reading and writing. I really do not know how long I shall be here yet or do I worry. The main thing is not to worry.

Yesterday on parade, they called for all men who had taken bombing courses, to fall out. So I did so, bombing is my hobby. Nothing makes old Fritz scream like a Mills No. 5. Rather cool-blooded remark, says you but it is so. I have heard him scream like a child although not hit, pure terror.

So a (Red Cap) Staff Officer came along and asked us all particulars. Says to me "Well my boy, you were a bomber in the 75th." "Yes Sir." "Where were you wounded?" "Vimy Ridge Sir." "When." "March 1st, Sir." You should have seen him smile ever so kindly. I don't know as yet what the idea is but no doubt will in a few days. Some say we are to take a new course for to be instructors. Hardly such good luck for me, I fear. Something tells me I shall be back patrolling No Man's Land before two more months are past.

You said in one letter not long ago something like this, "Will your life be the same to you as before the war?" No, it will not May. I sometimes feel as if I would like to get away back in the woods beside a clear calm lake, as close to nature as possible without losing any respect for civilization. Just to live there in a neat little log hut, away from all the mad whirl of this modern life. I have seen enough of this world's wickedness now to do me.[56] Then again I think if I only had been more attentive to my books when I had the chance, how grand it would be to continue fighting after this is over for Christ's Kingdom, which would bring a reward worth more than all the V.C.'s on earth. Of course I can't forget the home I left and how grand it would be to till the soil once more, to reap and sow, plow and mow. I think 99 out of 100 Canadians over here are in about the same state of mind. Let me tell you May, for I know I can trust you to keep it, that every man in the Canadian Army (except for a few well paid bomb proofers as we call them) are completely fed up with this war and wish it over. Not that they are cowards, but the "Red Tape" gets so disgusting at times. Of course we must have discipline but some officers not all seem to look upon a private as a thing with a weak mind and a strong back. In most cases of officers like this, they themselves have both weak minds and weak backs, but still they have a commission and superiors must be obeyed. I will admit that the boys of the Maple are hard to keep under control, more so than the Imperials. He frequently makes a break for a few days of liberty without the proper authority even though he knows that it means either a stoppage of pay or the next draft for France. In some cases both, but even if he does get both, a few more days of liberty and he will risk anything. Once in range of Fritz though and he forgets everything but his object. Of course there are always some men, in any army, who will shirk duty under fire, and you can't call them cowards. The fact that they are there answers that, but it is their nerves get the better of them. I have been in the same fix, ran with the rest, thinking to get out of danger when I may have been running into it, then just stopped to think "Well, what did you run for? One place is as safe as another." I am speaking of shell fire. To stand in a place exposed to

snipers and machine guns is a different thing. That would be suicide.
Yes, I saw about J. Scott being missing and the Greer you mention was
my bed mate all winter. Poor fellow, many a mile we tramped together
and many a listening post. He was first bayonet man in my bombing
section on March 1st. There were seven of us in the section. Here are
the names, Corp. Kenninger in charge, wounded in the knee; Craig
Greer 1st bayonet man missing; Scarf 1st thrower, bullet in breast,
serious; I forget the 1st Carriers name but he was wounded; second
thrower was yours Truly; 2nd carrier was Appleton, a fine fellow.[57] He
was severely wounded in the thigh with shrapnel. I bound it up with my
putties to stop the blood and started him back. I never saw him after.
The seventh was a rifle grenadier, missing. Seven out of seven leaves
nothing doesn't it.

Oh! here I must stop. It seems when I get started I can not write
about anything else and the thought has just come to me that perhaps
you do not care for this kind of news.

Tomorrow we have to sign some sort of cards for to help disposing
of the soldiers who return when the war is over.

I don't know of any more to write tonight so will ring off.

Hope you are having lots of fun.

Yours,

Herb

June 2: Fine. P.T. in morning downtown in the evening. Finished fire picket.

65

75th Battalion
1st C.C. Depot
Hastings Sussex
June 2, 1917

My Dear Mother,

Here it is Sat. afternoon June 2nd. How time does fly. I should have
written to you last week, but it seems I can't get around them all in less
than two weeks.

Well I hope you are well and that you are able to get out some now.
Surely the weather is warm there now. It is lovely here by the sea, not
too hot or cold.

I have been looking for a letter from some of you all week but none has come. Perhaps there will be one tonight. I sent a parcel last week. Hope you get it and that you will like the broach.

I wonder what you are all doing now over there in the west. I am longing for a drive with a horse and buggy. You never see any people with Canadian outfits here, all carts. Well, I did see one man with a buggy while at Ashcrofts.

I have been on fire picket all this week and have to stay in my billets after retreat so can't get out for a walk. There is no work in connection with it at all unless a fire broke out in which case we are to be ready to help the town firemen. I am still in physical jerks and in the lowest class. You see we work up just according as we become stronger until the Medical Officer thinks we are fit for service again. I am in No. 4 class and have to go through 3, 2, and 1 yet. No. 1 is fit.

A few days ago they called for all men who have been to the front, who had taken bombing courses. They took our names and particulars, but as yet have heard nothing more. Some say that we are to take a new course and become instructors. I hardly expect such luck as that, but it might be so. I like bombing and have always taken an interest in that line.

I don't know what is the matter that Ida and Jane do not write. Surely their letters would get through now all right.

I got Father's letter with Jane's enclosed. I suppose we shall soon have the Americans fighting with us in France. They certainly took a long time to decide so surely have chosen the right course.

What an awful loss of life and property this war has been. If all the money and labour had been for God's Kingdom what a difference it would have made and how many souls would have been saved. It is beyond our comprehension.

I am sending these letters of the next generation home for souvenirs. Put them away with my other papers.

God bless you and keep you Mother of mine.

Lovingly,
Herb

June 3: Went to Church.
June 4: Fine. Physical training.
June 5: Warm. P.T. as usual.
June 6: Warm. Carry on. Downtown in evening.

June 7: Warm. Bath parade in both A.M. and P.M.

June 8: Warm. Started to work in mess room. Went to station to meet friends.

June 9: Fine. Went for a walk in A.M. and to a show in evening.

June 10: Fine. In mess room so missed church parade.

June 11: Warm. Mess room. Wrote to father and J. Spalding.

66

75th Batt.
E. Co. 1st CCD
Hastings Sussex
June 11, 1917 7 P.M.

Dear Father and Mother,

I have beside me your letters of March 12, 22, and May 8th which found their owner a few days ago, at least the two March ones being addressed to France went there, and arrived here a few days after the one of May 8th.[58] So you can understand how uncertain my mail is and how hard it is to get them all answered correctly. Does mine take such jumps as that or do they arrive in correct rotation. I think I get all your letters sometime but as to papers I received one parcel of them from you about the middle of Feb. I know of three who sent me papers while in France but that is all that reached me. The transportation up to the front line, you know, is a problem and papers are sometimes left at the transport lines. It is appalling the amount of timber, sheet iron, iron posts, barb wire, steel rails etc etc which is used to consolidate a position to say nothing of ammunition and rations. So you see it takes an army to keep an army in the front line supplied. Many a mile I tramped last winter, in fighting kit—120 rounds of ammunition, rifle, bayonet and gas mask (a nice load in its self, but a man would not care to be caught by the enemy unarmed) and carrying perhaps a trench mat, it is like this

used to walk on in the trench or a GR frame

used to rivet a trench. They are placed about 5ft. apart and sheet iron put behind them to keep the sand from falling in. It takes all the powers of sight, hearing and touch, yes! and you get to be, in the dark, to almost smell a man. It is surprising how a hundred men or more will wind their way up a trench loaded with something in a pitch dark night and not have any accidents. I don't think I ever touched this subject before and am just telling you that in case I go to France again and don't get what mail you send me, just try and imagine the difficulties. Well we are getting lovely weather here now and a nice rain last night and everything is looking splendid. All appearances of a good crop here this year, which will be a good thing. Things are certainly an awful price in Canada and don't think they are so high here. I have always managed to get enough to eat, yet anyway. Did I tell you before that I weigh 163 lbs. I am working in the dining hall this week. I don't care much for the job but am not out in the hot sun. The hall is St. Peters Church Vestry, we have 8 tables each seating 26 men and two waiters for each table so the work is not very hard. It is better than France anyhow.

Was sorry to hear that both of Knowles boys were killed. I just saw Hugh once out there and Willie three times. I can see the place now where I saw Willie last—away out yonder behind Vimy Ridge. I was on a working party one morning and he came along, so we had a little chat. The 75th used to relieve the 102th (his Batt.) in the line. I have often thought of the last time I saw Tom also. I think I told you before it was about midnight Feb.–March in a tunnel under Vimy, we did not bid each other good bye as you might expect, but went out silently into the gray, black night to do our duty. I never thought then of being hit and I suppose neither did he. A man could not stand it, if he got that on his mind. While we lay in the <u>jumping off trench</u> (I don't suppose you understand that term)—for the set time to advance, I prayed that we might be successful in our attack and that the casualties might be small and that those who fell would be prepared. We went over the top at last and it was much easier to advance than be still, reaching the enemy barb wire we took cover in shell holes until our artillery would lift off his front line. This is where we lost heavily, a perfect hail of steel among us. My bomb carrier got a terrible wound in the thigh, so I sat up to bandage it, exposing my whole body. I knew that the moment I sat up, but forgot it at once and did my best to stop the blood. I took off his equipment and he started back slowly, each step so far as I could see him, I expected would be his last, so I knelt down and I said "Lord be merciful to we sinners." I have never heard of that boy since.

Oh, I must stop now, perhaps you don't care to read this kind of a letter. When I start a letter I tell myself not to get into that strain but somehow wander off.

Hoping and praying that you are all well. I will close for this time.

Your loving son,
Herb

P.S. I would rather you should not print what I say regarding other boys.

June 12: Warm. Went to park in evening.
June 13: Fine. Alarm at 12 noon. Air raid on London. Went to show.
June 14: Lovely weather. Went to station to see friend off.
June 15: Fine. Went for bath in the P.M. Wrote 4 letters to-day.

67

75th Batt. E Co.
1st CC Depot
Hastings, Sussex
15/6/17

Dear May,

I have here before me 7 letters of yours which I have not acknowledged. First, March 11 just before you heard I was put out of action. It and one of March 22nd just returned last week and although somewhat ancient are interesting never the less. First contained the snap and I think it is just fine. It could not be more like you and I like the dark finish. You asked some questions in that letter and I will just answer them here.

The Reserve Trenches are usually two or three miles behind the firing line. There is the firing line or front line trench and in some instances there are two such lines, the second a couple of hundred yards in the rear. Then 800 yards or so farther back are the support lines and third the Reserve Lines. Does that make it plain to you? Now here is the way we worked all winter. One Brigade (that is four Battalions) hold a given frontage, large or small according to the position, usually from 6 to 10 hundred yards. Well the 1st Battalion is in the front line, 2nd in supports, 3rd in reserves and 4th out resting. This in 6 day shifts make a 24 day round, with only 6 days in the one line, do you understand. This makes 18 days in the line and 6 out, for while in any line you are considered holding the front. Although not exposed so much while in supports or reserves, it is quite as big a strain on the nerves. Often 9.2's drop in reserves and then every night you get to go to the front line to repair trenches or perhaps into No Man's Land to put up Barb Wire. At Vimy we had five or six lines of trenches and it would have been impossible for Fritz to have broken through. The next is in answer to mine of the 28th of Feb. You guessed it correct although you say the censor erased it. Yes! May I wrote you that letter knowing that we were going over the top in a few hours and that perhaps it might be the last. Could you detect anything in it to that effect? I wrote to Mother on the 27th but they have not mentioned getting it. Next is April 23rd in which you speak of Tom and R. Wilson and of the Memorial Service for Col. Beckett and men. I wonder what it said about the Col. If I am spared to get home, May, I will tell you something of that morning but until then

_____.

I wonder which of my letters was in the Expositor. I never intended any of mine to go into print. I am not prosey enough and I just said plain things.

No May I never saw a tank and the Battle of Courcellette was fought before I left England. We joined the 75th just after they came out of the Somme. Courcellette is on the Somme and was an awful place.

Next is April 28th, I'll see if you asked any questions in it.

You were a little troubled in this one, about so many of our Perth boys killed in action. Well May an old sailor told me "What's to be will be," but it seems hard for one home to come to a double grief in the same day. I must write to Harvey.

If I had known it would have been no trouble for me to hunt up Jennie's brother at Epsom.[59] I would need his particulars though I might see him at Sandling.

Glad you got the photo and will be looking forward to getting yours.

Now May it is getting dark so I think I will soon call this off and turn in.

At present I am working in the Dining Hall. Hash Slingers they call us. I am not in love with the job but it is a change anyhow from P.T. Have to get up at 6 A.M. We usually have from 9 to 11 A.M. and 2 to 4 P.M. and done for the day at 6.

Tonight I had just started this letter when the General Alarm sounded, so had to fall in. They gave us a rifle and some ammunition and we marched about a mile, but apparently the scare was over so came back. Just three and a half months since I had a rifle in my hand, but although we are Charlie Chaplin's mob here we could give Mr. Fritz a hot reception yet.

Air raids are quite common this fine weather, but we are always on the Qui Vive for them.

It is too dark now May so I better stop or perhaps you will not be able to read this. Am expecting a letter any day now. The last was dated May 15th so there must be another pretty close now.

Excuse this pencil. My fountain pen has gone on the blink and it is too much trouble to keep an ink bottle, so easily broke. Good night and the best of luck.

Yours sincerely,

Herb

P.S. 1st post has just sounded 10 P.M., 9 by right time. The time was put an hour ahead on the 10th May.

June 16: Warm. Down town all afternoon. Payed in A.M.

June 17: Warm. Stayed in all day.

June 18: Cooler. Went to park in afternoon. Wrote some letters home.

68

E. Co. 1st C.C.D.
Hastings, Sussex
18/6/17

Just a line tonight Mother dear, along with these snaps. I intended sending these taken at the hospital long ago but neglected doing so.

I hope you are able to get out now and that you are enjoying yourself. Do try and not worry about me going back to France. I won't be there for some time yet and even if I do I shall not be alone. That Friend who sticketh closer than a brother is every where at all times. You spoke of Mr. Greig's attention to you last winter and I am so glad for he is a grand man. I had a card from him at Xmas and acknowledged it. I wonder if he got it. I would like him to write to me but I know he is a very busy man.

I got a box of sugar from Willie today and it has been on the way since April 28th. Some time eh!

Everything is much the same here. I think I told you that I was working in the dining hall now. It is quite an easy job. Looks like rain this evening and a shower is needed for we have had some hot days. A zeppelin was brought down not far from here yesterday morning. I would like to see one. Have seen every engine of war except a zeppelin and a tank.

It will be July before you get this and will soon be a year since I left home. My but the time has flown. A year ago last night I got home on pass from Kingston and you heard me downstairs at the strawberries and cream. Have you had any car rides this summer? And how is Tommy?

I wish Father and you would get a photo and send it to me. One about postcard size so that I could carry it. Now do try and get one.[60] Do you have many sore backs this summer and is your appetite good. You don't tell me very much at all.

Well Mother my stock of material for this letter is all done so I guess I'll have to stop.

Hoping and praying that you are all well. I will close now with love to all.

Your affectionate son,
Herb

P.S. Will write to Clara next.

June 19: Warm. Mess orderlies had photo taken.
June 20: Warm. D. Whelen and I went for a walk through the park.
June 21: Cooler. Same old story in the same old way. Downtown in evening.

68A

E. Co. 1st C.C.D.
Hastings Sussex
June 21, 1917

Dear Sister,

Have been looking for a letter from you this week but so far none
came. Got a letter from Willie's and a parcel of sugar this week, also a
nice long letter from a Miss Robertson of Pilot Mound.[61] She belongs
to the Rebeka Lodge and has been reading some of my letters in
the Era. She mentioned the one about Ginger and made some very
complimentary remarks on it. What did you think of it? I had nothing
to do one day at Dunsdale so wrote it out and addressed it to Mr.
Wilson and expected it would be in the Era. What kind of weather
are you having over there? It has been very warm here, but rained
some last night and is much cooler today. I am still working in the
dining hall. Everything is much as usual around the town. I think we
are going to have some sports on July 1st. Are there many festivals this
year and where is the 12th to be celebrated? A year ago today we all
had a great time at John's.[62] I don't suppose they had a doing this year.
Oh, those weddings will cause some stir won't they? May told me that
Elsie was to be married in June and I had a letter from Nellie Brunton
and she told me that Effie was getting buckled too. That's two good
times that I have missed, anyhow perhaps they are past now. Oh well,
I have seen something of the world and its ways since a year ago and I
think I shall benefit by the experience. If I have come through a lot of
hardship, have the satisfaction that I am doing my duty. I understand
they have conscription over there now anyway. Say! how does it catch
Morris boys? or any home when there is more than one man. There's
Devlin's and Caver's and dozens around Drummond Center. Oh! say
do you ever hear anything of Alex MacDonald? I had one letter from
Margaret[63] just before I left for the front last November and she said he
had joined the Medical Corps. I don't suppose she has come across yet.
I am like you Clara. I often look back to the times she and I had
together and think of what hopes we had for the future. She was the
only girl I ever cared anything for. (I guess you knew that before). So
like you, but to a far smaller extent, I have had my disappointments.[64]
I am looking for your letter in answer to one I wrote at Perth. I had an

answer to a card I sent Willies, from there, so yours must be pretty close now. I can pretty nearly tell when to look for mail now. I expect you know that May has written to me ever since I left for Barriefield and ever since coming across she has written at least every ten days. Have had three parcels from her. She is an ideal girl, don't you think so? I certainly have enjoyed her letters. Clara Penman writes occasionally and I get an odd one from Mae and Myrtle Darou, and several from Lena MacIntyre. Jack Spalding is the only lad who writes at all regularly. Just got a few from L. Cavers. I sent J. MacNaughton a couple of cards but got no answer. I guess he is too busy. Roy Keays does not write very often, I suppose he thinks one in the family is enough. So with all my own people and cousins and the outsiders, you see I have quite a list. In fact I can scarcely keep track of them all.

I wonder how my long epistle of the trip to Scotland will look in print. Say could you get an Era and send it to me? I would just like to see what one looks like now. I did not think I had much to write when I began but it is getting a bit lengthy. I started this in the forenoon but it came time to serve dinner, so had to go. We had beef steak and onions with Yorkshire pudding and gravy, boiled potatoes and some sort of other pudding and dressing for dessert, I don't know the name of it. Sometimes the grub is rotten (at least the way it is made up is rotten) for they make a sort of hash of chopped meat and something else. The boys call it "mystery." Well named too for it is a Chinese puzzle to know what it is. We have oat porridge every morning but without milk. The orderlies usually get an extra bit, so am living well this week.

Well how are you and Tommy getting along. Is he scared of autos this summer? and is he fat and glossy. Poor old Chappy, give him a slap for me and Charlie too.

Must stop now or they will be charging you at the other end. A new order came out to the effect that our letters go free from England as well as from France. This is the bunch of orderlies, except the black fellow, he is the slop man.

Love to all,
Herb

Write soon.

June 22: Showery. Boys went on a route march to-day. Two letters from Canada.

69

E. Co. 1st CCD
Hastings Sussex
22/6/17

Dear May,

Here I go, penciling again. Do you mind? Really it is a job to keep ink when knocking around so much. Yours of May 25th was almost a month on the road so I am answering it the same day. It was rather cool and showery today and this eve, the sun is bursting through the clouds every now and again, and shooting long rays of yellow across the sky. We had a hot wave and this coolness now is appreciated. How's the weather at home? Surely it was a late spring.

No, May, I was not long enough in Scotland to develop the burrs, but I love them yet and always will. I like Irish but I can't somehow agree with you altogether on their qualities of speech. I was at an Irish play last Saturday, "The Soldier Priest" and I certainly enjoyed it. I say again that I like to hear the real Irish spoken but still I'm Scottish "be gorra" and I am that ha ha r-r-r-r. We sing a song over here, one part runs like this "There's plenty of Scotchmen in the Irish Fusiliers."

Conscription, war and rebellion that sounds like Canada beware. I had hoped that conscription would never come in the land of the Maple but if it brings those other two it will be shameful. Canada today has the admiration of all the world and now when a glorious ending, or beginning rather, is in sight of her, is it to be trampled in the dust by a few thousands who are, I fear, trying hard to gain power long since lost. You know who I mean, no doubt. If they don't submit to conscription and step out and fight like men against what any sane man can see to be a just cause, I am afraid the silver light will not shine through the dark cloud, on Canada for many a day.

Say, I admire the pluck of Mr. Nesbit. A Commission in the Flying Corp no less, eh. I imagine a man with a mind so small as to say he would as soon shoot a farmer as a German, lucky for him that I was not there. I would have thrown him over the counter. His mind is bound up in town or city though and he doesn't know anything of the free and open country life so we'll excuse him there, but I can't get over the cheek of him to want a commission in the Flying Corps, right off the bat. He should have asked for his discharge before he tried to enlist, for he clearly doesn't want to fight, else he could find some place where they would accept him. Wonder how he would like to carry a 60 pound pack up to the front line and stay there for ten days and never dare to take his equipment (minus pack) off or have his rifle two jumps away, up to the knees in mud and nothing but bully beef and biscuit to eat; sleep, if he got a chance, on the firing step of a trench with the sky over head, or if lucky perhaps a sheet of steel trench rivetting, listening to the crash of shells and the rat-tat-tat of machine guns and looking at the fireworks over No Man's Land or crawl out into that place of wonders at dusk and stay until dawn, listening for any movement of the enemy. Well it is men of that stamp who make a success of the flying business. Just you remind Mr. Nesbit that a man must creep before he can walk and be a man before he can fly. Perhaps I am rude, you will say, but I'd like to get telling him a piece of my mind.

Why May, you have more grit than him. You are willing to take a step down to help along the cause, but he wants to get to the top of the ladder at one jump and if not that, stay sulking at the bottom.

Today you are going home for your holidays. I am sure you will enjoy them. Like you, I have ceased to worry to a great extent, since coming to England. We sing a song over here, perhaps you have heard it before but here it is. I hear some lads singing right now.

PACK ALL YOUR TROUBLES IN YOUR OLD KIT BAG

Private Perks is a funny little codger
With a smile, a funny smile
Five feet nine, he's an artful little dodger
With a smile, a funny smile
Flush or broke, he'll have his little joke
He can't be suppressed
All the other fellows have to grin
When he gets this off his chest

Chorus

Pack all your troubles in your old kit bag
And smile, smile, smile.
While you've a lucifer to light your fag
Smile boys that's the style
What's the use of worrying
It never was worth while
So pack all your troubles in your old kit bag
And smile, smile, smile.

There are two more verses but since I have not the music will not
write them. No doubt you have heard it anyway. We often sing it on the
march. It has a great swing. Well May I sure have made a scribble this
time. I never seem to improve in my writing, guess I am too careless
with it. I am still in the dining hall, am sending a snap of the bunch.

Tomorrow is Saturday again, really the time is flying away, over
five weeks since I came to Hastings and almost four months since I
was wounded.

Soon be a year since I saw you won't it? 7th August 1916 I left home.
Here's the best of luck, May from yours truly,

JHG.

June 23: Fine. Downtown in P.M. with H. Lamb, or in evening rather, had to
serve tea to-day but will be off tomorrow afternoon.

June 24: Cool.

June 25: Warm. Last day in mess and not sorry either.

June 26: Warm. Bathing parade in A.M. Put into graduation. Had a dental
inspection in P.M. Went to Ore in evening.

June 27: Fine. Started drilling once more, with rifle and equipment.

June 28: Dull. Payed in forenoon. Medical inspection afternoon and
marked FIT.

June 29: Dull. Route march to Battle. Viewed the spot on which battle of
Hastings was fought 1066.

June 30: Warm. O.C. inspection in A.M. D. Whelan and I went to Ore in P.M.
and to Alexandra Park.

July 1: Warm. Grand Church parade in cricket grounds. 1st, 2nd, and 3rd
C.C. Depots.

70

Hastings Sussex
July 1, 1917

Dear May,

Yours of June 6th was a long time on the way, just got it yesterday.

So you were home for two weeks. I bet you had a fine time, wish I
could drop in for a fortnight. I don't know what is the matter with my
mail again. I have not heard from home for three weeks.

I am a soldier again, May. Marked <u>FIT</u> and am leaving here for my Reserve Battalion next Tuesday. No telling how long I might be there and of course the next address will be "you know what." Yes, up the line and over the top with the best of luck as the boys say. Went for a route march last Friday to Battle a distance of six miles each way. It was my first march for four months but did not mind it for I was well repaid. I can say now that I have stood on the most historical piece of ground in the British Empire namely Senlac Hill where the Battle of Hastings was fought. You know all the history connected with it so I need not say much. When I get time I will write about it and if you wish you may have it in the Expositor. The keeper, a typical Englishman, showed us about and told us many things of interest. I am not much on reporting but I'll try to make it interesting. A few views in the mean time.

Today all the soldiers in Hastings went to church parade together to commemorate the Fiftieth Ann. of Canada's Confederation. We had three bands and about 5000 men. Tomorrow we hold sports and a number are going to London for the celebration there in Westminster Abbey. I would love to go.

So Elsie and Leo will be settled by now I suppose. I am sure they will miss her at home. Who will be next I wonder?

What changes a few years make in a neighbourhood. Every day nearly I meet another 130th man just in and also hear of more who will never return.

How is recruiting coming on now and what are your views on that matter? Well I did intend to keep that subject out but I see it has slipped in. Force of habit you see. All for today May, and good luck.

Sincerely,
Herb

July 2: Fine. Holiday.

July 3: Fine. Left Hastings at 11:45, arrived in East Sandling at 3:30, put into isolation camp for 10 days.

July 4: Rainy. Went on parade in A.M. but came back. Lecture in P.M.

71

75th Battalion
B. Co. 12th Reserve
East Sandling Kent
4/7/17 (July)

Dear May,

Oh ha ha. Changed your address eh![65] Well I doubt if you have the fever as bad as me. You see I have changed once more so you can direct a few here at least.

So you think Ottawa is alright.[66] So do I. Wish I were there for awhile. I know all those places you speak of and although I have seen some fine places there is no place like home. I suppose you are back to work again, holidays and wedding over and the same old routine again. I am glad you got two weeks any how and I glory in your pluck. If all the girls were as good and pure as you May there would be less temptation for the soldiers. You speak of and ask me of those temptations and I can tell you that all you hear is true, but it is too big a subject for this time so I will not attempt it.

Yes, here I am at Sandling, once more. Everything is the same except the 12th Reserve is in East now in place of West Sandling. There is a deep valley between the two camps. Came yesterday and we are C.B. for ten days, just in case something should break out. We do not do much drill so are quite contented. I am A III now and six weeks drill will make me AI and you can guess the next move. I was sorry to leave Hastings, had such a good time there but we are out to win, aren't we? Oh we casualties have fun watching the Umpty, Umpties drilling, forgetting of course that we were once in the same stage. The 255th Batt. is here fresh from Canada. Have not seen any of the 240th yet. Quite a number of the 130th are here. Some have not been to France yet. I saw three of our old officers here last night.

Oh I was going to tell you of my trip to Senlac Hall. When I went to Hastings I planned to visit the place of that famous battle fought in Oct. 1066. It so happened that we had to do a route march before leaving for the base so although I had to march out with equipment, rifle and pack on, did not mind it for I was anxious to see the place. We followed the old London road, over which the Norman army marched from Hastings where they had landed the day before the battle, and through Black Horse on Telham Hill where they camped that night, while across the valley on Senlac were the English. On the eve of the battle, William told his men he would build an Abbey in commemoration. So Battle Abbey was built on the ground occupied by the English Army and is now surrounded by the town of Battle. The Abbey is surrounded by a high stone wall but the keeper, a typical Englishman, met us at the gate and showed us around. His story of the battle and buildings was very interesting as he told it in his quaint way, dropping an "H" here and adding one there. The English, 10,000 strong, were formed up in solid ranks, 12 deep. The front rank used the long handled battle axe, the 2nd used the spear, 3rd cross bows and the rear ranks short handled battle axes which they threw at the enemy. Everyone of the company, which numbered about 30, all Canadian soldiers, was very much impressed by this ancient form of fighting and thought of the havoc which machine guns or shells would work on close formation of troops. Most of the buildings have fallen but the foundations still remain. The church was built over the place where Harold and his body guard stood and William placed the High Altar on the exact spot where the English banner stood. About twenty yards from the front of it stands a huge cedar of Lebanon, supposed to have been planted by William, where he slept the night after the battle, as he chose to sleep among the slain. Between the tree and altar is the foundation of the bell tower from which curfew was tolled for centuries. The old man took great pride in telling us that curfew had been tolled over Senlac from the building of the Tower until the Zeppelin raids of the present war and we told him that it would not be our fault if he did not hear it tolled once more.

Well May I guess this is all. I told you, you could have this printed but have changed my mind. It does not seem to be worth while, so perhaps you better not.

I expect it will be a week before my mail finds its way here but eventually it will.

Good bye May.
Best wishes,
Herb

72

East Sandling
Kent
July 4, 1917

Dear Father,

Yours of June 10th received and glad to hear from you again, and
that you were all well. We certainly have reason to be thankful for all
the mercies which God has shown us. We might be worse off than we
are. You are all well there and here I am over four months since I left
the fighting and the heaviest too, of this war. Almost four months in
England doing nothing practically. Arrived here yesterday and am
quarantined for ten days but that does not mean that there is any
disease in camp. It is merely a precaution against any possible outbreak
for those coming in. After the ten days are up we go back to the Reserve
and start training once more. My Reserve (the 12th) has moved from
West to East Sandling since I left here last fall. Of course it is all the
same place, just a deep valley between the two. The boys here tell me
that the drill is very stiff here, but I am not worrying about that until I
get at it. I used to worry about the drill but France took that out of me.
The best way is just to take what comes. Col. Pellat of the 12th when I
was here, has gone to France and they say the one who is in Command
now is very strict. He hands out punishment like a man without a
conscience. Well I have no crimes against me yet although I was up
before the Company Commander once in Canada for staying over pass
last August and once in France for being absent from sunset until sunrise
but neither offenses count as crimes. And I don't want any either.

Well so much for this place. I was sorry to leave Hastings. It was
such a good place in fact it spoils a fellow for camp life.

I am glad there are prospects of a good crop this year. Perhaps
there will be more for the soldiers then. I suppose you will be started at
the hay now. How is help, is it scarce? Yes I think I get all your letters
sometime but quite irregular. I told you a couple of times at least that
I got both letters with the money so you surely do not get all mine
either. Yes we get paid before going on Furlough. As yet I have not got
Maggie's letter which you speak of. It sometimes happens that I write

to you one day saying that I have not got mail for a long time and the very next day I get some. I did not know that Milton Stewart was killed. I have not got the papers you sent. Where did you address them to. Be careful to put the exact address I give you each time. If you happen to put B.E.F. it goes to France every time so unless I am over there don't put that on. You speak of Russia and I had the same opinion of them as you. But there is good news from that quarter now and the Yanks are keen to be at them.

I like to hear about your livestock. You must be getting quite expert in calf feeding.

I promised to tell you of my visit to the place where the Battle of Hastings was fought so I'll do it now.[67] When I went to Hastings I had planned to see that historical Senlac Hill, but as time went by and it came near my time for leaving and still I had no chance to get there, I was quite disappointed. But luck still favoured me. Before leaving we all had to do a route march and that was where the Col. chose to go. We left Hastings about 9 A.M. by the old London Road, along which William of Normandy led his men on the day before the battle. It is a beautiful road lined with huge oak and beech, through Black Horse on Telham Hill where the Normans camped for the night while the English camped on Senlac Hill just across the valley. After dinner we went up through the little village of Battle to Battle Abbey, built by William on the ground which was occupied by Harold's men at the commencement of the battle. It is surrounded by a huge stone wall, but the keeper, a typical Englishman, met us at the gate and showed us around and told us the exact formation of the two armies. The English were about 10,000 strong and stood shoulder to shoulder 12 tier deep. The first line used long handled battle axes, the second the spear, the third cross-bows and the rest short battle axes, which they threw over the others heads, at the enemy. This formation baffled all the attacks of the Normans until William feigned a retreat. The result was that the English followed, broke ranks, leaving openings for the enemy cavalry who galloped in and so won the victory. Most of the buildings are torn down now, leaving nothing but the foundations so I will not describe them. You will see them on the cards I sent a few days ago. William built his church there and put the high alter on the spot where the English banner stood and where Harold fell. The most historic spot in England passed into the hands of the Normans, October 1066. Near this spot stands a huge cedar of Lebanon supposed to be on the spot where William chose to sleep among the slain and between the two is the foundation of the Bell Tower from which they tolled the curfew for generations. The old man told us in his funny English, dropping an "H" here and adding one there, that the people of Battle had rung curfew from the time the Abbey was built until the start of the Zeppelin raids of the present war. And "Now boys," says he, "all the soldiers whom I have shown over the grounds say that it will not be their fault if I do not hear it rung out over Senlac Hill again." We all gave him a hearty clap and passed around the cap for him, for which he was very grateful. You see civilians have to pay one shilling entrance fee, which goes to the old man's wages but soldiers are admitted free, but all England knows that the Canadians are generous.

I hope you get those cards alright. Did you get the pictures I sent you taken at Epsom?

Well I guess this is a pretty fair size of a letter so I better stop now.

Your loving son,
Herb
75th Batt.
B. Co. 12th Reserve
East Sandling Kent

P.S. I looked up Luke 21:19 and would liked to have heard the sermon.[68] Jerusalem is compassed about with armies again. Patience is something that we do not all possess.

July 5: Fine. Did some bayonet fighting.

July 6: Fine. Went to Hythe beach for bath at 6 A.M. Had a lecture in P.M. Went on guard at 6:30 P.M.

July 7: Warm. On guard. Air raid on London.

July 8: Cool. Church service at 10 A.M.

73

12th Reserve

East Sandling
Kent 8/7/17

My Dear Mother,

Here I come to visit you again by letter. I have no news only that I am well and only hope that you are the same. I wrote to Father the other day saying that I was in quarantine—will be getting out next Friday. This has been a rather lonesome day for we can't get out to go anywhere. We had church service in the A.M. Chaplain Gilmour, text Acts 27, 25, "wherefore, sirs, be of good cheer, I believe in God." It was a good sermon and I enjoyed it as we stood under the spreading oak trees. This afternoon I slept all between dinner and tea. Now Jim Trail and I are lying side by side on our bed, each writing to our mothers. Jim and I were hit the same morning and were together for a couple of hours at the dressing station, separated, met again for a week at Epsom and then landed in here, he Monday and me Tuesday. So we are together and likely to be for awhile.[69] Jack Stewart of "Tin Groove" is here too, also a number of others. Almost every day another 130th man comes in.

Were you at church today? Did they fix the sheds this summer? Do you get to those meetings often?[70] I suppose the same bunch are in the choir yet. How often does Mr. Greig come to see you? Were there any new members this summer? It is just some queries for you to answer this time, you will be thinking, but really I have no news. Did you get the pictures I sent? Here are two more cards for you to put in my bunch. They were stamped so plainly in France that I am returning them.

Well good night mother dear and may God keep you safely until we meet again.

Your loving son,
Herb
XX

July 9: Rainy. Met Sgt. Simpson, now Lieut. P.T. and BF and bombing.
July 10: Fine. Working party to West Sandling did about 1 hours work. The old place seemed quite familiar and we thought of the day we left.

July 11: Fine. Bombing in A.M. Half holiday for all casualties.

July 12: Warm. On guard around camp.

July 13: Warm. Sea bath in A.M. Out of quarantine, attached to C. Company.

74

C. Co. 12th Reserve Batt
East Sandling
Kent, 13/7/17

Dear Sister,

Well Clara, I am a soldier once more. My four and a half months holidays have left me a bit lazy perhaps, but no doubt I shall get over that in a short time. The ten days in quarantine were rather dull but are over again and once more we are out with the boys. Was paid and attached to C. Company today. This company is all casualties from the 3rd and 75th Battalions and I have met a number of old pals already. Some who have never been to France yet to do their bit and of course they are not quite such heros as those who have, we still like to meet them. There are some in the band, pay office and some instructors. Captains Douglas, Duemany and La Moine are here also Lett Simpson has returned with Lieutenant's uniform having taken out his commission. Just was talking to him for a few minutes. At present I am in the Club and just by this table a piano and violin is going while the boys are singing popular songs. Just wish you could hear us sometimes. We do have some fine music and singing.

It is going to be a bit hot drilling but they treat the casualties pretty well, giving them three afternoons off per week. A new order has come out too, to the effect that casualties are not to be sent to France unless there is no others to fill the drafts required, so don't worry, I shall be here for a couple of months at least.

Have been looking for a letter from you for a month. Perhaps I am not getting them, never got an answer to the one I sent you from Perth. Did you not get it? You don't write very often do you? I don't write to you often but I try to address them to the three of you in turn and expect them to do you all.

How is Mr. _____ of Powasson? Has he made a trip to Balderson yet? Well if he comes don't let him walk back as Maggie E. did. Ha

Ha. I had another letter from Edna Paul must answer soon and one from Mae Darou, type written, what do you think! Nice girl Mae, any how what think you? Do you have many visitors? and do you do much visiting? I suppose you will be doing something at the hay are you? I hope to be home for haying next year. By the look of things now there are hopes of the end being this year or early in next. Russia has started again and now that the Yanks are into it, Germany must either give in or take an awful punishment.

I must write to Jane and Ida once more. Can't understand why they never write to me. Never had a scratch from Ida since I enlisted and but one or two from Jane while in Canada. America is an allied country now so letters should come. Edna Paul gave me young Cowie's address so I wrote him the other day.

I wonder if G. Brownlee has got across yet. I think H. Mather is at Shorham. Has Scott signed up yet? What are all the boys doing now conscription has come in? I bet some of them are turning gray already. I sure pity them for they will get the sweat drilled out of them when they get across here. The 255th are here with us and they get it hard enough. We like to kid them and call them Umpty, Umpties. Some of the boys took off their wounded strip and told them they belonged to the 331st. "Oh you do," says they, "we belong to the 255th." Their numbers run into the millions. I know we should not make fun of them, once we were the same, but you see some of them are so swanky, you can't help it.

I am thinking of taking a course for an instructor, but have not decided yet. It is a rather tiresome job but it is bomb-proof.[71]

I suppose you had a big time at Elsie's wedding. Hope you got to Effie's.[72] Two good times that I missed but I don't suppose many there would miss yours truly. I never danced much anyhow. I bet there was a swell supper at Uncle Bill's that night. A supper would kill me now I think. It would be too much of a shock after army rations.

Well Sis it is getting late so must ring off for this time. Hope to get a letter soon giving me some account of the doings around Harper. Address as above.

Your loving brother,

Herb

July 14: Fine. Got kit and equipment completed. Holiday in P.M. Had a bath but stayed around camp.

July 15: Windy. Church parade in A.M. Saw W. Ashby.

July 16: Fine. Did nothing in A.M. Started course on machine gun in afternoon.

July 17: Fine. At school in A.M. Writing and reading in afternoon. On inlying picket at night.

75

C. Co. 12th Reserve Batt.
East Sandling
Kent England
17/7/17

Dear Mother,

Just a line today to say I am fine, hope you are the same. We are having beautiful weather now, neither too hot nor too cold. I guess it will be hot in Ontario now—hay time once more—wish I were there to help for a few weeks. I am taking a machine gun course now and just work in the forenoons, read and write afternoons.

I got these cards when at Huntingdon but never got an envelope large enough to send them in so today I cut a piece off them. Have seen Bill Ashby several times here. He expects to go home to Canada anytime now. He lost his left eye, but otherwise is fine. I am still looking for mail. It must have got stranded at Hastings.

Well goodbye for today. Love to you all.

Your loving
Herb

July 18: Raining some. School in morning. Spent afternoon writing.

76

C. Co. 12th Reserve
East Sandling
Kent
July 18/17

Dear May,

Hello! How is business, pretty good? Are you handling lots of "tin" these days and have you any new juniors to break in?[73] I guess the bank is a pretty warm place some July days, is it not? Where did you go for the 12th? I was on guard around the quarantine camp, at least I was supposed to be; sat under a big oak tree most of my time on duty. I got over here last Friday and Monday started on a machine gun course. We just work in the forenoons, some job, just the kind I like. Much better than general drill you see, for we sit around and have lectures, learn the parts of the gun etc etc. I hope to get a bombing course also and kill more time. It is mighty hard for us who have been to France to do squad drill and bayonet fighting—things that are never used in the trenches. We all get a weeks course in first aid too, which is a fine thing. I had a little of it at Valcartier but not near enough to be of much use. Here I am rhyming off a lot more military stuff, you must be sick of it by now. But really there is nothing else to write about here for I am not seeing anything new. War, War, everywhere, of course that is our trade here.

Jim Trail is across the table, writing too and I suppose he is using the same line of material for his letter.

Well, I think we must be winning now, we got some strawberries for tea the other day, but say, I shall never be able to look another fish straight in the face, when this war is over. I don't suppose you have tasted war bread yet. Ha ha. The Col. gave us a short lecture on trench warfare this morning and says the few things he wished to point out to us, might be of use to us when we go back to the front. Oh, you should have heard the undertone that ran through the group. They all say "We don't want to go to France anymore," but if necessary, they will be right there with the goods. I am still waiting on the letter, giving me an account of the great wedding. Surely it will soon be here.

Are you having many auto drives now? Is there any sports going on in town? I hear that Caldwell's mill had been burned. That will leave a lot of people in Lanark out of work. The mills are their meat there. Trail has broken his pen and is in a little scrap of his own. I better keep quiet, else he will be reaching out for me. He and I have some awful times together. Jack Stewart from Lanark is another one of the gang.

Another page started May but I don't believe I can find enough of stuff to fill it. Jim has his pen fixed now and we have been recalling old times for the last ten minutes.

It has been raining a little all day. The Umpties are doing bayonet fighting in their huts.

I think I will take a trip to Folkestone this weekend. One of my chums, Orville Gorman is in Shorncliffe Hospital near Folkestone and I must go down and see him. I think I told you of him before. We used to sleep together, over yonder in the mud and do lots of tough jobs together.[74]

All for today.

Your sincere friend,
Herb

July 19: Warm. School in forenoon.

July 20: Warm. At school in A.M. Sham battle on hill in afternoon by troops of 12th battalion.

July 21: Warm. Gun drill in A.M. Sports on Battalion parade ground in afternoon. C company won the relay race.

July 22: Fine. Sent to YMCA on fatigue. Wrote letters.

July 23: Fine. Machine gun course.

July 24: Warm. Firing on range with Lewis gun and finished course.

July 25: Warm. Digging trenches in forenoon. Pass in afternoon. J. Trail and I went to Folkestone.

July 26: Fine. On an entrenching course. Payed in evening. Some boys on the weather.

77

C. Co. 12th Reserve Batt.
East Sandling
Kent
July 26/17

My Dear Sister,

You wrote your letter on June 26th and I am answering it on July 26th. It was a fine fat one and I have read it I guess a dozen times. The clippings, I enjoyed. It is a real good way to send news. Glad to hear that you were able to get to Effie's wedding and Mother got to, but it grieves me to hear that she is not improving this summer. I think she must be worrying too much about me. Tell me if she does. We got paid this evening and the effects of it is quite apparent in this hut. One chap especially (Gibbs is his name) is pretty noisy. Oh that old drink makes a fool out of a man. I am thankful that it does not trouble me anyway. Some of these chaps get paid one day, a pound or two perhaps, and are broke in two days. Gibbs is at present betting that he can drink more whisky and beer than some other lad, and a bunch outside are singing.

Friday morning.

The lights went out so I had to stop last night. I have had a wash and shave and am waiting on breakfast now. Don't need to shine my buttons etc. this morning as I am on an entrenching course. Some course too. The bunch are all casualties and know as much about building trenches as the instructors do, consequently we put in an easy time. It is just a sort of a refreshing course though for us to put in the time and it sure does bring back memories of dark nights, muddy trenches, star shells and machine guns.

Third spasm, 27th 6 P.M.

We have moved today into another part of camp, a change not for the better either, not so nice a place as we had before. Tomorrow is Sat. again and I think I will go down to Moore Barracks hospital to see O. Gorman, my bed mate of last winter. He was wounded in May. We casualties get a pass every Wednesday from noon until midnight so last Wed. I made a trip to Folkestone, Jim Trail and I. We went down on the bus and home on the train. It is a very nice town but the beach is not very pretty. They have German air raids quite frequently.

I am so glad you got the box and everything suited, especially the ring. I thought it would be near your size anyhow. And you got a brand new watch eh! I have none now, I broke mine in the trenches last winter. I should say your assortment of jewellery is 1st class. A twenty dollar watch, five dollar ring and five dollar gold piece. I must try and get something for Mary Ellen now.

I bet you had a fine time at the wedding. I bet Pearl cut a dash, eh! So Miss Nettie is training for a nurse. Say, do you ever hear anything of our lady Margaret MacD. I don't. Wonder if she is married yet or going to be. Did I ever tell you that I got a letter from her before leaving Canada and she said "I am sorry you are in the army now." But I don't think she was and I am not worrying anymore. Yes, I am a bit surprised that you and "Mr. Powassan" have broken off already, gee, but it is a year now since you were up there. All I can say to you is to keep heart. Perhaps the time will come when you and I can either live together or get a partner of our desires to live with us. Thomas' are certainly having a lot of trouble this summer. I have not had a letter from May for a long time now. And you did not get to Elsie's wedding after all, too bad they came on the same date. As yet I have not heard any particulars about it. This is the longest spell without a letter from that party.[75] In fact I have not been getting many from anywhere lately. Had an awful rush after people knew I was wounded and in England but have forgotten now I suppose.

I think this is all tonight so good night and love to all.

Herb

P.S. I have not received the parcel yet.

July 27: Warm. Entrenching.

July 28: Warm. Entrenching. Went to Shorncliffe, Sandgate and Hythe. Very warm walking. Had tea in Hythe.

July 29: Went to Church parade and got wet.

July 30: Cloudy. Started on bombing course. Easy time.

78

A. Co. 12th Reserve Batt.
East Sandling
Kent England
July 30, 1917 6 P.M.

My Dear Sister,

Just received your parcel today. Many thanks. It was in good shape and sure is a treat. My mail is all going to Hastings yet and is delayed of course. Mary E. said the Poland ladies had sent off a box to me, but I have not received it yet. It will likely get through alright.

Well what have you been doing today? Busy as usual I suppose, haying and harvesting. The women over here are doing a great deal of work on the farms. There are two ploughing in a field just by where we drill. They have a gasoline traction engine and a three furrowed plough. One runs the engine and the other the plough and can handle them well. They dress in breeches, leggings, blouses and straw hats. A great many work at railway stations and docks, to say nothing of the thousands employed in the munitions factories.

Haying is almost over here and the grain is beginning to colour. I went for a walk last Saturday afternoon. Went to Shorncliffe—Sandgate and Hythe. The two latter places are on the seaside. When we go to Folkestone (5 miles) we can go by train or bus. It is a nice trip by bus. The road is right along the shore and is like a street.

Were you to Church yesterday? We had a Brigade Church parade and the Bishop of New Westminster was to address us but it rained and he did not come, so the Chaplain went through the usual service and we came home pretty wet. I went to service in the Club in the evening.

Well Clara, I wrote you just a few days ago so I have nothing else to say. This week I am taking a bombing course and having an easy time.

Hoping you are well as this leaves me O.K. Love to all.

Your loving brother,
Herb

P.S. Note we have changed from C to A Co.

July 31: Raining. Lecture in hut but throwing rings and reading half the time.

Aug. 1: Raining all day which spoiled our afternoon off. Got letter from May and answered it.

79

A. Co. 12th Reserve Batt.
East Sandling
Kent England
August 1, 1917

Dear May,[76]

Just received your welcome letter of July 6th. I had looked for it for some time and it strikes me there is one somewhere between here and Perth, because you never said anything about how the wedding came off, as you promised to do. You keep all your promises so I conclude that one at least has gone astray. It may turn up. Yes May, I got the first one you wrote after you heard I was wounded and have kept it, the only one I have not burned in the campfire. It is impossible to save old letters here as I used to do at home.

I am glad the explanation of the trenches was satisfactory, but remember those lines had been consolidated in 1915 and consequently were permanent. The French, in 1915, lost 70,000 men trying to take that ridge, got half way up and stopped, the British took over that section and lost three trenches of it in June 1916, leaving our front line just on the brow of the first steep slope, where we found it in December 1916, held all winter and finally drove the enemy clean off the Vimy Ridge and some two or three miles out on the plain behind. Perhaps I have told you this before, if so please pardon me for chewing my cabbage twice.

Conditions are all together different at the front now though, since the advance has started. The British and French started another push yesterday morning and so far have gained their objectives. But I do pity the poor chaps out yonder. It seems every time we start something, the weather turns against us. We had splendid weather up to yesterday morning. I believe the bombardment must bring rain. It has rained continuously since yesterday morning—a cold easterly rain and doesn't look a bit like clearing up tonight. Perhaps you could imagine what it would be like to be soaked through and then lie out in a shell hole all night. It makes me shiver to think of it. When a man gets into those conditions too, he becomes more reckless, and wishes almost for a short way out of it all. However, we are surely but slowly winning. We have right on our side at least and have not dishonoured our name by any acts of cowardice or torture.

Conscription at last eh! I hope the people of Quebec act like Canadians and not make a fuss to spoil our good name. The French-Canadians we have over here are good fighters, second to none.

No, I did not know that J. Phillips had enlisted, nor do I understand why you are sorry for him. Did he not want to leave his girl?

Ding is still following the big brass band eh. It is wonderful what a band will do to draw a crowd. Yes, and it would surprise you how it lightens a pack on a route march.

The evening mail has just come in and brought a letter from J. Spalding. His was on the way since June 29th. Has been chasing all over the country after me.

Well May, I am putting in an easy time around here, taking courses you see and sit or lie under a big oak most of the time listening to lectures (at least supposed to be) but a good deal of the time is spent talking of experiences in France.

We casualties get a pass from noon to midnight every Wednesday but today the rain has spoiled it. I went to Folkestone last Wednesday.

Tonights paper says "The day has gone well—every objective achieved in great Flanders battle. Ten villages taken, 3500 prisoners taken in first day."

We have some crowd in this hut—jolly but sorry to say too fond of gambling—two games going now. A few of them get on the weather every pay day too. A Scotchman is sitting at the table just now cleaning the brass on his equipment and singing—

Just a song at twilight, when the lights are low
And the flickering shadows, softly come and go
Though the heart be weary, sad the day and long
Still to us at twilight, comes love's sweet song
Comes loves old sweet song.

A pretty piece it is and is often sung in bivouac and on the march.
Good evening now and good luck all the time.

Herb

P.S. I mean to get some photos before going to France again, but will be
looking for yours.

J.H.G.

Aug. 2: Raining.

Aug. 3: Raining.

Aug. 4: Fair. Lecture in A.M. E. Monk and I went to Hythe in evening and
to show. Very warm evening.

Aug. 5: Church in YMCA. Was to bible class in P.M. and to communion
in evening.

Aug. 6: Fair. Bombing raids for practise.

80

A. Co. 12th Reserve Batt.
East Sandling
Kent
Aug. 6, 1917

Dear Father,

Just one year today since I left home. I wonder what another year
will bring. We have had a good many things to be thankful for in that
time, haven't we. A good many trials and temptations, hardships and
narrow escapes. So I try to thank the "Giver" and lead a better life.
Was to Church yesterday morning. All the C of E men went to one
club room and other denominations to the YMCA.[77] Then in the
afternoon I attended a Bible Class at the Y. The Capt. is a young man
and a fine fellow so we (about 15) had a nice talk together, sang hymns
and afterward the Capt. treated us to cocoa, sandwich, cake and kisses.
At 7:30 P.M. there was another service. Capt. Lambert addressed us,

from the 61st Psalm and Mrs. Lambert sang a couple of solos. After the service there was communion. About 20 were there. It was the best Sunday I have had in a year. I enjoyed the Bible Class especially.

I think I can explain the difference in time between those letters. Mother's, being censored, was delayed a couple of days perhaps so missed one boat, while yours just got in time to catch the next and so went right along.

Glad to know that the crops are going to be fair and that everything is fine. That was quite a loss for Caldwell's and certainly a bad thing for Lanark.

You are surely getting expert in the art of raising calfs. That was quite a price you got.

Say, how often is my photo to be in the papers. Must be a half dozen times now. It is a terror how those stories do start isn't it. Quite a number left here today for Canada but I guess I will travel to Canada via France, unless those peace talks come to something pretty soon. Now I have no other news for you. Camp life is much the same day by day. Don't work too hard and don't worry about me. I will be alright for I am never alone.

Good evening and God be with you till we meet again.

Your loving son,
Herb

Aug. 7: Fair. Pulled off some more raids. Lots of fun. One chap got a blighty by a dummy cartridge.

Aug. 8: Fine. Throwing live bombs in A.M. To Hythe in afternoon and to show which was good. "Romance of Red Cross."

Aug. 9: Fine on Q.M. Fatigue. Washed 10 dixies in field kitchen.

81

A. Co. 12th Reserve Batt.
East Sandling
Kent England
August 9/17

Dear Sister,

Your two nice long letters arrived last night. The last one came the quickest of any I ever got. Just two weeks coming, of course the other one went by Hastings. They certainly contained a bunch of news—have read them three times already. I was out until 11 o'clock last night so as lights were out, I had to wait until morning to read them.

I don't think the picture is very good of Pa and Ma but the snap on the back is good of Mother.[78]

Busy haying eh! I thought so. You will be harvesting now, which will be easier and then you will not need to work hard after that. I hope to be home for the next crop anyway. We can always hope and pray for the best anyhow. Was somewhat surprised to hear that our people were invited to J.C.'s wedding. I thought since they had a Ford that butter would not melt in their mouth. Am glad that old thing has been forgotten. I hope Father's eye is better now. I hope he does be careful among the animals.

A conscripted army in Canada eh! Well I pity them when they hit this burg. Very regimented in this camp—hand out punishments here like oat cakes.

Well I thought our Alex was across long ago. I half expected that Miss M.P. would not keep her promise, let by gones be by gones. So you had a visit from Clara. She sent me a snap of herself. I wondered often why J. McNaughton never wrote. He could easily have got the address from you, so I will just wait now until he writes.

When you speak of buns my teeth water. We don't get too much to eat and every thing is so dear to buy. We went down town last night and before I started home went into a restaurant for a lunch. Had 1 cup tea, 3 cakes, 1 piece pie—cost eight and a half pence, or 17 cents. In Folkestone, ham and eggs, cup of tea, 2 thin slices of bread is one and eight pence or 40 cents so a quid does not go far. It comes quite natural for me to count in English money now. A quid is 1 lb or $4.96. My pad is done, so I got this sheet from E. Monk. He is from Franktown, by the way. Speaking of porridge, I use that sugar on mine and it goes good, just one cake left now.

Still what's the use of worrying. I am putting in a good time here and am contented. I may as well tell you now, so that you will be prepared for it, that I expect to go to France, perhaps in September. Yes, just in time to meet the mud and rain. I must not complain though, for as you say I have been very lucky, soon be six months across.

I am sorry you have had difficulty in the club. Surely it will smooth over and that you have not taken your name off yet. I never cared about a dance or anything of that sort, but if it drew a little money for we chaps why it is a little good. We must look over some things you know.

There is nothing new to write about. I have just been out for the mail for this hut but none for me tonight.

I am going to a concert in the Y tonight so will have to get a wash and my boots cleaned and get away. We have some fine concerts here which make the evenings a bit cheery.

Here's hoping you are all O.K. and try to enjoy yourselves. How many fairs are you going to this year?

Your loving brother,

Herb

Will be looking for a snap of yours. I have not got a single one of yours alone.

Tra La La.

Aug. 10: Warm. Route march all day. Dinner at Stouting.

Aug. 11: Warm. PT. and B.F. in morning. Slept and read all afternoon.

Aug. 12: Fine. Church parade and to Bible class.

Aug. 13: Warm. Shooting in Hythe ranges. Scored 40 out of 40 points.

82

A. Co. 12th Reserve Batt.
East Sandling Kent
August 13/1917

Dear May,

This is Wednesday afternoon "casualties half holiday," so I have made my bed and made myself comfortable and will do some writing. I have 6 letters of yours here, dated from June 29th to July 29th. Six a month is pretty good and do you mind me speaking my thoughts just here? You certainly are the best friend I have May. You don't ever forget me for more than ten days at a time. I appreciate your thoughtfulness very much and although I do not write so often, still I think of you every day. I often think of a certain night over a year ago, especially when the moon is young. I wonder sometimes if we shall ever drive out to Playfairville again. But say, May, may I ask you why you never told me about the wedding. Is it possible that it went astray, and also did you get a parcel I sent you from Hastings in May? I sent Clara one at the same time and she got hers alright.[79]

You bet I would like to see Perth now, although this is a pretty country. No place like home.

No the Twelfth is not celebrated here very much. There was a bank holiday a short time ago but did not affect us.

Ethel must be quite a, well I was going to say flirt, but won't. How many does her charm bring home I wonder. Ha Ha. Of course I don't expect you to tell me.

Yes I remember the 27th of November well. I looked it up in my diary and saw that I had been up on Telford's hill entrenching that day and it was wet. I had not that item down but when you mention it I remember we bought the corn in the Salvation Army and the milk in Sir J. Frenchs club. Tom and I left for France the next week. Jim is a good chap and a crack shot, but I don't see why he has not gone across. There are lots of lads over there under age, who are not nearly so big as he is. Of course I don't think it is right but if a chap signs up he should do a turn in at any rate.[80] That snap at Valcartier was taken with my camera and I am next to James. Roy Wilson snapped it. Jim was Sgt. of the Guard and Harold, Corporal. Most of the boys here are in favour of conscription, of course, but it is to be hoped that they manage it better than they did in England. Too many exemptions, red tape and graft.

So you think those are a nice bunch of Canucks eh. Sorry but I don't know that chap's address.[81] I did know his name once but have forgotten it. Seeing so many, one can't keep track of them. He belongs to the Medical Corps anyway.

Don't flatter my notes on trips and places too much May or like you say I might have a tumble also. I do wish you could see Beachy Head from Hastings. It is lovely. By the way you speak there does not seem to be much sport there this summer in the baseball line. We have lots of sports here and the Canadians are starting to play cricket a good deal. I like bowling and tennis both are very interesting. Did you ever try them? Now I have looked over your letters and I think have answered any questions so any I have missed just tell me.

Camp life is much the same. We had a route march last week, were away all day. The field kitchens went with us. The pack seemed pretty heavy after five and a half months with out carrying it.

This week I am at the ranges. Went down this morning but it started to rain so we "about turned." I like shooting, although not much of a shot. So far have only made 74 points out of 95.

The most of the boys are playing poker at present. We got payed the other day you see and for a few days gambling is all they think of until they, one by one, go broke and then it's over until next pay.

Good afternoon and believe me to be yours sincerely.

Herb

Aug. 14: Warm. Shooting. Application 17 out of 20. mad minute 17 out of 45. Total 34 of 65 points.

Aug. 15: Raining. Went to ranges but could not shoot. Writing letters in afternoon.

Aug. 16: Fine. Shooting.

Aug. 17: Fair. Shooting 5 and 600 yards with R.E. Rifle. Classified 1st class shot.

Aug. 18: Fair. Shooting in gas respirators and on the advance at disappearing targets. Had good sleep in afternoon.

Aug. 19: Fine. Church parade. Went to Shorncliffe to see Or. Gorman with G. Janes.

Aug. 20: Fine. Route march in A.M., drill P.M.

Aug. 21: Fine. Drilling slow march. Missed P.M. parade so was put on Hythe picket.

Aug. 22: Fine. Air raid in A.M. Entrenching in P.M. Staff inspection so casualties did not get half holiday.

Aug. 23: Fine. On square A.M. E. Monk and I went to Folkestone in P.M. on half holiday. Went to show.

Aug. 24: Rainy. On butts in A.M. and machine gun in P.M. Got letter from father and answered it.

83

A. Co. 12th Reserve Batt.
East Sandling Kent
August 24, 1917

Dear Father,

Your letter came across in good time, just 16 days. Just to think that we are over 8,000 miles apart and two weeks would cover that distance and still <u>so</u> far apart. Still we keep on hoping and praying that the time is getting near when Canada's men will be home and peace among nations.

At present the Allies seem to be making good progress on all fronts. We had an air raid here the other day over Dover. It was just about noon when the alarm sounded on the coast and we all hid in trenches dug for that purpose. You see no troops stay near the huts for Fritz likes to get a camp. Well, they came just near enough that with the naked eye they looked like a flock of crows, when our planes and guns engaged them. Three were brought down and the rest turned back. There were a few killed and a number hurt in some of the coast towns. They don't come very often now though because our airmen are keeping them busy at home.

Well, I guess you must have worked hard to get all that hay off so early. I bet you were finished before some of the neighbours, were you not? The harvest would be easier and you must not go to the mill or corn cutting this fall. Try and hire a man for the threshing. And if you don't plough up any sod there should not be much ploughing to do.

I am awful glad that Mother was able to take a visit to Dalhousie. I hope it did her good. I wish you could both be here by the sea for a while. It certainly agrees with me. I have such an appetite. Yes, I heard of Jim's sickness and have written to Jane since but did not hear what was the matter. Seems to be serious though when he is going to hospital. I have also had a letter from Tows. Tells of the rather poor crops out there. Too bad for we need the wheat. Have not heard from Willie or Mary Ellen for some time. I suppose they are busy and like myself have not much news to write.

There is one thing I have been thinking about lately. It is that Will I made out. Is it all right the way it is or should a lawyer have signed it to make it good? Let me know next letter.

Now I think this is all for tonight so I will close this and get it posted tonight. I go to Goodnight service in the YMCA and Church of England club at 8:30 P.M. Goodbye.

Your loving son,
Herb

Dear Mother,

Just a few lines to you now to say how glad I am to hear that you were able to get out some. I hope you will just keep like that. Try and avoid colds, of course I know you will wrap up well when you go out. Get the stove in early, there is plenty of wood is there not? I think there will be a hard time here this winter for coal, but people in Canada are all right for fuel. I guess yours will be the next letter. I'll write it next week some day.

Heaps of love to you and take care of yourselves.

Lovingly,

Herb

Aug. 25: Fine. Firing machine gun. E. Monk and I went to Folkestone to play entitled "Damaged Goods." Letter from May and C. Penman.

Aug. 26: Fair. To Church and Bible class.

Aug. 27: Showery. On special P.T. class. Training for brigade competition.

84

A. Co. 12th Reserve Batt.
East Sandling Kent
Aug. 27, 1917

Dear May,

You say your last letter did not contain much news but I think just the opposite for there was "lots" in it and then your usual cheerful way of putting things. Please don't say that any more. Your letters are all just fine.

I must say this time that I have not much to write about and what little military news I put in, others will have to be cut out. I see something to that effect in the orders. I can't imagine how the little I put in could do any harm. However there is nothing new just now only that I have started on a special physical training course today. It is a little stiff at times but I like it and it is good for a fellow. We are to compete against four other classes at Brigade Sports. Will tell you later.

Have been having a bit of sport lately. E. Monk, a 130th from Franktown, and I went to Folkestone last Wednesday and Saturday afternoons. Wed. we just went to the pictures but Sat. we were to see the famous play "Damaged Goods." Perhaps you have heard of it before. It has taken a big run in the country. It has a splendid moral—clean living to put it in a nut shell. After the matinee we had tea and went to see Charlie Chaplin to end a pleasant afternoon.

I like to hear of you having plenty of sport or at least some for I think you must be working pretty hard. I hope you are O.K. again and that Jason Buck has done good work. Poisoning is such a serious thing. Do be careful May![82]

Say, I don't blame you for not liking that club.[83] Bombers carry them to finish off stunned or wounded. Being few in numbers bombers take no prisoners. I didn't like the idea so dropped mine before I had a chance to use it.

Supper is up so will halt! for a few minutes and load up. Perhaps I'll be in better humour after tea for writing and perhaps not so good, all depends on what the army has given the cooks.

We use no china.

Well thats another job over. It doesn't take long. We had beans, bread, butter and tea—also shall I say fruit, not without a slight hesitation—I had, (now don't tell anybody) three gooseberries. I am afraid I will be sick tonight. Ha Ha.

However so long as the money lasts we will not starve. One would be rather out though if he could not buy a cup of tea or coffee and some cake in the evening.

How many fairs are you going to this fall? Go to a couple for me will you? Gee, but I could enjoy a good social now. I don't often let myself think of such luxuries. Do you really think you would like to venture across the Atlantic at present May? I sure admire your pluck, but if you don't mind me expressing my opinion in plain English, you are better off where you are. It would be a grand experience for you no doubt but as regards doing more for King and Country, you have done or are doing quite your share, by relieving a man for the army. There are a great number of women enlisted for service in France now. They drive ambulances, clean aeroplanes, cook, work in store depots, pay offices and record offices and lots of other things thereby relieving men for the front. The women are certainly winning a place in the Empire, which will not be forgotten when peace comes. I think they will have no trouble getting votes after.[84]

All for now. Good luck.

As ever your friend,
Herb

Aug. 28: Raining. Kit and medical inspection marked fit. Fatigue in afternoon. Payed.

Aug. 29: Fair. No passes issued on account of dirty huts. Battalion competition in P.M. Won in bombing team.

Aug. 30: Cloudy. Warned for inoculation but did not need it so did nothing all day.

Aug. 31: Fair. On the square in A.M. and beat parade in afternoon for a change.

Sept. 1: Showery. Through gas school in forenoon. Went to Hythe in afternoon. Got some pictures taken. Went to show.

Sept. 2: Fine. Church in A.M. Bible class in P.M.

Sept. 3: Fine. O.C.'s inspection and route march in A.M. Inoculated at noon.

Sept. 4: Fine. Having a good rest to-day.

Sept. 5: Fine. Pte. Monk and Quackenbush and I went to Folkestone to play "Betty" and to show. Home by train.

Sept. 6: Hot. Fatigue in A.M. Acting Fritz in practise attack and sham battle in afternoon.

Sept. 7: Fine. Working in company mess. Six letters today.

Sept. 8: Fine. Fatigue in A.M. Writing letters P.M. Pte. Monk and I went to Hythe. Got the photos.

Sept. 9: Fine. Church parade inspection picket.

85

A. Co. 12th Reserve Batt.
East Sandling
Kent England
Sept. 9, 1917

Dear Mother,

It is time I was writing you a few lines isn't it? There is very little to write about for I get tired telling you of military affairs.

We had our usual church parade this morning, but owing to a kit inspection at 1:30 P.M. I was prevented from going to the Bible class. I'll get out for evening service though.

Even over here our Sundays are taken up with duties of one kind and another. The whole Battalion is C.B.—confined to barracks this week, we being duty Batt. So will not be able to get out anywhere. Was down to Folkestone last Wednesday afternoon and evening for a change.

I think I said in the last letter that I was on draft but other than being fully equipped to go, we have heard nothing further about it, so will possibly be here a couple of weeks yet. I am feeling fine, although I have failed some since starting to drill. I suppose I have developed some muscle. You can judge for yourself by this photo. The boys think it is real good. Do you?[85]

Wonder how you are spending your Sunday. You will be just at dinner now.

Just here we had to leave our huts. An air raid alarm rang. Nothing happened however so we have had supper and perhaps I will get this finished now.

War is truly Hell. Even here we can't have a peaceful Sunday. Of course in France—well I'll stop here—.

The Canadians are doing some heavy fighting around Lens now. I expect to hear of them taking it any time.

I had a letter from Janet the other day. It was a long time since I had heard from them. Also had one from Jane too, for the first time.

Well Mother I hope you are keeping well this fall. I would love to see you all now. I often dream of you and of being home also often of being in the trenches again. They say dreams go contrawise but that can hardly be so for many reasons. Oh Mother I must tell you of one dream I had. You know I never believed in telling of dreams but I must tell you this one or two. I was in the front line and who do you think was with me? You, yes you, and I was telling you to keep down for we could see the Germans quite plainly. Believe me I was glad when I woke and found it untrue. Another dream was that I was on the boat in dock at some Canadian port. John came on board to help me off and I could see you all standing on the dock. Dreams are funny aren't they.[86]

Well I think this is all for now. I hope this finds you all in good health and quite at ease. Will be looking for a letter some of these days telling of your trip to Dalhousie.

Good bye. Love to all.

Your loving son,
Herb

86

A. Co. 12th Reserve Batt.
East Sandling
Kent, England
Sept. 9, 1917

Dear May,

This is Sunday and a dull, foggy day it is—real English fog. I don't know whether it is that or not but some how I don't feel very spry today, got a bad cold in my head.

The Col. has just been through on his weekly inspection of the huts. For a wonder he had no fault to find today. Two weeks ago he made a terrible report, everything was dirty and out of order, so he just stopped our Wednesday pass as punishment. He is very regimental and severe. We sent a draft to the 3rd Batt. last week and they certainly told him what they thought of him. The night before they left they would not go to bed but raised a particular cane in the hut. Finally the company officer went in and tried to quiet them but twas no use, so the Col. went in. I would not like to repeat what they told him but perhaps you can guess, when I say that he went out and cried. "To think" said he "that my men will treat me so, after all I have done for them." They also left a letter for the Company Officer containing their "best regards." It takes a good man to keep a Casualty Company the size of this one in hand. The thing is just to take them the right way. They want to be treated as men not as raw recruits. 75th draft is the next to go and I expect another "big night."

Well, May, I received your ever welcome letter of Aug 11th last week and of course pleased to hear of all the doings around Perth. Yes, I heard about the Tovey–Closs wedding. I knew her when she taught school, some kid too she was. He must have been under the weather when he went to tea without her. I wonder how she felt about it.

So the Col. is to be married all right, silly old thing, is what I say. Anyhow, I give him credit for what he did over here and in France. I hear that Col. Ed. Watt has or is returned to Canada. Cold feet eh. The Perth Red Cross should present him with a couple dozen pairs of socks.

Lett. McCallum of the 75th has returned to Smiths Falls. He and I came down to the Clearing Hospital in the same ambulance. He was a fine fellow.

Had a letter from J. Spalding yesterday saying that Miss Noonan was going to teach at Harper. Say has she found some common sense yet. He never mentioned Georgina at all. Where is she hanging out her shingle? Pte. Monk, Quakenbush and I went to Folkestone last Wed. afternoon and attended the Matinee.[87] "Betty" was the title of the play or rather musical comedy. It was fine, well acted. At night we went to the pictures for variety. The others wanted to go to the Central and see Charlie Chaplin on the screen but yours truly mutinied and would not go. I am completely sick of Chaplin. So we went to The Play House. Dinner is up so I'll ring off now. I'll call you up after dinner.

Hello! Perth this is Sandling—after dinner. That meal consisted of potatoes, beef, onions, soup and bread with the smallest bit of plum duff as a savory. Some dinner.

Orville Gorman, my old pal, and I went out to one of the tea rooms and had tea, cake and fruit. Results, excellent.

Now we are to have a kit inspection at 1:30 so I will be interrupted again. We had church parade as usual at 10 A.M. Text was from 1st Corinthians.

The mail call has just gone, wonder if there will be any for me.

The officer has commenced the kit inspection at the other end of the hut. I have mine laid out so will just proceed with this epistle until he reaches here. This is third for me since last Sunday. Had a special one during the week when I was put on draft.

Oh! no mail for me. What a disappointment but more so for Monk. A parcel came in to him but alas different initials and number which makes all the difference. Oh well, I got seven letters in the last three days so by the time I get them answered perhaps more will arrive.

Kit inspection is over, but I understand we have to draw some rifles today yet. Yes, here it is, the Corp. has just come in and warned us to "Fall in."

Well that is another job done. So you see even in England one scarcely ever has a Sunday in peace. We are duty battalion all this week too, so will not get out of camp until Sunday afternoon.

I got some photos taken last week. The boys say they are good but I will leave you to judge for yourself.

We have a Kazoo and a mouth organ here and I think I have laughed more in the last twenty minutes than in the last month. Did you ever hear a Kazoo played?

Now I have written todays events as they occurred. Tell me what you think of a day in the army.

Good bye for now May and I hope you are not working too hard. Remember me to Laura and give Lottie my congratulations.

Yours sincerely,
Herb

Sept. 10: Fine. O.C.'s inspection in A.M. on fatigue in afternoon.

Sept. 11: Warm. Route march to Etching Hill. Practised raid and came home.

Sept. 12: Fine. Fatigue in A.M. O. Gorman and I went to Hythe in evening. Visited Mrs. Man and went to show.

Sept. 13: Cloudy. Special platoon all day. Payed in evening. On picket.

Sept. 14: Fair. Special platoon.

Sept. 15: Warm. Went to amphitheatre to practice new wave formation. Monk and I went to Hythe after tea. Went for a row on canal.

Sept. 16: Cloudy. Church parade.

87

A. Co. 12th Reserve Batt.
East Sandling
Kent England
Sept. 16, 1917

My Dear Sister,

Here I am still in Sandling camp, and no more signs of moving than when I last wrote. Still drilling and doing a few route marches and sham battles for variety.

It has been quite hot this week, quite as hot as July, but the nights are very cool. Of course they always are here beside the sea! The grub was pretty scarce for a few days last week. They started a new system of dining and for a few days it was awful. We put up a howl though which brought them to their senses. Even the Col. came to see what we were getting and said himself that the rations were small. All this week the meals have been gradually getting better and today they were good. But this is all in soldiering and owing to the war.

Monk and I went to Hythe yesterday evening. We got a boat and spent a couple of hours rowing on the canal. That is about the only sport in which I take any pleasure. It is a fine pastime.

Sunday today is just like others. Church Parade at 9:15 A.M. but by the time we polish up, stand on parade for an hour and are inspected twice by Capts. and Col. no one seems to care whether they listen to a sermon or not and many are the drooping heads to be seen. The text today was John 6–68.[88] Was prevented getting to Bible class again by Kit inspection and will not be able to go to evening service on account of being on picket. So you see how Sunday is taken up.

Tomorrow I start on a First Aid course so will have an easy week. All the 130th boys that are here are getting their photos taken next Sunday. Capt. Douglas 130th is getting a camera to do the job.

Well Clara I have been looking for a letter all week. Was expecting an account of your trip to Dalhousie but I guess another boat has gone down. Friday was Lanark Fair day wasn't it? I could not help thinking of the times we used to go to the Fair. It was a wonderful day when we saw the first balloon going up, and a few men in kilts, with pipes and a brass band was simply glorious. Now it seems like a dream. What did Mother think of the dreams I told her last week? and the photos too? Say I wish you would send me one of yourself.

Must ring off now as it is near tea time. Hope to get a bunch of mail soon.

Love to all,
Herb

P.S. How's Chappie?

> **Sept. 17:** Cloudy. Started on first aid course.
>
> **Sept. 18:** Rainy. Find 1st aid very interesting work.
>
> **Sept. 19:** Dull and some rain. 1st aid in morning. Intended going downtown but rain prevented. Letter from Clara, May, and Edna Park.
>
> **Sept. 20:** Fair. First aid lecture in evening at YMCA by Capt. Cameron. Subject habits.

88

A. Co. 12th Reserve Batt.
East Sandling
Kent England
Sept. 20, 1917

Dear Sister,

No Canadian mail had come in for about two weeks, until last night. It brought three for me, yours included, and two today, one from Maggie and one from Clara G.P. from Toronto. I was beginning to think that a boat had gone down. I always think of that when mail comes in long intervals. I was delighted to hear of your trip to Lammermoor and that you got some fruit. Gee, but berries and cream would go good. We buy fruit here occasionally but like all other things are dear. Large plums are about 2 for a penny, apples and pears 2 pence each for the large.

I am glad that Tommy is good and faithful to you this summer, so that you are not tied at home for want of a driver.[89] Seems as though half the people in that part have auto's now. Does Pa ever speak of getting one? You could soon learn to run one, lots of women over here run large lorries and steam engines. Large numbers have gone to France to drive ambulances.

So you had a visit from Violet. I suppose you had a fine time recalling days gone by. Does she speak much of Jim? I can easily guess the kind of life he is leading in this country and in France, unless by chance he has reformed a great deal.

It takes a strong will to keep out of trouble here and this is where I find the benefit of a good father and mother and all they taught me. No doubt they often thought that all their efforts were in vain but not so. There is plenty of opportunity to do good here, but I never say anything unless a good chance occurs. You know the old proverb saying "actions speak louder than words." I did not know that anyone took any notice, until a few days ago when one chap turned to me during a heated argument and told me that I, being a truth believing chap, should settle it. The majority of the boys do not take God's name in vain so much but have taken to Tommy slang (Tommy = English soldier) and have, I might say, multiplied it by about ten, until it is simply disgusting the expressions they come out with.

Old St. James looks just the same, I suppose, and is Watson Corners still a thrilling center?[90] Young people must be scarce in that part now compared with ten years ago. By your letter, I believe Jim Pauls have a car. Raymond will be hitting the high spots this summer. Who is he rushing? How is Fairs getting on, did you see any of them?

I had a letter from Edna Paul yesterday with a snap of she and Mabel, also had one from my new friend Miss Robertson, with a snap. Isn't it funny how people I never saw before write, while my first cousins never seem to think of it. Gracie writes pretty regularly. I sent her one of those pictures the other day. Also had a letter with snap enclosed from my faithful little friend in town—you know who.[91]

Now I wrote only a few days ago so will leave off now for I want to go to the YMCA to hear Capt. Cameron of Toronto. He was a preacher there and has spoken in every Canadian camp in England and to every Canadian Batt. in France. He has a fine singer from London with him too.

Here's hoping and praying that you are all well and that we shall all meet once more to exchange experiences.

Love to all,

Herb

P.S. Have no word of going to France yet. Am taking a course in First Aid this week. It is very interesting work and may come in handy some time.

> **Sept. 21:** Fair. First aid. Moved into number 3 hut. Some men transferred to C Company.
>
> **Sept. 22:** Fair. Examination in first aid. O. Gorman and I went to Hythe. Rowing and went to show.
>
> **Sept. 23:** Church parade and lecture by Capt. Cameron. Service in evening also.

89

A. Co. 12th Reserve Batt.
East Sandling
Kent, England
Sept. 23, 1917
Sunday 1 P.M.

Dear May,

Now I shall endeavour to pen you a few thoughts, just to let you know that my heart is still in its proper place. ha ha. No doubt several times last winter it was not, but six and a half months in Blighty has brought it right again.

Last week I spent studying our "Make and Aches." Such a life, one week you learn to kill men and next bind them up. I found the First Aid course very interesting work and perhaps next time I go across "yonder" it may prove very helpful. This week I am on Butt Party. Quite an easy job it is, just score the hits and plug the bullet holes. The biggest part is marching to and from the range—a distance of about two and a half miles. I thought I was failing in this camp, but got weighed yesterday and was surprised to find that I had gained some. Just tip the beam at 170 lbs now.

Well yesterday was Saturday. So after we got our bunks and floors scrubbed and cleaned up personally, four of us hiked off to Hythe.

Proceeded to the canal and hired a couple of boats. Well talk about fun! We tried races, took snapshots, wet each other and it is a wonder someone did not play submarine. It is dandy exercise rowing. Do you ever try? Next time you go out just try, that is if you are not already an expert.

This afternoon I was over to the "Y" to hear Capt. Cameron of Bloor St. Toronto, preach. He was here three nights last week, but owing to engagement of regimental import, was only able to attend one night. He is a fine man. Has spoken in every Canadian camp in England and to every Canadian Batt. in France. His subject Thurs. night was "Habits." He brought out some points very forcibly and I think they went home. The Y. was packed and not a man went out. He spoke of the awful habit of taking the Lord's name in vain. I think I have mentioned that to you before. Men just out from the trenches seem to curse as if it had become a second nature. Taking no thought of Him who watched over them during long vigils on listening post and without whom we can do nothing. Today his text was "Say unto the righteous man that it shall be well with him." He likened us unto a ship setting sail and as he watched her head out to sea and become smaller and smaller until at last she is gone. But the vessel has not become any smaller and by and by someone watching on the other shore sights her and cries "she comes." So we travelling on should see to it that our friends already on that other shore will one day be able to say that of us.

Was indeed sorry to hear of Laura having to undergo an operation. I hope it was not very serious, but of course an operation in the throat must be a delicate job and I trust she has recovered completely. Speaking of lost letters May, it is quite evident that you don't get all mine and I don't get all yours. Sorry I did not get your account of the wedding and that you did not get my parcel.

I did get the sugar O.K. and wrote next day telling you. I shall thank you again for it, twas just grand. By the way the little gift I sent you was a book of Scottish poems, bound in tartan, which I got in Perth Scotland. Don't worry about it May. I'll send something else. Say what would you like? I find it hard to choose articles. Now don't be afraid to say. You said you were glad that you could trust me and I am sure that I can trust you, so let us just be quite frank with each other.

Why do you say "perhaps I shouldn't write so often for your sake." If you want to write every week, I shall be only too pleased to get them and will try to answer them all. Don't mind what I said about bring someone around, was only joking. You know what I said one night, about not asking you to make any promises. I say the same yet, but still you are my truest friend, if no more.

A few of the boys have started to play cards—poker—on the table, so I cannot write and listen to them so will call off. I am going over to service in the Y at 7 P.M. Remember I am also just the same as you knew me a year ago, only like yourself, have seen a little more of the world and its ways. Some more of our old 130th boys have called to see me, so excuse me May, I want to have a chat with them.

As ever,

Herb

90

A. Co. 12th Reserve Batt.
East Sandling
Kent England
Sept. 19, 1917

Dear Sister,

This is a beautiful afternoon but I am not going out any where today, for we just returned last night from a three day route march and manoeuvres.

We left on Wed. morning about 6:30 and marched 9 miles, had lunch and then went 6 more and bivouacked for the night. Of course you know what that word means. Well although it was cool and rather like rain we slept well, having a rubber sheet, 2 blankets and our overcoats. Three of us got together and were snug as bugs in rugs. "Fall in" went at 5 A.M. and we marched off to meet the "supposed" enemy, engaged them about 3 miles further on, took several prisoners and fought a rearguard action back to a town called Eythorne. Here our company held a very strong position, winning compliments from the referees. From here we retreated back about 2 miles and bivouacked for the night. Next morning we started out to retake the village again, which we did by 9:30 A.M. and by 10 A.M. had the enemy in full retreat. The enemy were all Imperial soldiers distinguished by white bands on their caps, while we Canadians were 5 infantry brigades or 20,000 men, 3 batteries of artillery and several other corps. It was great fun fighting but the long march had its effects. However, we have had all day today to rest. The object was to see how long it would take the troops in this area to meet an enemy force "if" they were to land on the East Coast. Forty-eight hours is the time figured, but of course that is quite unthinkable for we still have a fleet. So that has been our work this week and next Tuesday I expect to go to Seaford for a three week course in entrenching.

Your letter and a few others were awaiting me last night so I got into bed and read them there. One from Janet came today with a snap of the three kids. It is rather dark but I can see a great change in the girls and think the lad is all right.

Glad to know that you were all well and going to attend some of the fairs. Wish I was there to get some of that jelly and cake. You will have an awful time keeping that kind of stuff when I get back. Do you know I am longing for some nice mashed potatoes and fried pork. Most of the food is boiled and I am sick of it. So the West is getting some help from the East this fall again. It sure will be a good trip for Roy but Pa Pa will have to work pretty hard I am afraid.[92]

You were wondering what I was doing the Sunday you wrote this letter. Well I'll tell you. In the morning I went to church and in the afternoon to the Bible class. Capt. Manning who runs the YMCA has a Bible Class every Sunday at 1:30. I go every chance I get. He is a fine young man and so like Rob. Nairn.

Well Clara, I am lonesome too at times, like you are, but of course I don't get as much time perhaps to think about it all. A year ago today we were in mid-Atlantic and the old Lapland was sure rolling about and I was sick. So in one week more, I shall have been across one year and only three months at the front so I consider myself lucky.

It surely won't last much longer and then we will all be home again. There will be an awful time when the Canadians are let free again.

Good bye for now and just address your letters here and they will be sent on to Seaford to me. Hope this finds you all well.

Love to all,
Herb

Sept. 24: Fine. Butt party Hythe ranges. [Butt duty was to score the hits on the targets and then plug the holes for the next round]
Sept. 25: Fair. Butt party to ranges. Preparing to go on route march.

Sept. 26: Fine. Left camp at 6:30. Marched 9 miles and stopped for lunch then 6 more and bivouacked in park near Eythorne.

Sept. 27: Fine. Went out to engage enemy. Took some prisoners and fought a rear guard action. Back to Eythorne. Retreat and bivouacked.

Sept. 28: Fine. Advanced and retook Eythorne by 10:00 A.M. and started home. Arrived at 7:00 P.M.

Sept. 29: Fine. Resting up and writing letters.

Sept. 30: Church parade and bible class.

91

A. Co. 12th Reserve Batt.
East Sandling
Kent England
Sept. 30, 1917

Dear May,

Here I am this lovely Sunday morn to have a chat with you. I sure did enjoy that little Sunday evening chat and when you mention roaming over the hills, it brings me back to other days, days of peace and freedom. Again I come with one letter for your two. You see yours of Aug. 19 went to France and just arrived here with the one of Sept. 2nd. You won't mind me telling you of your slight mistake in addressing it—you put on the 75th instead of the 12th, with above results. The 75th is my unit in the field alright, but am attached to the 12th Reserve, and all letters with 75th on them go direct to France to that unit. Now I have explained, you will not make any more mistakes.

So the two letters were here for me on my return from a three day route march and manoeuvres, I'll tell you about it.

We left camp at 6:30 A.M. Wed. and marched nearly east across country in the direction of Dover. Nine miles out we stopped for lunch, then did about six more and bivouacked for the night. Real old time campaigning it was, sleeping under the stars, knapsack for a pillow, beside long rows of stacked rifles and the sentry silently walking up and down.[93] We were all tired enough to sleep the sweet sleep of a soldier and dream of other days. In the gray dawn we rose and had breakfast, buckled our equipment, shouldered rifles and marched off to meet the "supposed" enemy who were "supposed" to have made a

landing on the coast between Dover and Ramsgate. The good old 12th
led in the operations of our Brigade and of course were the first to
engage the enemy. By 10 A.M. my company had captured a company
of cyclists and retired to the second line which was held by Kilties of
the 2nd Reserve. Here we were just in time to support them and drive
the enemy back, until our troops could withdraw to a third line. Again
we lined a railway embankment and wiped out a whole company, after
which we retired to a pretty little village called Eythorne, where we held
a very strong position, but were finally driven out of it to our fourth line.
Night came on and we bivouacked again, still holding this position in
imagination. Gray dawn comes again and with it we make a counter
attack, retake the village, also a strong point at a colliery and finally have
the enemy in full retreat. Operations closed at 10 A.M. and we start on
a 12 mile march for home arriving at 7 P.M. Now May I suppose all this
is Latin to you, but I have tried to explain. The enemy were all Imperial
troops and were marked by white bands on their caps and not so
numerous as we who were perhaps 30,000 strong. Of course we all used
blank ammunition and there were no bayonet charges, otherwise it was
just like the first days of the war before trench lines were dug. Referee
on each side scored marks in much the same way as any sport. It sure
was great fun and if I had room to tell you of the march, getting apple
showers along the way, etc. etc., you would laugh.

Now the object of this was to see how long it would take the troops
of this area to mobilize and meet an enemy force, should they effect a
landing, which I don't think is possible. In 24 hours we could meet them
with infantry, cavalry, artillery etc. etc. Yes and we had the field hospitals
in full swing although there were no Blightys.

Quite a bunch have gone west eh! It will be a fine trip for Roy, but
I bet your father misses him. So Laura is teaching. I believe I have seen
her school. Tell her not to use the cane too much. ha ha.

I did not know until you told me of J. Walters being killed. I
knew him well and he certainly was a good fellow. Too bad, do you
know May, he went through an operation to get into the army. Yes,
I remember you speaking of Mr. Smith and it is fine that he has got
home. As to Ed. Watt, I'll not say anything here. I expect you know my
feelings towards him without.[94]

Well May this is getting rather lengthy isn't it and I believe dinner
will soon be up and of course we can't miss that—more fish likely. Oh
yes I am leaving here for Seaford on Tuesday for a three weeks course

in pioneer work. I will see some of the 38th boys there. Will write this weekend and tell you of that place. Just address your letters here. I'll be back before your answer to this anyway.

Good-bye for now.

Yours as ever,

Herb

Oct. 1: Fine. Left for Seaford for pioneer course. Arrived at 2:00 P.M. Drew blankets.

Oct. 2: Fine. First day very strict on discipline. Takes about 10 minutes to dress on square. Sand bagging and wiring.

Oct. 3: Raining in A.M. On redoubt. Went to sports in P.M. at north camp. Feeling rather tough.

Oct. 4: Rainy. Lecture in hut and PT for half hour.

92

Pioneer School
Seaford, Sussex
Oct. 4, 1917

Dear Father,

It must be your turn now to get a letter so here it is. First of all, I hope it finds you all well as it leaves me all right, although yesterday I felt rather out of usual. A touch of grippe I guess but am much better today and a good nights sleep will fix me up. It rained today so we did nothing, which was fine for me. Also yesterday being sports day did not work in the afternoon. I came here last Monday and will be here until about the 22nd of this month. The course consists of field fortifications, their defence and supply. It covers a great many points which one not in the job would think of. Experience in France taught me a great deal but still there is always something to learn, always some new scheme for safety and comfort being discovered. At first the Allies copied trench fighting from the Germans but now I believe we are superior.

This is a sea coast town about the size of Lanark and the camp is about 2 miles out. And I might say also too far West to be troubled about air raids. These moonlight nights have been fully taken advantage of by Fritz. Last week they came over almost every night. One passed directly over our camp at East Sandling. It was like old times to hear the guns going. Now I have no more news so will have to stop. I see that Capt. Cameron is to be here all next week so I will have a chance to hear him again. I am sorry to miss our Bible Study Class for three Sundays. Am enclosing a booklet of the studies.

Good bye for now and may you have good health.

Your loving son,

Herb

P.S. Don't address to here.

> *Oct. 5:* Fair. Systems and defence of C. trenches. Sham battle at night. Runner to O.C.
>
> *Oct. 6:* Fair. On barrack fatigue A.M. O.C. inspection at 11:00 A.M. Very minute. Pte. Quackenbush and I went downtown in P.M. to show and concert.
>
> *Oct. 7:* Rainy. Church parade in YMCA.

93

Canadian Pioneer School
Seaford, Sussex
Oct. 7, 1917

Dear May,

Hello! another new address, but don't answer to this for I shall be back to Sandling before you get it, in fact I am looking forward to that day already. In short I do not like this place, far too strict in regards to cleaning brass. It takes about 20 mins. to get formed up on parade to suit them. The first day here of course, we were a bit slow and they had the bunch out half an hour earlier next morning. The whole staff is "rotten" absolutely. Then again I have been here a week and don't know anymore than when I came. Experience over yonder is a good teacher and one doesn't forget what he learns there. It may be alright for men who have never been across but I am "fed up" with it pure and simple.

Now May, I know you won't care to hear all this "grousing"[95] but I am telling you plain facts.

The camp itself is about 2 miles from the scattered little town of Seaford. An Imperial Con. Camp lies to the north so you may have an idea how full the place is of troops. Yesterday Pte. Quakenbush, whom I think you have met, and I went down to see the sights. It was very cool so the beach had no attractions. Well next best is theatres. In vain we hunted for a play house but found none so were content with a picture show, which proved very good. Tea came next. We had eggs and tomatoes, pie with cream and lemonade. In the evening we took in a sort of concert in the hall. It proved very good also so we did spend the afternoon quite pleasantly. Today was quite rainy but nevertheless we went to church at 11 A.M.

After dinner I had a nap, then supper and now I am in the Y doing this. Mr. Quakenbush is by me and just now we were speaking of a certain dance at Drummond Centre in 1916. "Compre." Gee, I would not mind a drive and a little dance like that now. Pte. Q. was speaking of Miss Phillips and I wanted him to write to her. He sends his respects to you. Some guy he is, very fond of candy. We have just finished a box of Creme de Menthe.

What's the rush in Perth? Getting like fall I expect, as it is here. Won't be long until skating begins. You learned last winter didn't you? I have not decided yet where I will spend the winter. Ha ha. I may take a trip to the Continent. If so I shall find the deepest dugout and stay there. A draft has left for the 75th since I left Sandling—just missed it. Oh! I have met several 130th boys here. H. Edwards and O. Noonan, T. Moore and others. All are fine and making the best of it.

Have you heard this song over there?

Where are the boys of the village tonight
Where are the boys we knew
Round Piccadilly or Leister Square
No not there, no not there
They have taken a trip to the Continent
With rifles and bayonets bright
They have gone across the water
To see the Kaisers daughter
That's where they are tonight.

Spoke shaf[96]
Well good night, pleasant dreams.

Herb

Oct. 8: Rainy. Taking down wire in A.M. Had a rest in afternoon.
Oct. 9: Fine. Wiring. Getting good food here. Went on a tramp through trenches at night.

Oct. 10: Fine. Building roads. Pte. Quakenbush and I went over to 7th reserve and afterwards to the show.

Oct. 11: Cool. Reservoirs. Lashing spars and tying knots.

Oct. 12: Fair in A.M. Working on cut. Rained in P.M. Had lecture on grousing causes and cures. J. Saunders called.

Oct. 13: Rainy. Inspection in morning. J. Saunders, H. Quackenbush and I went downtown to show and concert. Called on Cpl. Dack.

Oct. 14: Fine. Went to hear Capt. Cameron.

94

Canadian Pioneer School
Seaford Sussex
Oct. 14, 1917

Dear May,

Hello! beautiful day "is it not!" "Oh ripping" "Shall us take a walk on't beach's afternoon?" "Oh I say, Rather." ha ha. Can you read this? Well it is a mixture of Lancashire, Yorkshire, Cockney and Canadian so I don't wonder if you don't "compre" it. It is amusing to listen to some of these Blighters talking.

Anyhow May, it is a dandy afternoon and I just wish you were here to take a walk with me down by the sea. Let's go anyway. Shall we start down by the New Haven wharf and go east. Yes, we will walk along the promenade in front of Seaford's summer hotels, now vacant, then along the pebbles and sand. We will walk right where the last wave came in, now watch the next one or you will get your shoes wet, those waves have a habit of creeping in farther than you expect.

Now we will climb the cliffs and get a good view from the top of one of the Seven Sisters. Away out to sea, well I'll have to leave you here, the censor comes in for his share, so look landward across hills and valleys, with its farmsteads, roads and by-paths, villages, camps lying peacefully under the October sky. Just close your eyes to the Military Camps and you would not know that there is a war on. The machinery is stopped for a short while but in the morning again, every place is astir with troops training.

Say I can almost smell that corn boiling when I read of the roast. Many a good night I have spent too, roasting corn on a stick.

They are improving greatly in Perth eh! Well I shall get off at Glen Tay then and walk across to Harper, guess I will know that thrilling center. ha ha. Looks good to me be it ever so humble.

Did I tell you that a draft had left for the 75th since I left Sandling. I had a letter from Jim Trail last week and he said he was leaving next day. We counted on going back together having come across the same time, but here I am at Seaford, but perhaps I shall catch him up yet.

I don't care how soon I go back to France now. I am fed up with soldiering here. This "chocolate soldiering" gets monotonous. Perhaps I shall be lucky enough to get another "Blighty." When I think of having been in the army over one and a half years and did so little, I feel ashamed of myself. Others have done so much heavy fighting while I only saw one little scrap. Capt. Cameron of Toronto is speaking in the Y tonight and as I want to go and hear him and it is now almost supper time I will ring off for now. I will write again soon as I get back to Sandling.

I saw A. Dack yesterday, that is Annie Sinclair's friend. He looks pretty good. Have not been speaking to H. Edwards yet. I also saw Tommy Caldwell yesterday (T.B. son). He is O.C. of the 6th Reserve here.

Wishing you health and happiness.

Yours Sincerely,
Herb

Oct. 15: Fine. Building trenches for 16th reserve. Went to see D. Stefanin and to hear Capt. Cameron.

95

Canadian Pioneer School
Seaford Sussex
Mon. Oct. 15, 1917

Dear Father,

Received your welcome letter of Sept. 11th, a few days ago and glad to hear that you were all well. I am fine, had a little cold in my head but it is better now.

As you see, I am still at this school, expect to finish this week and get back to Sandling about the 23rd. I like the place a little better than I did at first. One thing is we get good food and lots of it. I told you of the work in my last letter so will not take space with that.

This is a lovely day. Have had some wet weather but of course we do not mind a few wet days—get a rest then you see. Yesterday went to church at 11 A.M. then to Bible Class at 2:30. I enjoyed it. We went out in the fields and sat by a stone wall. There was one Army Chaplain and the Capt. of the YMCA. Had a nice talk on Phillipians 1st. Then at 7 P.M. I went to the large YMCA to hear Capt. Cameron. Last night was the first of his address here, which will continue all week. The Officer Commanding the troops here, introduced him. Miss Harley of London sang and it was worth going a long piece to hear. I never heard "Nearer My God to Thee," sung so nice before. She was accompanied by Miss Wood, Toronto pianist and so Capt. Cameron said he was pleased to have a real live Canadian girl on the platform. Cameron is certainly a clever speaker. I wish you could have heard him last night and saw the crowd of boys that were there to hear him. The place was packed. I went about 6 o'clock in order to get a front seat and then I was back about 8 rows from the front. He spoke especially to the boys who have been to France, whom he spoke to there. He has studied conditions at the front and knows a soldiers thoughts, out of the line and in. He is quite comical too and just brings in enough jokes to make the crowd sort of lean forward to hear what he has next to say, which is always rock bottom truths. Will try and get a pamphlet and enclose for you when I go over tonight.

Well take care of yourselves and do not work too hard.

Yours lovingly,

Herb

Oct. 16: Rainy. Had two lectures and half hour PT. Got letter from P. McNicol and answered it.[97]

Oct. 17: Rainy. Fixing firing trenches on the ranges.

Oct. 18: Fine. Working on tunnels all day. To lecture at night. 2+2=4.

Oct. 19: Fine. Tunnelling. Digging jumping off trench at night.

Oct. 20: Fine. Inspection in A.M. Visited Alfriston and Lilington. Very pretty places. Saw old inn where Alfred the Great burned the cakes.

Oct. 21: Fine. Orderly. O. Noonan and H. Edwards called.

Oct. 22: Fine. Tunnelling in A.M. Fatigue in P.M. Went to cinema.

Oct. 23: Rain in morning. Getting ready to return to Sandling. Fine. Left at 2:00 P.M. Home at 9:00 P.M.

Oct. 24: Fine. Short route march. Wrote some letters in afternoon. Parcel from Mary E.[98]

96

East Sandling
Kent
Oct. 24, 1917

Dear May,

Here we are again, returned in perfect safety from our three weeks stay at Seaford, to find the Reserve still in the same place. Got back at 9 P.M. last night and found your letter awaiting me. Glad to hear from you of course and to know that you are still happy.

You said you had not much news. Well I differ with you but also assure you that mine will contain less by about half.

Well we left our old pals at Seaford quite well. Did I tell you that O. Noonan and H. Edwards are going to the Flying Corps.

What do I think of the war ending? Well I hesitate to say when, but I am sure that we are in for another winter in the trenches. Will Germany be able to stand our drive next spring is another question.[99]

It is a good move to get the Canadian people to save food, all is needed and plainer food would be better for lots of people if they only knew it, take a soldiers rations for instance.

Was glad to hear that Roy likes the west, but perhaps you have lost him. ha ha.

Some of my pals went to France while I was at Seaford.

Like you, I too, am writing by the fire while outside the rain pours down and I am thinking of the lads out yonder in the shell holes on outpost.

Conscription at last eh! I hope I am to France and back again before they come over or better still to meet them right in the front line their first trip in. "Some of them," I say, you know who I mean.[100]

Well Tra La La. I am going to have a game of draughts now—getting to be quite expert. Am enclosing some cards so will make one page do.

All the time,
Herb

97 (envelope)

[This envelope was addressed to Clara Gibson. May had written "Oct. 24/17" on it. It contained a picture of duckboards, but there was no letter inside.]

> *Oct. 25:* Cool. Squad drill and short marches. Payed at 6 P.M.
>
> *Oct. 26:* Cloudy. B.F. A.M. Route march P.M. Wrote some letters. Got Courier from Mae Darou.
>
> *Oct. 27:* Fine. Bombing in A.M. Scrubbed bed boards afternoon and cleaned equipment.
>
> *Oct. 28:* Cool. On quarter guard.

98

East Sandling
Oct. 28, 1917

Dear May,

I wager you never got a letter written in a place like this before.

The much respected "Guard Room" of the Battalion. Some place, believe me, to spend a Sunday. Never-the-less, duty must be done. Oh no, I am not a prisoner. Guess I am too scared of the punishment to do anything wrong. ha ha. Well, I am very lucky since this is the first quarter guard I have been on since I left Canada just over thirteen months ago. Your letter came to me here this afternoon and sure was doubly welcome under the circumstances. It sure put some sunshine into an otherwise dull time. 5:30 P.M. "Fall in the relief." 7:30 P.M. The relief "fell in" forthwith and has done its two hours sentry duty so now I shall endeavour to finish this epistle, before going on again at 11:30.

So it is just three weeks ago since you wrote this letter. As yet I have not received the one written in pencil but hope to soon. Yes it must be nice to get home for a couple of days even short and sweet, eh. You are having some cold weather too. Well we also are having a share of it now. Cold and dull here and I see by the papers that there has been snow in Scotland. Of course we can't expect anything else at this time of year.

Sure I know Ray Paul and have seen Miss Pretty but don't know her personally. He must think a great deal of his aunt, to have her help pick his outfit. Say just here I can't help adding I could pick a suit for him from here and best of all it would not cost him a cent. I believe he is driving a car this summer too. But still we can't all be soldiers, some one must stay at home.[101]

By the way, I have learned to play Five Hundred too. Rather interesting, is it not? Some fellows buy farms for a blind eh. Well, a poor excuse is better than none, then again we must have wheat and bacon.

Yes I knew that R. Watt was home. If I were him I'd go away and hide somewhere in the bush. Not that he is yellow but something far worse.

Say May, I am getting quite curious to know who conscription is bringing in from that part, do you wonder. You know how a person gets sort of bound up in their work whatever it may be. At the same time I hate the very idea of conscription, but since they won't volunteer to do a bit, I guess that's the best plan. I am glad you told me what you would like for a keepsake. First chance I get I will see about a silver _____ something.

I did not go downtown Wed. or Sat. afternoon. Sort of fed up going out so stayed in and wrote letters for a change.

I got a *Courier* the other day and had a great time reading it.[102] Think I read every bit of it. All the Councils, sales, marriages, etc. etc. I notice that Fred Bell has sold his farm. Where is he going to live?

Well here's wishing you luck and the best of everything.

As ever,

Herb

Oct. 29: Fine. Off guard at 10:00. Route march afternoon.

Oct. 30: Rainy. B.F. and squad drill. Clothing exchange. Letter from May.

Oct. 31: Fair. Route marching. O. Gorman and I went to Hythe in evening.

Nov. 1: Rainy. Did very little of anything today.

Nov. 2: Fine. On butt party.

Nov. 3: Fair. Bombing in A.M. Saltwood picket at night.

Nov. 4: Fair. Coal fatigue.

Nov. 5: Fine. Shovelling coal. Two letters from home. Wrote to Mother and M.E.[103]

99

East Sandling
Kent, England
Nov. 5, 1917

Dear Sister,

I have just been looking over some old letters and I notice that the last one I got was written on Sept. 11., over a month before yours of Oct. 8, so now I am convinced that I do not get them all. I do wonder where they get to. Any how it can't be helped I suppose. I guess you do not get all of mine either.

Well, Clara, I spent Thanksgiving at Seaford and it rained most of the day. It was not much like other Thanksgiving days.

I am sorry to hear that Pa and Ma have not been so well but I hope they are as usual again. You want to watch and not get the old trouble this winter.

It must be fine and cheery in the kitchen with that new range. Does the wood fit it all right and will there be enough to last all winter? Does the hard water pump work all right and did you do anything to the cistern?

Gee but chicken, tomatoes and citrons seem good to me. But I should not complain now for the food is much better lately. One could do on the army ration but I always buy a cup of tea and some cakes in the club in the evening.

So there was lots of corn to cut this year. Perhaps I could have got a few jobs eh![104] Seems like a dream to look back to those days and I sometimes think I must have been somewhat of a fool to try to run as a outfit alone. However we did some good work with it and perhaps some day will be running the hasher again.

I was indeed surprised to hear of Mrs. McDougall's death. I never thought she was anything but healthy. And Raymond is married. He wrote once and I answered but never got a reply. Thomas's are certainly having a lot of trouble this year. How did Jack get hurt?

Well I am glad to hear that you and Mrs. McTavish are so chummy. There is no need for me to say more for you know I always liked them too. It is nice that they are not afraid to use their car to give you a drive.

The ink in my pen is NA POO.

Middleville people should change the date of their fair, I think for they get so many bad days. It must be about six years since I was at a fair there. I guess you remember that day as well as I do. Someday alright—snow and mud and something else.

And you were talking to Henry! I suppose he did not mention yours truly? Do you ever hear from Margaret? Say what is Alex doing so long at Kingston? Got a "bomb proof" job I suppose. You are about right in your thinking of M_____ too. She will never leave Ottawa, I guess. It seems that I can't collect my thoughts tonight to write so if this letter rambles please excuse. I wish I had something new to write about but tonight I have not.

Tell Father to take good care of himself and that I will write to him next.

Good night and pleasant dreams.

Loving,
Herb

100

East Sandling
Kent England
Nov. 5, 1917. 4 P.M.

My Dear Mother,

Received your welcome letter at noon today so am not long answering am I?

Was awful glad to hear from you again. I guess I think as much of your letters as you do mine. Do I write often enough Mother? I try to sort of distribute them around but may leave some long intervals sometimes.[105]

I am glad to say that I am feeling fine. I am very much afraid of you getting laid up this winter again though. Do take care of yourself and don't worry about me too much. I certainly have been lucky to have been so long in England while the heavy fighting is going on. Sometimes I feel as if I were not doing my duty but it is not my fault. Anyway I hope now to spend this Christmas in England. I would like very much to but of course one never knows.

Now I hope you keep well and may God bless and keep you until we meet again.

Your loving son,
Herb

Nov. 6: Rain in morning making the job very nasty. Washed some articles in afternoon.

Nov. 7: Fair. Muster parade at 9:00 A.M. So did not get finished before noon.

Nov. 8: Fair. Coal heaving. Draft called for 3rd Battalion.

Nov. 9: Fine. Coal fatigue. Prepared photo to send to Canada.

101

East Sandling
Kent England
Nov. 9/17

Dear May,

Pardon me, for the long space of time between letters for really, May, there is so little to write about. I am afraid my letters are some what of a bore, are they not? Just the same old story every time, of my own doings.

Your letter in pencil was more welcome (if such a thing were possible) than any other in ink, for it tells me that there is nothing conventional between us. We are just plain friends May, are we not? You know that I don't want gilt edged paper or anything of that sort. I am glad you liked the picture but whether I look more like a soldier now or not, I can't tell. I feel more like one at least.

By now you will be quite settled in your little white room and I am sure it will be almost like home with your Aunt.

And how is business at the Bank? No signs of it busting is there? ha ha. Don't work too hard anyway.

Say I hope you have a better pen that this. I would not part with it though for you see, I have carried it for sixteen months steady, through thick and thin. The top came loose in my pocket a few times, consequently the point got injured, broke its nose as it were.

Oh, I must tell you what a "draft" means. It is any number of men proceeding overseas to reinforce battalions at the front. "Drawing" rifles simply means getting them out of Quarter Master stores for use. Is that quite clear to you. Oh yes, I knew Ray Paul since we were _____ babies. Was quite surprised to hear of him getting spliced though. Oh perhaps I mentioned that before.

There are two large drafts picked for France now, to reinforce the 3rd and 75th. As yet I am not booked to go, for reasons which I will tell you later. Perhaps I shall be here for Christmas yet. If I get a decent length of leave, I intend going to Ireland, sure and I am.

Well I think I will quit this scribble now. Its raining tonight as usual and I am in the Jellicoe Club.[106]

Good night, sweet dreams.

As ever,
Herb

Nov. 10: Fair. O.R. Gorman and I went to Moore B. hospital to see G. Janes. Sent photo home.

101A

East Sandling
Kent England
Nov. 10, 1917

Dear Sister,

Just a short note today as my pal, Orville Gorman and I are sending a couple of pictures. We tossed a penny to see who would send them so it fell to me. I hope they do not get broken and I want you to forward one to the address below. Mrs. A.G. Gorman, Stittsville, Ont. The officer is Capt. Crawford, twice wounded 3rd Batt., Sergt. Major Grant 75th and the others are 3rd and 75th men.

It has turned quite cool this afternoon but is clear. I had a nice bath and general clean up since dinner and after tea Gorman and I are going down to Shorncliffe Hospital to see G. Janes, an Appleton chap of the 130th.[107] We may go to the Picture Palace after. We go there about once a month for there is nothing else to go to when out, now since the cold weather has set in. I have been on Coal Fatigue all week and next week will be Hut Orderly. The name explains that, just keeping the hut clean and tidy. Will be getting a new uniform next week too and the week after I intend applying for a pass.

We have had frost one night. How many have you had? Reports say that there will be no coal shortage here this winter which will be a good thing. I think the food situation is looking pretty bright too, so we are not beaten yet, are we. I see a report saying that the Germans have to take their drafts up the line under escort. A large draft left here yesterday morning for France and as usual they woke us with their cheers! Compare the two. This is all today. Hoping you are all well.

Love to all,
Herb

Nov. 11: Fine. Fatigue in morning. Scrubbed hut. Picket at night.
Nov. 13: Fine. Hut orderly. Received some letters and answered some.

102

East Sandling, Kent
Nov. 13, 1917

Dear Father,

Just a line today to say that I am well and as you see still in England.[108]

Everything is much as usual around camp and in the country in general. Now and again there is a commotion of one sort or other such as some new plan of food conserving, recruiting, etc. etc. but people have got used to these things now and nothing seems to excite them any more. As to the war, you know as much as I do. Very little is printed here and the papers are very small on account of paper shortage. We are settling down to another winter campaign anyhow and I think there is still another ahead of us.

Supper is over so now I will finish this. We had some very good sausage and pudding tonight. I am hut Orderly this week and have not very much to do.

There is a concert in the YMCA tonight and I think I will go to it.

Had a letter from Willie's today and expect some more Canadian mail tonight. I got a new suit of clothes today and am going to try for a pass next week. Think I deserve one now, have just had five days since I was home, of course Sick Furlough does not count as a pass. The weather is getting quite cool now and plenty of rain and mist. What kind of weather are you having. I hope the winter over there is not so stormy as last winter, like wise over here. The ground will be all frozen up there by now I expect.

I was talking to a 130th man from Pembroke the other day. We were in the same platoon in France. His brother was killed in April and his Mother is at home alone on the farm. She has asked the Authorities in Ottawa to let him go home. One of his chums is going home under the same circumstances. I expect he will at least get a six months furlough. They have revised the scheme over here and will not take men for the army if managing a farm. I expect lots of men are hiding in Canada, under the head of farmers, who don't own farms.

Well I must close now and get this posted for tonights post.

Love to all.

Herb

Nov. 14: Fair. Medical inspection for draft. Through Q.M.S. for equipment.
Nov. 15: Fine. Sewing buttons on great coat in morning. Inoculation in afternoon. Paraded for passes.

103

East Sandling
Kent, Nov. 15/17

Dear Father,

Your letter of yesterday and I feel very down hearted indeed to get such news as it conveyed. But I must bear up and trust in God to spare you both yet awhile and bring you both back to your usual. Mother in bed again at this time of the year has some significance to me and the why she took it indicates the old trouble.

I hope the Dr.'s treatment of you has good results and that nothing further develops.

I can not say very much in this letter but you know that I am thinking hard. My one comfort is that if we do not meet again on earth we will meet across the great divide where there is peace for ever more.

I trust the other two boys will do all in their power to comfort you since I am far away. I know I came away against your will but I would have been called up by now anyway which would have been almost as bad. No, I am not hiding behind the excuse. I firmly believe in pre-destination. A man's career is cut out for him and he must live it out. I know you will not want for anything that can be had and there is peace in that land. You have good neighbours there too, whom I know will be willing to help, as you both have helped others when in trouble. In spite of all I feel that I should be there to help. Not that I could do anymore but the mission I am on, calls so much of your strength to bear the anxiety.

I don't know how soon I shall be sent back to France, so now I am preparing you for that news which I hope will be broken as easy as possible. This is all I can say today and may God watch over and keep us all and bring us safely through.

Goodbye, Love to you all.

Affectionately,

Herb

103A

Dear Clara,

I wish I could but give you a few words of consolation in your time of trouble and anxiety. But all I can say is to look to God for help as you have always done and He shall bring all things about to His glory.

It is a hard time for you, Clara, I know and please don't think it is not for me although so far away.

Try and look on the bright side of the cloud and if anything should happen, God's will be done.

Goodbye now. God bless you.[109]

Herb

104

East Sandling
Nov. 15, 1917

Dear May,

I sure have a job ahead of me this time, two long letters of yours to answer. The second came before I got a chance to answer the other. I don't feel much like writing though May, for I had rather bad news from home in yesterday's letter. Mother is in bed again and Father is not well either. You know how one feels when anything goes wrong at home and so far away. But we must try and bear these things and trust in God, who will bring all things for the best. I may never see my dear parents again on earth, May, but one hope and comfort is that we shall meet in a better land where there is no war, sorrow or parting. I want to ask you May, if you will call on Mother at your first opportunity. I know she will be glad to see you and perhaps you can give her a word or two of comfort for me. I shall be exceedingly grateful to you if you will. Your letters were both newsy and I am glad to hear that you have had a visit from your cousin. He will be able to tell you lots of things that I could not. I am sure I would be pleased to meet him over here or in France. Most likely it will be in France, for in a few weeks time I will be "up the line." By the way, what Battalion is he in?

Glad to hear of your being in the First Aid Class. It is real good for anyone. I don't wonder at Eva getting the bones mixed up, there are so many. Can you give the "points of pressure" yet?

So there are some men on "exemption" eh! Now those are men who were eager to soldier when there was peace. I call them "Heroes when there is no war"—"Cowards when there is." Serg. Maj. Smith did the right thing to ignore those people, I would do the same. Pte. Quackenbush leaves for the front tomorrow, I will see him tonight and convey your compliments to him and tell him to write.

Now May, I think I have not missed anything in those two letters. It doesn't seem a big job after all to write this much but you will please excuse me for this time.

Hope this finds you in the best of health.

Sincerely,
Herb

Nov. 16: Fair. 48 hours light duty. Moved to headquarters company. O. Gorman and I called on Mrs. Mann and had tea.
Nov. 17: Misty. Through gas in A.M. Went to Folkstone in P.M. Went to picture house and to pleasure gardens. Got home at 12:00 P.M.
Nov. 18: Dull. Church parade.
Nov. 19: Fair. C.O.'s inspection and went to the ranges. Kit inspection.
Nov. 20: Fair. Final kit inspection by Lieut. Douglas. Bayonet practise. Writing letters.

105

East Sandling
Kent England
Nov. 20, 1917

Dear May,

Hello! Perth this is us! As I have some spare time this evening
_____. Just here a couple of our 130th came along whom I had not
seen for twelve months. One Cpl. Griffiths used to be a Serg. of ours
now in the 3rd batt., Pte. Penny of the 130th, the 3rd and now in the
C.A.V.C. also Pte. G. Farr of the 75th. Well, as we were saying, some
time to spare so Gormon, Monk and I came over to the club to write.
At present the two are playing checkers. We have some great combats.
I have just challenged the winner.

The weather man has been very good to us lately, but we miss the
wet days to have a rest. The nights are dark now so we have not had any
air raids to speak of. It is disagreeable getting about though, but we do
not mind much. Was downtown on Wed. afternoon and evening. First
we took a stroll along the beach to the pier. There were four of us and
two went into the roller rink but Gorman and I not wishing to risk our
necks just looked on awhile and then went to the pictures. Then went to
the YMCA, had supper and read the home papers awhile. They have
newspapers from all parts of Canada there, arranged alphabetically so
I looked up all the local papers and had a half hour at home. Auction
sales, births, marriages, entertainments, minutes of Councils and a dozen
other things were quite as they used to be. I read most of the Prize lists
of the Fairs and saw who made the best bread, and cookies etc. etc. By
this time we, having made arrangements with the other chaps to meet at
the Theatre, we had to go, arrived there only to find that they had been
to the first house. We were out for a good time so took seats in the upper
circle. T'was a very good night. The opening act was a young lady who
did a few good stunts on the swinging bar and rings. She was a marvel
of muscle and suppleness. The rest was a troop of four stars and about
20 girls of 15 or 16 years. We enjoyed the evening to the fullest, caught
the 11:17 train home, arriving at 12 o'clock. Tomorrow afternoon we
get another rest and half holiday but I think we will just go to Hythe,
for a change. Last Sunday evening we were out to tea with a cousin of
Gorman's, Mrs. Mann. She was a trained nurse before the war. Married

a Doctor and he has been at the front for two years nearly but is coming to England to work soon. Her home was in Stittsville but she trained in Winnipeg. Orville made the toast over a coal fire in the grate and I buttered it, mind you with real butter too, while Mrs. Mann made the tea. It sure was a treat to have a tea in a dining room with china, silver, white table cloth and all the rest of it.

You see this last week, we have been making the best of our time for it won't last long. Two days more and we leave for the front. Have been on "draft" for a week and today had our final tests in bayonet fighting and gas. Tomorrow we have kit inspection by the Brigadier, then we are all ready. I packed my outfit tonight. Perhaps it would interest you to know what we take in Active Service Kit. I think I have it all off by heart now. Web equipment, blanket, rubber sheet, 1 suit underwear, 1 top shirt, 2 pair socks, sweater, coat, gloves, towel, soap, razor, comb, tooth brush, knife, fork, spoon, clasp knife, mess tin, hold all, house wife, canvas shoes, oil can, gas helmet and gas respirator. Equipment is bullet pouches, water bottle, pack sack, haversack and entrenching tool. Besides there is what you wear and a great coat. All this with a rifle and 120 rounds of ammunition makes some load. Would you like to have a walk, say out home and back, with it on. I guess not, and I hope you never see anyone else carrying it. But we don't carry all this in France. They make you take it all from here alright and many a dollars worth is thrown away. The bare necessities alone are kept.

So May, the answer to this will find me perhaps with the old address 75th Canadians, B.E.F. France. I will drop a line before we leave here but the next letter of any length will be written "Somewhere in France." I shall think of you always over there May and believe me

Sincerely,
Herb

P.S. Mailed a small gift the other day. Hope you get this one.[110]

J.H.G.

Nov. 21: Fair. Brigadier's inspection in morning. O. Gorman and I went to Hythe in evening.

Nov. 22: Dull and warm. Went to ranges and fired. Battle practice. Letter from Father.

Nov. 23: Fine. Filled a few sandbags in morning. Packed kit in afternoon. O. Gorman and I went to Hythe.

106

East Sandling
Kent England
Nov. 23, 1917

Dear May,

I leave for the front in the morning. It is almost lights out and we get up at 4 A.M. so I must make this short. Tomorrow night I shall hear the guns but May, I shall always think of you and try to live up to the same high ideals that you do. You have certainly been a great help to me by your cheery letters. I trust you may have all good success in your work. I will drop a line at the first opportunity and of course you know the old address.

75th Canadians, B.E.F. France
Wishing you the best of luck.

Sincerely,
Herb

Nov. 24: Fair. Left E. Sandling at 6:00 A.M. and marched to Folkestone. Embarked about 4:00 P.M. Had a very rough passage. Men all sick. Landed in Boulogne at 7:00 P.M. and marched to rest camp.
Nov. 25: Fine. By motortruck to Etape by noon. Drew rifles, helmets, etc.
Nov. 26: Cool. Through gas school. Wrote home.

107

75th Canadians
B.E.F. France
[Etape]
Nov. 26, 1917

Dear Father, Mother and Sister,

This time I will write to you all at once to save time and material.[111] Also will have to remember the censor now.

Well, I have set foot on the Continent once more, arrived Saturday night after a very rough voyage. Everyone was sick I think but the sailors. I was not quite so bad as I was the last time but sick enough believe me.

However we had not far to march after landing and had a good nights rest, after which we had a long ride on motor lorries up to this camp. I do not know when we shall join the Batt. nor where. Felt rather weak yesterday and today but will soon be myself again. It will be some time before I get any mail and will be an anxious time, but I am hoping and praying for the best and I am sure God will be the same great Protector to us all as He has been in the past, if we but trust Him. I hope you are all keeping better now and that you will not worry too much about me, although I am in France.

I am quite near the hospital that I was in last spring and marched along the same road today as I rode in an ambulance then.[112]

Will write soon again if I go up the line. Hoping to have some mail soon and that it brings good news.

Will close now.

Your loving son,
Herb

P.S. Please send me a pair of good mitts, a small neck muffler and a suit of silk underwear if you can get them.[113]

Love to all,
JHG.

108

75th Canadians
BEF France
[Etape]
Nov. 26, 1917

Dear May,

Here I am on the Continent once more. Arrived Sat. night after a rather rough voyage. Yes, rough with a capital R. Was I sick, no that's only a rumour, ha ha. Everyone was sick regardless of rank. Was not quite as bad as the last time but plenty enough though.

We had a little march out to rest camp, had a good sleep and thence by motor lorries to this camp, which is a long way behind the line, but will be going up the line in a few days. The weather is cool and windy but will soon get a wetting likely.

Will write again when we join the Batt. so in the mean time don't work too hard.

All the time,
Herb

Nov. 27: Cool. Resting. Packed kit to proceed up the line. Monk and I went to cinema.

Nov. 28: Fine. Left at 7:00 A.M. Landed at Calonne at 3:00 P.M. Monk, Askew, Lennox, Waters and I went to Aucheul.

Nov. 29: Fine. Marched to Gauchin en Gal. No billets or blankets. Four of us slept in grain mow. Madame raised cane.

Nov. 30: Fine. Marched to Maisonville Bouche. Went to Camblain L'Abbe at night, to cinema.

Dec. 1: Cool. Inspection in morning. Trail and I went to Gouy Servins to see chums in 3rd who were out on rest there.

109

Somewhere in France
[Maisonville Bouche]
Dec. 1, 1917

Dear May,

Bonsoir, how are you this evening? Fine I hope and as for me, I can't complain.

We arrived here yesterday after a very good trip up the line. We only marched about 25 kilometres and the rest by train and lorries. We only carried our packs a short distance too, which made it a lot easier. We are in the same district as I left last spring, so the country is quite familiar. Yes the beautiful scenery _____ I don't think. Have not seen our Batt. yet and don't expect to join them for a while. Are in billets in huts and quite as comfortable as can be expected.

I saw about twenty of the old boys today—among them Ed. McKerracher, looking very much alive, also Strang, Blair, Bygrove, Scott and a lot of others. They are out for a rest and look fine. Strang was wounded and down the line for 8 months.

Jim Trail and I are together again and looked them up today. It is great to see so many familiar faces again.

<u>Sunday Morning</u>. My candle went out last night so had to ring off. It is quite cool this morning. We have just been paid and now we are going to church service. Such is life in sunny France. I can hardly realize that this is Dec. 2nd—just nine months yesterday since I left the line. Some rest eh!

Well I suppose Perth is just the same as usual, only three weeks until Christmas. Gee, I hope we get a better dinner this year.

Will be looking for a letter from you in about a month so in the meantime,

Au Revoir.

Sincerely,
Herb

P.S. O. Gorman sends his compliments.

JHG.

Dec. 2: Cool. Payed. Went to Gouy in afternoon.

110

France
[Maisonville Bouche]
Dec. 2, 1917

Dear Father and Mother,

Now I have an opportunity to write a letter, and when I start a letter my first thoughts are always, I wonder how the folks are at home. Yes! Dear Parents, I wonder how you are tonight. I can see you there all the time but can't tell if you are suffering sickness or pain. Then my thoughts turn to that One who sees and knows all, who will not burden us over much. So "God's will be done." This is just the second letter I have written since leaving England, we have been on the move so much. We had a very good journey up the line by train and motor lorries, only marched about 25 kilometres and that without packs, arriving here yesterday. We have not seen the Batt. yet and do not expect to join them for sometime. I suppose we will get some drill around here just to keep in trim. We are billeted in huts and are quite comfortable. It is the same front that we were on last winter, so I know the country fairly well. Saw about 20 of the old chums today, some were reported killed, others were slightly wounded and the rest have never got a scratch. Some of them are McKerracher, Strang, Scott, Bygrove, Blair and quite a few others from Renfrew and Pembroke. Jim Trail and I are together again. Ed McKerracher looks fine. Ronald Scott has been recommended for a medal I believe. It does one good to see so many familiar faces again.

We are quite near the cemetery where Tom Butler is buried and I intend to try and visit his grave.

Well I hope to get some Christmas parcels this year, I lost so many last year.

You will not know yet that I am out here again. I think it is just a little over a week since I wrote telling you. But don't worry, I will be alright. I would like to be home to work the farm next spring but there doesn't seem to be any signs of peace yet. Voting of the troops is being carried on here at present. As yet I am undecided as to what I will vote for.

Now I hope you are both improving and will continue to do so.

I am praying for you daily and trust that God will hear and answer them.

Au revoir,

Your loving son,
Herb

P.S. My pack is my writing desk tonight.

Sunday Dec. 2nd

Birthday greetings Mother dear.

JHG.

110A

Balderson Ont
Dec. 6, 1917

Dear Herbert,[114]

I got a letter today and one yesterday, the one I got yesterday was dated Nov. 15, one today was dated Nov. 13/17. Clara got the photos also. Well did know that those last letters of mine would cause you anxiety but how could I help it. Well, Mother is not well and I don't suppose you expect to hear that she is altogether well, but for quite awhile she has been down in the kitchen mostly every day which is a wonderful difference to us. I was very sick for about 2 weeks. I could not eat, my stomach refused to take anything of any account, but I have got over that now and eat fairly well, but if ever I get over the heart trouble it will be some time. Sometimes it doesn't trouble me and beats quite regular. The swelling had gone out of my feet and legs, but last night my feet was a little swelled. If I go out and work, I am worse. I don't like to have Clara do the work in the house and at the barn too. I was thinking of selling the colt, it would be one less to look after, but Mother thinks, and Clara too, that I should keep it for a driver.

Well, we had a very cold Nov., over 10 inches of snowfall, but so far in Dec. it has been mild. I do hope it keeps so. You might not need to do much fighting this winter. There is prospect of an Armistice between Russia and Austria so it might possible come that all the Powers join in, and it might possibly work around to peace, but we are so apt to get hold of anything along that line.

You said you were thinking hard, the greatest thing you can do to us and yourself is to pray. I am praying every day that God will heal Mother and I, give us strength according to our years. God is the hearer and the answer of prayer, we may not get all that we ask for but a great blessing comes to us in talking to our Heavenly Father.

Well, Mother and Clara gone to bed. It is a quarter to nine o'clock. So you can look away across the seas and see me sitting alone at the table. We had Mr. and Mrs. Colin McNicol here last night. They are fine company. They left about nine o'clock. Some nights I don't go to bed till eleven or twelve, can't sleep all night. Not long ago for 3 nights, I only slept 2 hours in all that time. It was my nerves was the cause. Since that time had some good sleeps.

Our kitchen is very bright and cheery this winter with our new range and it seems to me that we don't use quite as much wood. Wish you were here to enjoy it.

I think this is all for this time and the Good Lord keep you safe where ever you are and bring you back again. If we could all trust the Divine Power more it would be better for us. May He have mercy on us all is my constant prayer.

Well goodbye for now.

Father

Thurs. morning Dec. 7

I had my breakfast and Mother is at hers now, 8 o'clock, lovely winter morning. I may go today to see the doctor. I am fairly well, can eat good, but my feet is and legs is the trouble with me.

Well, dear boy, keep right with God, every day and your prayers will be effectual.[115]

> **Dec. 3:** Cool. Started to drill, squad drill PT. and platoon drill.
>
> **Dec. 4:** Fine and cool. Squad drill on the double. Went to Four Winds113 to see W. Ligary. Did not see him.
>
> **Dec. 5:** Cool. Left to join battalion. Got ride in truck from Estree-Cauchie to Bruay. Arrived Camblain Chatelain and attached to C. Company. Voted after supper.
>
> **Dec. 6:** Fine. Fired on ranges in A.M. Got our Christmas pay in P.M. (70 Francs) Downtown for supper.
>
> **Dec. 7:** Fair. Went to M.O. for inspection in A.M. Did nothing rest of day.

111

France
[Camblain-Châtelain]
Dec. 7, 1917

Dear May,

Here we are again. Oh! I forgot. Bonsoir. Yes I am picking up a few words again—very few though, for a Scotch Canadian makes a very poor Frenchman.

Well, I have joined the Batt. once more after an absence of 9 months. Am in C. Co. again and I find very few of the old boys still here. They all look fine though and were glad to see us, at least in one sense of the word.

We are billeted in town of course and the little corner which is "Home Sweet Home" for the time being is up in a typical French garret. Not the usual farm house buildings with the rectangular smell [*sic*] in the middle, but a regular town property in the residential part.[116] On the whole this is about the best town I ever struck for billets. It is somewhat cleaner than the common run. There are any amount of Estaminets[117] and cafes. "Cafes" after a style which I would hardly like to try to describe. The main menu is eggs, chips and coffee with chips and eggs for a change. Christmas is just posted for the miners and they sure have been having some celebrations.

We all voted the other day. I wonder what the result will be.

Have not received any mail since coming across but I expect some soon so will ring off until I get some to answer.

Best wishes.

Yours as ever,

Herb

Dec. 8: Rainy. Route march Ourton to Lacompte and back. Had a rest in afternoon. Wrote some letters.

Dec. 9: Dull. Some PT. Started to clean for model platoon.

Dec. 10: Fair. Inspection. 9 platoon won com. competition.

Dec. 11: Cool. Went to shoemaker, tailor to get some repairs done. Shooting on ranges.

Dec. 12: Fair. Some drill. Preparing for Battalion inspection. Shining, scrubbing and shooting.

Dec. 13: Fair. Inspection. 13 platoon won the competition. 9 failed in shooting. 6 letters.

112

France
[Camblain-Châtelain]
Dec. 13/17

Dear Father,

My first mail since coming over reached me tonight.[118] Very glad to hear that you and mother were no worse, whatever better. I don't know much about that trouble but think the swelling going down is a good sign and I hope the Doctor's treatment continues to help you. Glad to know that Mother has some appetite, which surely will, with the medicine, bring back her strength. Of course, I know that years are against both of you, but I trust and pray that God will spare you until we meet again. I am fine with the exception of a slight cold, caused I think by the change of climate and surroundings perhaps, although we are very well billeted here.

We are having some excitement these days, through a competition between platoons for the best in the Batt. Today was the final inspection and we are all anxious to hear the verdict which will soon be given. My platoon (No. 9) was ahead in everything but Musketry and I think we have a pretty good score in that also. The best Platoon in the Division gets a six day pass to Paris.

I would like to be there to help you dispose of some of the fresh pork, new butter and cream now but perhaps it will not be long until we shall all be home.

I don't know how that application will turn out but I am quite willing to accept anything.

Had a letter from Mr. Greig tonight and one from J. Neil, Moderator of the General Assembly, both of which were very encouraging. Well, Father you don't know how glad I was to get your letter tonight. I had such bad luck with my mail last year but now I have got some I am sure of it all coming through. Good Night and God keep you all safely.

Your loving son,
Herb

P.S. Your letter was dated Nov. 4th. We heard of the terrible calamity at Halifax.[119] Wasn't it awful!

113

France
[Camblain-Châtelain]
Dec. 13, 1917

Dear May,

Yours of Nov. 5th came through tonight and was doubly welcome, owing to it being the first this side of the pond. Seven weeks seems a long trail but now my mail has started I will get them all right.

My chum, Gorman, and I have just had some eggs and chips. After a rather busy day, we felt we should have something better than army fare. Of course this is quite a nightly procedure for us but today we were really busy.

You see there is a competition on for the best Platoon in the Division. My Platoon (No. 9) won in our Company and today was Battalion inspection which brought us up against a platoon from each of the other four companies. As yet I have not heard the decision but

last I heard we were several points ahead, with a fair chance of winning.
We have a good Platoon officer and I like the boys fine. I think we have
a better company than when I left it last spring. These competitions
are very exciting and sure keep a chap tuned up. We also have plenty
of sport.

So Elsie has had a trip home. I bet she thinks often of the old 8th.[120]

You were saying you would like to see England but as yet you have
not expressed the same desire of this country. I guess most you hear of
France is its poor qualities. Just wait until I go to Paris, then I'll tell you
the tale! I suppose Roy is home now so you will be able to get home
oftener, won't you?

I have not heard from him often but he seemed to like the country
fine. Is J. Spalding home yet? Pleased to hear that you were down to
visit Clara and hope you find time to go often. Gorman says "tell her
you are not as young as you used to be." I don't quite catch on myself, a
couple of them are passing a few remarks on the writer and guessing at
the receiver.

Well so long. As B4,

Herb

P.S. Who did Jennie marry?[121]

> **Dec. 14:** Dull. Bombing in A.M. Wrote some letters. Downtown for chips.
> **Dec. 15:** Cold. PT. Extended order. Went to YMCA in afternoon and
> wrote letters.
> **Dec. 16:** Dull. Church parade. Payed at 2:00 P.M.
> **Dec. 17:** Snowing. Parade in full marching order. Cancelled. Gorman and
> I bought a watch each from refugee of Lens.[122]

114

France
[Camblain-Châtelain]
Dec. 17/17

My Dear Sister,[123]

Monday morning and the first touch of winter. Started snowing last
night and is still at it. About half an inch of soft snow has fallen—just
enough to make lots of slush when it gets mixed up. We turned out in

it but the parade was called off, so while I have an opportunity I'll write you a few thinkings.

I am down in our stopping place kitchen, sitting by the window with the pad on the sill. Some joint this. Washing day has this small kitchen a sight for sore eyes. There is Madam and a girl of about seventeen, one girl and two boys at school and two little girls. The second youngest is a rather nice little thing but the youngest is crying nearly all the time. The old man is a miner. So you can imagine with a dozen soldiers tramping in and out, what a place it is. We have to go through the bedroom to get upstairs. She scrubs about twice a day (at least mops). The floor is tile but two minutes after there is another trail across the floor.

Yesterday was payday for the troops so one of the neighbours arrived early in the day to make pancakes for the Canadians to buy of course. These French are all after the money. Two cents for a pancake that you could take at one bite.[124]

I think I told you of the prize platoon competition. We were beaten in the Batt. by No. 13. Fell down in our rapid fire on the range. Tough luck but we have to hand it to the best shots.

I got a parcel from the I.O.D.E. yesterday with a couple of pairs of dandy socks, chocolate, cocoa, this pad and 25 envelopes and some other small articles.

I wish now that I had sent home last summer for a pair of high top boots or moccasins but its late now. Would be almost March before they could arrive.

I heard something to the effect that our old Batt. funds were to be used to send those who are left a few articles. They might as well do that now rather than keep it for them on their return. None of them will think anything of $25 or $50 then.

Well Clara I wonder what you are doing this morning.

Is Mother lying upstairs yet? I think it would be much nicer for her and easier for you to have a bed in back of the dining room. She might not be so lonely as away upstairs. Have you many visitors this winter or do they visit you over the phone?

Father was saying that M. MacNaughton spent a weekend with you. I have yet to receive Jim's letter along with several others who promised to write. But it is a good thing to always have something to look forward to. I am almost sure that we are up against another Christmas in the trenches. We move tomorrow for some unknown destination. I was lucky though to join the Battalion while they were on rest.

Now I hope Father and Mother are much better and you are enjoying the best of health.

Love to all.

Your loving brother,
Herb

P.S. Don't forget these letters are for you all although addressed to one.

Dec. 18: Cold. Marched to Chateau de la Haie. In beehive huts. Went to cinema. Father entered rest.
Dec. 19: Cool. Marched to Neuville St. Vaast. Roads slippery. In bee hive huts.
Dec. 20: Foggy. Came up to supports near Petit Vimy. Fair dugouts. Ration party.
Dec. 21: Fair. No working parties here. Only rations at night. Very quiet.
Dec. 22: Clear and cool. Nothing to do but eat and sleep. Wrote to May. Went to YMCA for biscuits and milk.

115

France
[Near Petit Vimy]
Dec. 23, 1917

My Dear Mother,[125]

It is almost noon and I have just had a good wash and shave. We did not get up until almost 9 o'clock this morning, so after breakfast, I went out and got some ice from a shell hole, melted it down in a petrol tin and it served as a bath tub for about a dozen of us. Had not had a wash for several days and I sure feel the better of one.

I wonder how you are this morning. I hope you are much better and able to be up at least a while each day. It is my first thought in the morning and last at night, that you and Father may be restored to health again and I pray that we may all meet once more at home. Won't it be a joyful meeting for some when the troops go marching home and at the same time a sad time for those whose dear ones do not return. But they shall be worshipped rather than pitied, those boys who came so far to fight for their friends and died in a foreign land.

We are having a very easy time this trip, only eat and sleep and bring the rations each night. As yet have had no working parties which is something new for me. The rations are much better also. We have lived on one loaf of bread between seven men, now we get one third and sometimes half a loaf each. Get bacon and tea each morning, soup at noon and rice and tea at night, besides jam butter and cheese. There is a YMCA about five minutes walk from my dugout, where we can get milk, biscuits, chocolate, fruit, etc. etc. So you see life in the trenches is not so bad.

My chum Gorman got a parcel last night, so we had a feed today. I made some cocoa and he supplied the cake, then had candy for dessert.

I'm looking for some parcels now, hope to have better luck than last Christmas. The weather is clear and cool with a little snow on the ground and of course moonlight nights. It is a very quiet front so don't worry about me, Mother, I shall be alright.

It is very hard to get any material for letters out here so don't mind these short ones. I'll try to write often and let you know how I am, which I suppose is the main thing you want to know.

I trust this finds you much better. God be with you till we meet again.

Your loving son,
Herb

P.S. How is John getting on this winter? Have not heard from them for a long time.

JHG

Dec. 23: Clear. Got up at 9:00 A.M. Washed and shaved. First working party.

116

France
Dec. 23, 1917

Dear May,

On receiving your letter of Nov. 15th, I sent you a "Whizz Bang" and perhaps you noticed on it a line saying "letter follows at first opportunity," so I guess this is the opportunity.

Once a fellow said "Opportunity knocks once at every man's door." "Yes" says the other fellow, "and then beats it like the small boy after ringing a door bell."

It is now 9:20 P.M. Everything is quiet, except for a couple of chaps chewing the fat about something. One is a bomber and the other a machine gunner so the usual good natured, vocal barrage is going on. I can scarcely write for the noise. Occasionally a dull "crump" breaks in to remind us that the guns are not altogether idle. You see they fire an odd shot to keep the bore clean. Ours, too, are doing the same, sending Fritz's iron rations over. However we should worry, here twenty feet underground. So far this is the best trip I ever did in the line, eat sleep and bring the rations. A year ago it used to be "Fall in" for the working party sometimes twice a day. It seems funny to be here on land that Fritz held a year ago and to look at the other side of, shall I say, the world almost. To me "No Man's Land" seems to be a dividing line between Good and Bad and when one sees the destruction wrought this side of the "original" front line, it looks as if some great storm had swept everything in its path.

So you have lost your soldier visitor. Yes! I am sure it must be hard to come back after spending a few holidays in good old Canada, but I hope he has the same good luck to get home again and next time for good. You want to know if I smoke yet. Well, I do a little when there is nothing else to do, but don't worry about the package of fags. I have lots of chums here who will be pleased to smoke them if I don't. Of course since you sent them, I will have to smoke them myself. Hope to receive it soon, perhaps I will get it just in time for Christmas.

Now May, perhaps I will write another page tomorrow. Will spread my rubber sheet and blanket now and have a sleep.[126]

Bonsoir, Mme.

Herb

Dec. 24: Dull. Working party at night. Parcels from IOOF and B.W.W.[127]

Dec. 25: Fair. We had counted on having a good dinner, but shell hit cook house and spoiled it. Two casualties. Dinner at 9:00 P.M.

Dec. 26: Snow. Worked awhile in A.M. Party at night to front line. Some shell and machine gun fire. Clear moonlight nights.

Dec. 27: Foggy. Some shells coming over. Washed and shaved. Working party to front line.

Dec. 28: Clear and cold. Went to Neuville St. Vaast for bath. Rations and water. Two letters and parcel from [sister] Clara.

Dec. 29: Foggy. Worked in Gertie trench. Rations. Parcel from May.

Dec. 30: Fair. Into front line. Fritz raid on our right.

Dec. 31: Cold. Quiet on listening post every night. Mother passed away at 12:15.

Notes

1   Catarrh is an inflammation of the mucous membranes of the nose. "Livestock" are lice.

2   Herb got very few parcels that Christmas.

3   See diary entries for January 31, 1917, and January 4, 1918. See also letter 31 regarding "got hit on the back."

4   May said Herb told her that the Germans kept shelling the well, but when he saw an officer going to the well, he decided to go too, taking a number of canteens and walking across the duckboards. Just as he reached the well, a shell burst and he was hit in the back by an object, which may have bounced off his entrenching tool. The officer was hit, however, and died instantly in front of Herb. His jugular vein had been severed. See diary entry for January 3 for a description of duckboards.

5   T. Earl was Herb's friend Tom Butler. Roy Wilson was among the first of the 130th boys from Perth to be reported killed on March 1, 1917.

6   This letter had been opened by a censor. The box to which he refers came from May, and was likely made of corrugated cardboard. The boxes held quite a bit—May always put in writing paper and envelopes, gum, Life Savers, chocolate bars, cookies or cake, taffy, and cigarettes, but matches were not permitted. Under normal conditions, Herb would never work on a Sunday.

7   Here the censor has removed the hours.

8   The *Era* was the Lanark newspaper, while the *Courier* and *Expositor* were Perth papers.

9   December 21, 1917, was May's 22nd birthday.

10   Iris remembers singing "Mother" on a Mother's Day in the mid-forties with her Sunday school class. The song was new to her then, and she had no idea Herb would have sung it under such conditions thirty years earlier. It must have been a haunting moment for him to hear us.

11   "Get a blighty" meant being wounded and sent to Britain to recover.

12   Jennie K. was the sister of Willie and Hugh Knowles.

13   Herb's father sent "tracts"—religious readings.

14   A very descriptive letter illustrating the duties of a "scout" or a "bomber." On listening post, he told May, he was so close to German lines that he watched an officer stamping around on the parapet to keep warm early one morning, but dared not give away his own position. He likely refers to this event in letter 34, too.

15   The censored letter from "near home" would have been from May.

16   "Rugby dump" likely means food dump.

17   From being employed as a "Junior" at the bank, May had moved to Current Accounts. They had accounts for Wampole, Perth Shoe, and Jergens.

18   Here he speaks of a man who tried to go to the United States to avoid enlisting but couldn't get "across the line."

19   May did not get the handkerchief mentioned in this letter; perhaps that is what he was referring to in his previous letter of February 2.

20 "Whiz-bangs" were shells fired from a smaller-caliber field gun—specifically to the sound of the shell exploding. The term also referred to postcard-like messages that could be sent home quickly and easily.

21 In saying he has "failed some," Herb means he has lost weight.

22 The censor has removed the date of this letter—February 28. The raid would happen the next day.

23 Names mentioned here are neighbours and chums. Herb knows he is going "over the top" soon.

24 He later described the hospital to May as being a tent within a tent.

25 There is no record of a letter being sent from Fred Adams, a soldier chum, but there is a whiz-bang that Herb sent. Adams was the son of a photographer in Perth who took a lovely picture of May—a side view with her hair highlighted. Fred Adams returned home.

26 C.C.S. = Casualty Clearing Station, Bruay, France.

27 Field Clearing Station: Villiers de Bois.

28 Casualty Clearing Station, Bruay.

29 See letters 50, 57, 59, 64, 66, and 67 for more details about Herb's bombing section on March 1, 1917.

30 Rice pudding was one of Herb's favourite dishes. Maple syrup and sugar were favourites, as well.

31 Mr. William Ashcroft, of Abbots Ripton, Huntingdon, was a brother of Towers Ashcroft, who married Herb's sister Maggie. They lived in Manitoba, and their children were Effie, Emily, and Willie.

32 Herb liked to read, and he enjoyed poetry too. Robert Service and Robbie Burns were favourites of his.

33 This was written on a postcard depicting Dunsdale, Westerham.

34 Arthur may have been Arthur Gibson or Arthur Ashcroft, both young nephews. Herb's sisters, Jane and Ida, were in North Dakota. Jane married a cousin, James Gibson, and Ida married Hugh Harper.

35 The chaplain was wrong. The 75th was badly broken—with 687 casualties out of 1,700 attackers—but was reestablished.

36 Herb did not yet know that the battle had started. The Battle of Vimy Ridge was fought on Easter Sunday, April 9, 1917. Herb was wounded in the March 1 trench raid, which preceded the larger battle by five weeks.

37 Notice his description of the weather and its similarity to that in France when the Battle of Vimy Ridge was fought.

38 Herb asks his father, "What do you think of the war now? You never say?" He may have been looking for some indication from his father that he had done the right thing by enlisting.

39 "Strippers" are cows not in calf.

40 The cheese factory at Balderson, Ontario.

41 A "driver" is a horse broken to drive a cutter or buggy.

42   The *Citizen* is the Ottawa newspaper.

43   Roy Keays, May's brother, tried to enlist but was classified B2, and was not accepted for duty. In the British Army's medical categories, B2 meant "able to walk 5 miles, see and hear sufficiently for ordinary purposes" (see http://www .epsomandewellhistoryexplorer.org.uk/MedicalCategories.html). Whether he was rejected for health reasons or because he was needed to work on the farm, we do not know. He stayed on the farm and married Winnie Gilmer in 1928. Their children are Joyce and Raymond.

44   This letter is dated April 2, but we believe it was written later—perhaps April 22, since he had received a letter from his father dated April 2 and since he had left Seven Oaks and was at Epsom. Also, the envelope is dated "Epsom April 30."

45   Here he refers to his photos and maybe his letters appearing in the newspaper.

46   Before he went overseas Herb gave May a small brass 130th Battalion pin, which she proudly wore during the war.

47   May Keays wrote this poem after Vimy, when the casualty lists were heavy.

48   May had a photograph of Pte. Lamb and Herb in their convalescent blues. Pte. Lamb was also wounded on March 1, 1917.

49   *Belle fille*, perhaps?

50   Herb's sister Clara was very discouraged living with her parents. He sent her his army cheques for her own use, and told her if he didn't come back the farm would be hers.

51   The bridge to which Herb refers would be the Forth Bridge.

52   Towers Ashcroft married Margaret Gibson, sister of Herb Gibson.

53   This letter was published in the *Perth Courier*.

54   We believe the address of the "dwelling house" in which Herb was billeted was 47 Chapel Road, Hastings (see diary entry of May 18, 1917).

55   Clara's birthday was August 11, and she was 33 years old. Written on the back of the envelope:

> To greet you on your birthday morning
> With all my heart I wish you joy
> Dear friend of mine.
> May all that's best in life be yours.
> And love light all the way
> With sunshine may your path be bright.
> May all the shadows fly.
> And happiness in greater store.
> Be yours as years go by.
> 24/5/17

56   This is an important letter. When Herb returned from France in 1919, he visited around Perth until July. He then sold the farm and went west. Mary Ellen and Willie were at Poland, Ontario, and Lammermoor; Jane and Clara were in Walhalla, North Dakota; John was in Winnipeg; and Maggie Ashcroft in

Sinclair, Manitoba. Herb stayed in North Dakota the winter of 1919–20, clerking in James Gibson's store, but moved to Winnipeg with Jane and Clara in the summer of 1920 (Jane had sold her house, as her husband had died in 1917). He returned to Perth in 1923, but went back to Winnipeg again. May's mother had died in 1921, and she went back to the farm in the spring of 1922 to look after her brothers and sisters: Art (9), Ena (11), Ivan (14), Neva (19), Lottie (21), and Laura (23). Mother was 25 and Roy was 27. Herb eventually left Winnipeg and worked at the Celia Jeffery Indian School, at Lake of the Woods, and plied the supply boat between the town and the Minaki Lodge resort hotel. In a way, he did get to do as he said he would do in his letter: "live by a clear calm lake." He always regretted that he had not gone to high school longer. Herb had started high school in Lanark, where he boarded with his sister, Ida, and several other girls, each of whom had a room—but having just a cot in a hall, he was discouraged and left at Christmas, ending his high school career.

57   Herb calls the second carrier "Appleton"; in fact, his name was G. Janes and he was from Appleton, Ontario. He was a bomb carrier and badly wounded the morning of March 1. Dad dressed his wound with his putees (leg wraps). Craig Greer, for his part, was taken prisoner.

58   This is an important letter, which tells of the night before the March 1 raid. See also letters 64 and 101A.

59   Jennie Wilson married Fred Keays, May's second cousin. They lived in California and came home in 1929. Roy was married and May was working in Perth again, so when they asked her to go to California with them that summer, she did. May was working at Perth Shoe, because bank jobs had gone to the returned soldiers. Jennie's brother Earl was killed in France. The Zeppelin raid on London of June 13, 1917, was the most destructive of the war, with 160 deaths.

60   The photo was taken, and May had it. It is a very nice image of both of them, with Herb's father standing and mother sitting.

61   The Robertson sisters of Pilot Mound, Manitoba, read Dad's letters in the *Lanark Era* and wrote to him. Their brother had been killed.

62   "Great time at John's" refers to the reception they held in Herb's honour before he left for Valcartier.

63   Margaret MacDonald was Herb's first girlfriend (1908–12). She was a teacher at Lammermoor, and then trained for a nurse in Ottawa. She married a member of the Dumbells.

64   Clara's fiancé had died of typhoid fever, and her second friend from MacDonald's Corners drifted away.

65   May's change of address refers to the fact that she had moved from a rooming house on North Street, Perth (Mrs. McVeety), to the house of her Aunt Charlotte Paul, Stella's mother. Ethel and Stella worked at the Merchant's Bank, Perth.

66   May had gone to Ottawa with Stella Paul and Ethel Armstrong to see the Prince of Wales. They stayed at the YWCA, and went to cathedral service on Sunday morning.

67   Herb would never pass a historical marker or plaque without stopping to read it, as he was very interested in history.

68   His father must have written about a sermon he had heard or given.

69   Jim Trail from Lanark was later killed.

70   These meetings would have been meetings of the Church or the Women's Institute.

71   "Bomb-proof" was a joking expression meaning a "safe" job.

72   Clara would not have been at Elsie Keays's wedding because they did not hold a dance reception for friends and neighbours. Also, Effie Brunton's wedding was the same day. See the List of Persons for others mentioned.

73   "Handling lots of tin" may refer to handling lots of money. May's bank salary was twelve dollars a week, and she paid her aunt four dollars a month room and board, which was supplemented by vegetables, etc., from the farm.

74   Orville Gorman was a good soldier friend. He was very young and transferred to the R.A.F. He lived in Smith's Falls after the war, and Herb regretted not seeing more of him.

75   By "that party" he would mean May.

76   This letter was opened by a censor. The Battle of Flanders had begun a few days earlier, on July 31, 1917.

77   "C of E" = Church of England.

78   Herb carried this picture of his mother and father in his wallet.

79   May did not get the parcel. Herb must have written May about getting corn, etc., and she wrote back to him about it, and he refers to it again in this letter; or May went to see Clara on November 27 and asked him what he was doing that day.

80   The Jim mentioned here is Jim McVeety. Enlisted, age 17; killed August 28, 1918, age 19.

81   "That chap's address" likely refers to the soldier to whom May gave three pieces of lemon pie when he stopped at Balderson for dinner on a route march in 1916. She called him her "lemon pie soldier."

82   May must have had some kind of ailment—an infection she ascribed to handling dirty money and cheques at the bank—yet she was not off work.

83   Herb's reference to a "club" likely referred to a trench club, used by soldiers in close combat during trench raids. The club could be used to bludgeon enemy soldiers.

84   May was part of St. John Ambulance, and one woman had gone from Perth to serve in France. Also, Herb was correct: women got the vote in 1918.

85   A nice photo in uniform, seated on a long railing.

86   Herb was preparing to go back to France. His dreams are very interesting.

87   Col. Ed Watt returned to Perth to help raise another battalion. He met a returned private who had been wounded, and said, "You are home"; and the private said, "Yes, Sir, I wouldn't revert"—a slap in the face, as officers could revert or take a lower rank in order to return to Canada. Lett McCallum, who was wounded on March 1, returned to Smith's Falls in 1917 because of those wounds. May met Hubert Quackenbush at a dance at Drummond Centre, where he gave her his pass as a souvenir. He was killed in action on September 1, 1918.

88 John 6:68: "Simon Peter answered him, 'Lord to whom shall we go? You have the words of eternal life'" (New International Version).

89 A "Tommy" is the driver of a horse-drawn buggy.

90 St. James's is the church at Hood, near Watson's Corners.

91 A reference to May. May recalled seeing Herb for the first time: he was sitting on the bench in front of John Gibson's store in Harper. She was about 16 (it was 1912) and he would have been 22—a little out of her league, then, but she remembered his fine head of dark, curly hair.

92 Roy is Roy Keays, who was heading west to harvest on the harvest excursion train. Before combines were introduced, the prairie harvest required large numbers of men. "Harvest trains" moved men west for the harvest.

93 Herb liked to go hunting deer in the fall, and we think a large part of the attraction was in tramping through the woods, having a fire to prepare food, and "scouting."

94 See letter 86 in regard to Ed Watt.

95 "Grousing" meant soldiers complaining.

96 We are not sure what "Spoke shaf" refers to.

97 McNicol was a cousin of Herb's.

98 Herb's sister, Mary Ellen.

99 Conscription was a contentious issue in Canada during the war. Needing more men to fight, the Canadian government passed the *Military Service Act* in July 1917. Men working farms might seek exemption from service to help with the farming, although this exemption was later revoked to increase the number of recruits. Some men went to the United States to avoid conscription, while others stayed home on the farm—sometimes even when there were already two or three men on the farm (i.e., more than enough labour to do the work). Some Canadians felt that those who stayed on the farm were trying to avoid service.

100 The British launched a new offensive in Flanders on October 12, 1917.

101 Ray Paul was Herb's first cousin; his fiancé Minnie Pretty came to May's Aunt Charlottes' for supper (May was staying there). Aunt Charlotte's husband, Alex Paul, was also Ray's uncle. Charlotte must have helped him to pick a suit for his wedding. Because she was a dressmaker, he likely valued her opinion. Ray did not enlist.

102 The *Courier* was the Perth newspaper.

103 Mary Ellen Paul, Herb's sister.

104 Before the war, Herb contracted out with his corn-cutter; hence his speculation that he "could have got a few jobs."

105 This would be the last letter his mother received.

106 The Jellicoe Club was a place for soldiers to relax and write letters.

107 G. Janes of Appleton was Herb's bomb carrier on March 1, 1917. See letters 64 and 66.

108 Herb's twenty-eighth birthday was on November 11, but he does not mention it, either here or in the diary.

109 Herb's father received this letter. Herb knows that he will soon be leaving for France.

110 His gift to her was a mother-of-pearl Maple Leaf pendant with "Canada" engraved on it.

111 His parents were both dead before this letter could reach them.

112 The hospital he speaks of was likely at Bruay or Camiers. He landed at Boulogne on November 24, 1917.

113 The silk underwear was to help prevent lice.

114 This is the last letter of Wm. R. Gibson to his son Pte. J. Herb Gibson. It was written in answer to Herb's letters of November 14 and 15, and Dad carried it in his wallet until his return to Canada. His father died on December 18, 1917, aged 69 years.

115 "Four Winds" is described in W. Bird's book *Thirteen Years After* as a crossroads, and Cambligneul was on the left.

116 See letter 27 for a description of such a farmhouse.

117 Estaminets were small cafés that served alcohol.

118 Herb's father would not have received this letter. His father had applied to have Herb return to Canada on leave because of his parents' poor health and because he was the only son to look after the farm. It is interesting to consider what might have happened had his parents survived long enough for him to return home.

119 The terrible explosion that Herb refers to was the Halifax Explosion, which was caused by two vessels colliding, one of which carried a cargo of munitions. It exploded with such force that two thousand people were killed outright with another two thousand maimed or injured.

120 Elsie Keays Block came home to the Eighth Line from Chapleau, Ontario, where she lived with her husband, who worked for the CPR. Roy was home from the west after the harvest (see n. 92). May had called on the Gibsons, as Herb had asked her to.

121 Jennie was likely Jennie Knowles, sister of Willie and Hugh, both killed. She married Morton Publow, and he and his brother were killed in late 1918, with word of their deaths arriving only after November 11, 1918.

122 This was the luminous watch that made Herb so popular up and down the trench, and frequently greeted with "What time is it, Gibby?"

123 His father had a stroke on December 17 and died the following day. The funeral was on December 21, which was also May's twenty-second birthday.

124 These small pancakes were probably crepes.

125 His mother died December 31, so she did not receive this letter.

126 This letter seems incomplete, as Herb had indicated he would write further, but sent the letter as is.

127 IOOF = Independent Order of Foresters. B.W.W. = Balderson.

1918

Jan. 1: Fine. Spent the day in Funk hole.[1] Made cafe au lait and dined off May's parcel. Fritz raided 54th.

Jan. 2: Cold. Everything as usual. Parcel from E. Robertson. No letters. On listening post every night.

Jan. 3: Clear and cool. Slept some today for must keep keen lookout for the enemy.

Jan. 4: Fine. Relieved in front line and came back to supports. Good dugout. Thirty feet deep. Patrol in white suits.

Jan. 5: Fine. Had good rest. Carried some wire at night. Letter from Mae Darou and parcel.

Jan. 6: Fine. Had breakfast at 10:00 A.M. Wrote some letters.

117

France
[Reserve Dugout]
Jan. 6, 1918

Dear May,[2]

It is Sunday afternoon so I think I will come up for a little chat. I suppose the first subject is the weather but really I do not know much about it, being thirty feet below the surface. So will let that go for I want to tell you that I received your parcel OK. Just the night before we went into the front line. So I carried it up with me intact. It was New Years Eve too and I landed a listening post right off the bat. After first relief, I crawled into my funk hole and undid the wrappings, had some cake, etc. etc., put on the socks and had a sleep. It was a splendid parcel, May and came just when I most needed it and I thank you from the bottom of my heart. I have had more parcels than letters lately, but of course I expected a few gaps in the line.

Well how's Perth? Are you skating much and are the boys playing hockey? I see by the paper that it has been very cold all over Canada, but did not say if there was much snow.

I can hardly believe it is 1918, can you? The fifth year in which the war has been going on. I wonder how many more?

I just wish you could see us now May! Imagine, if you can, a room about 10′ by 30′, thirty feet underground, lit by candles, occupied by some thirty men, some of whom are washing and shaving, reading or writing, sleeping or playing cards. There is a banjo and mouth organ going now, the happy side of life you see. "Are You From Dixie" generally leads, followed by some other popular songs.

Well all for now so Au Revoir and God knows what will happen before I write to you again.[3]

Sincerely,
Herb

118

France
Jan. 6, 1918

Dear Sister,

Just a short note today Clara, you know I can't write much, but am glad to say that I am in good health which I expect is what you most want to know.

I received your parcel in good condition and at a good time too. I think it was Christmas night. All the things were fine and I must thank you very much. I had lots of eats both Christmas and New Years. Got 5 parcels in five days. This is Sunday afternoon and I am here in a thirty foot dugout. Oh, I wonder what you are all doing and how you are. All I can do is pray and hope for the best.

Have you heard anything of the application you put in?

Had a letter from Mae Darou last night, said she had sent a parcel but it has not arrived yet. Well Au Revoir, Dear Sister, for today and Love to all.

Your brother,
Herb

Jan. 7: Fine. Nothing doing.

Jan. 8: Snow. Nothing doing all day but went over to see the Germans at night.

Jan. 9: Snowy. Tired. Relieved at 5:00 P.M. Walked to Neuville St. Vaast. Light railway to billets at Chateau de la Haye. Arriving 3:00 A.M.

Jan. 10: Mild. Slept to noon. Had dinner and slept after. Went to YMCA cinema.

Jan. 11: Fair. Cleaning rifles and equipment. Went to concert at night. 4th division "Maple Leafs" played "Aladdin France."

Jan. 12: Fair. PT. in morning. Rest of day cleaning up. Picture show at night.

Jan. 13: Cool. Church parade and bath.

119

France
[Château de la Haye]
Jan. 13, 1918

Dear May,

Again I have two letters to answer in one. One addressed to Blighty
and one to France. I hardly expected one direct so soon and it was sure
welcome as the flowers in May. I wrote one from the line telling of
getting your parcel, hope you got it.

Since, we have come out for a rest and have been busy cleaning up
and also catching up with some lost sleep. First night out I went to the
picture show in our old standby, the YMCA. Second night the whole
Batt. were paraded to the large concert hall. The 4th Division concert
party "The Maple Leafs" played "Aladin France" and it sure was
grand.[4] For two hours we forgot the war and all our troubles and were
back home having some of the happy side of life. You could not wish
to see a better play every minute was full of life. There were two good
impersonations, the Princess and the Widow. You looked twice before
you saw they were really masculine.

Last night we went again to the pictures, which were very good.

Today, being Sunday, we went to church service at 8A.M., had
dinner at 11:30 and then went to the baths. The routine scarcely stops
on Sunday, even when at rest and of course Sunday is the same as
Tuesday in the line.

It was a nice sunny afternoon and after returning from the baths,
Lett Miller, who just returned to the Batt. a few days ago, and I took
a walk down to the cemetery to see where some of the 130th boys are
laid. The only one you would know is Tom Butler. Perhaps you can
imagine my feelings May, as I looked upon the grass covered mound
and wooden cross. Here, standing in a foreign land, beside the grave
of my chum, neighbour and finally comrade in arms, my thoughts
flashed back to the quiet peaceful homes from whence we came, on an
errand the full consequences of which we did not realize then. When
in a mood like this I always think of the first line in one of our hymns

"God moves in a mysterious way His wonders to perform" and I have no doubt that He has not a great blessing which could not come without this Great war.

So we must keep on running and faint not. Well, May, I suppose your busy time in the Bank will be passed now and I hope you will have plenty of time for more pleasure. Don't work all day and study First Aid all night either. "All work and no play _____" you know the rest.

Say, is it Jack Phillips that is married? You just said Jack. That's rather hard on Georgina isn't it? She seems to have poor luck with the bowers (Jacks)! I had a letter from Spalding the other day and he gave me a list of some of the classes. There doesn't seem to be many getting exemptions.

That was a bad accident at Trenton[5] but wasn't the Halifax explosion terrible. It certainly is a great loss to the country, but I see the USA were almost first on the scene with relief. I don't think they can be beaten for promptness in a case of that kind. Canada has done well for the Victory Loan indeed and I only hope this will be the Victory Loan.

Like you, I too am tired of the war and there are millions like us. But both sides still seem confident of the outcome.

I am glad the little article was to your liking. You know I never had any experience in purchasing gifts for ladies ha ha.

I am sure Dick Leighton would be glad to get home, he put in a long spell out here. Say do you know where Miles Hughes is now? I never hear from him at all. I suppose he too is ignorant of my whereabouts. I expected to hear of Russel's marriage before this, really I did.

I wonder what you would think if you could step in and see us in our little beehive hut. We have lots of smoke from our stove (which is made of two five gallon cans on end) mingled with smoke from issued cigarettes, some singing, some music on mouth organ and banjo, arguments to no end and once in a while a draft when the door is opened. Gee! look how long this is getting, I best stop now and like the rest of the chaps have a lunch and go to bed for we have O.C.'s inspection in the morning.

Au revoir,
Herb

120

France
[Château de la Haye]
Jan. 13, 1918

Dear Mother,

I have been out of the line for four days now but have not written to you. You see I was waiting, expecting a letter from you every day but so far have been disappointed. I can't understand it, for I have been getting letters from all around written about Dec. 10th and I think your last one was about Nov. 18th. Strange isn't it.

But I know from their letters that all must be as usual at home. Mary E. said she had a card from you, saying you were some better, so I am hoping the improvement is still going on and that you are able to be up.

I am fine. Our twenty day trip in the trenches was easy compared with some times. T'was quiet and the weather fair. Was to church this morning and I certainly enjoyed the service. It was held in the large concert hall and we were comfortably seated and warm. The sermon was from Corinthians and the Chaplain spoke of the great race we are running and encouraged us to run it so as to obtain the reward.

We have just had dinner—mulligan, tea and hard tack. Then my chum and I had a can of peaches and some biscuits between us to finish off with.

We are going to have a bath this afternoon so you see how Sunday is spent in France. Only for my pocket diary, I would hardly be able to tell Monday from Saturday. Every day is so much like the last.

I hope the weather over there has moderated a little. I hear it has been very stormy. I hope you have plenty of wood.

Well Mother, I don't know what more I can say this time.

I would love to see you all now but each day must be bringing that glad day closer, whether it be on this earth or in the life to come, it is coming, so we must keep up our hearts and put more faith in God.

So Long Mother and May God bless you all.

Your loving Herb

121

Dec. 19, 1917

Well Herb,

This is Mary E. that is writing from home. I am writing for them and I don't know how to begin to tell you what has happened here, but I suppose you will have an idea by the letters Pa has written to you, this while back. Well, Herb, I will have to break the sad news to you that he is gone. He passed into his eternal rest Tues. 18th Dec. at half past six. Willie and I, John and Maggie were here. We thought of sending a cable to you but Mr. Greig thought a letter would be kinder. He took a stroke on Mon. about half past three in the afternoon. Clara was just home from voting and in from her chores. He was lying on the sofa when Clara noticed him talking strange. She went over to him and spoke, but he did not appear to know them, but he rallied a little and named us all. Clara phoned Willie, and we just happened to be at Poland voting when the message came, so I just got into the cutter and went with him. We got our supper and started. It was a bitter night but we put on lots of clothes. We were awful glad we came that night, for he would not have known us the next morning. He died very peacefully and Ma is keeping up wonderfully. Everything is being done for them that human aid can be done, and you know that they are trusting in a living God who do'eth all things well. We are all thinking of you. We all have kind friends here to sympathize with us, but our first thought was of you, but the same God is with us as with you. Ma says to tell you that she is sitting here at her breakfast, and to tell you how that we are all here and everybody has been so kind. Mr. Greig is such a kind man and good in trouble. We telegraphed Jane and she is coming. We are keeping him until she comes. We expect her Thurs. night 20th Dec. Funeral will be on Friday at half past ten. Ma said to tell you we noticed a change for two or three days for he just read the Bible and prayed and on Sunday night he said "Oh my, but I would like to see Herb once more before I die, I think we would have great prayers together."

Clara says she will write in a few days. Ma says to tell you that Willie dressed him and he looks so nice.

Keep up your heart dear Brother. Trust in the Lord for he is good, as you said in your last letter to me. He will not put upon us more than we are able to bear, and Ma says she thinks she has got strength from the Lord. I will close now.

From your loving sister.

Mary E.

As I asked Pa if he knew who was here, and he said "Yes, it is the one we called M.E." Goodbye Herb, and write soon.[6]

Jan. 14: Fair. Had a couple of parades. Received M.E.'s letter of Fathers death.

122

France
[Château de la Haye]
Jan. 14, 1918

My Dear Mother and Sister,

Today's mail brought me M.E.'s letter with the sad news of Father's death. You know how I feel without me writing a lot. I'm sad and lonely with no close companion in whom to confide except Jim Trail. The last letter gave me such hopes and I thought if he continued with the treatment that he might get better. I was afraid of him taking some sort of stroke, though. Well I am glad that you had the rest of the family there and that he knew you all. So he has gone to his reward and we are left to struggle on yet awhile and given another chance to mend our shortcomings.

I am wondering if you have heard any more of the application to get me home. Whether or not, Mother, you put in your claim right away through Dr. Hanna. And besides speak to Mr. James Watt or Rob. Wilson and the I.O.O.F. may do something (if the authorities don't grant it). My own application has gone to Brigade Headquarters, for a furlough but of course I do not know if I will get it or not. Let this be kept as quiet as possible.

One letter I got today spoke of a rumour that I was to be home for Christmas. How these things start beats me. I suppose some people's imaginations carry them away. Will Jane be staying long? I hope she will and that the old complaint does not trouble her. I know you would have lots of company for awhile but there is always a time comes when those must return to their own cares and the bereaved are left alone. Then all the thoughts come back.

I am glad Mother that you are keeping better and oh how I hope and pray that God will give you strength to withstand this trial. It may be that I will soon get home again. I don't see why they should not let me go, after almost two years of service and now since only sons are getting exemptions.

This will be all for tonight and may God watch over us and keep us.

Your loving son,
Herb

P.S. I am sending this across to England to be posted, with a lad who is going on leave.

Herb

123

Perth
Jan. 3, 1918

My Dear Herb,

What comfort can I offer you, I wonder, in this awful sorrow that has come to you. I am so sorry for you, away there in France, with so much to endure, and that this hardest of all, I know, must be added. I can only say "be British" still Herb and remember that you will never be tried more than you will be given power to endure.

I know that you loved your parents[7] and I can understand how you will long to have been with them to the last, and yet you must not grieve about that. I think you had one great cause for comfort now, perfect understanding with each other. You left because you felt it your duty to do so, because of your love for them, and your love for humanity too, that kept you unselfish and noble. Even to have been with them now would not have atoned to you for duty undone, would it. And they would not have you do so. They knew too, and it must always have helped much to know, that you faced cannons and eternity without fear. It is hard indeed but you haven't the regrets that would make it unbearable.

In a letter not long ago, you spoke of them after hearing their health was failing. I was sorry for you then. It seemed as though a premonition had come to you of this. I am sorry not to have written often to you now. I am writing this at the office at noon hour. I had a letter written when I heard of your mother's death so I did not send it.

I was down to see Clara on New Year's Day and found her lonely, but trying to be brave. It is great that her sister is with her now, and Mrs. Paul was there also. They were wondering if you would be able to get home now. Under the circumstances you should have a chance, but it would be a sad homecoming for you too. Do you think it will be possible? I have your letter of Dec. 2nd and am glad you have had some degree of comfort.

This is all today, Herb. I will try to write soon again. With all my sympathy.[8]

Yours,

May

Jan. 15: Rain. Parade in A.M. Marched to billets at Souchez. Working party at night. Rain and mud.

Jan. 16: Rain. Working party called at 10:00 P.M. Lots of mud and dark. Rode on light railway. Got stuck a few times.

Jan. 17: Rainy. Got in at 6:00 A.M. Had breakfast and slept till noon. Went to YMCA for eats.

Jan. 18: Fair. Working party in A.M. Home at 3:30 P.M. Went to bed early after having wash and shave.

Jan. 19: Fair. Wrote some letters. Respirators tested at Kings Cross.

Jan. 20: Fair. Church parade. Into line at Lievin.

Jan. 21: Fine. Living in cellars. Working party to front line at night. Muddy.

Jan. 22: Fine. Slept till noon. Same party at night. Shelled on the way up, mud to knees.

Jan. 23: Fine. Usual program, only later, got in at 3:00 A.M. Very tired but off all day and night.

Jan. 24: Fine. It is very lonely here and cannot keep from thinking of the folks at home.

Jan. 25: Fine. Slept until noon. Into front line. Few shells and gas.

Jan. 26: Fine. Stratch section established new post. Three hour reliefs and deep dugout, to stay in. Plenty of eats. Better trip than expected.

Jan. 27: Fine.

Jan. 28: Fine. Everything quiet. Clear moon light nights.

Jan. 29: Fine As usual. Got some mail at midnight. Read it by moonlight. Shocked to hear of Mother's death.

Jan. 30: Fine. Relieved. Walked to Lievin. Light railway to Petit Servins. Arrived 2:00 A.M.

Jan. 31: Foggy and rain. Slept until noon. Cleaned up some after noon. Had some eggs at night.

Feb. 1: Very chilly. Inspection in A.M. and bath in P.M. at Gouy Servins.

Feb. 2: Warmer. Pay parade and kit inspection.

Feb. 3: Church parade and route march in A.M.

124

France
[Petit Servins]
Feb. 3/18

Dear May,

I thank you for your kind letters and words of encouragement at this time of sorrow. I have put off writing because I could not think to speak of it all. It seems as though there were nothing more to live for now. I am just moving about like a machine without any object in view. Although written the same day, your letter reached me before the one from Maggie (they did not cable thinking a letter would be easier for me). It came to me about midnight the 29th of January as I was at my post in the front line trenches. The moon was full and I opened your letter of January 3rd, it being the latest one. The opening lines, I thought related to Father's death but when I came to that line "I had a letter written when I heard of your Mother's death" I thought my eyes were deceiving me and read it over and over again, before I could realize what it meant. It is so hard to think that my dear parents passed away in such a short space of time, and that they will not be there to welcome me home after the war. But I know they will be There to welcome me into that Eternal Home where there is no war, so we must submit to God's Will and try to understand His great works. I often think of that hymn "God moves in a mysterious way His wonders to perform." And how true it is, we feeble creatures cannot understand it and sometimes we do not try very hard to understand. May God give us strength to run the straight race and reach the goal.

This is all for tonight May and I hope this finds you in the best of health.

Sincerely,
Herb

P.S. We are out for a rest at present.

JHG.

124A

Winnipeg Manitoba
July 21 — 21[9]

My Own Dear May,

I wish I could drop in and be with you for a while this evening but since that is not possible I will try to write you a few lines.

But Dear, what can I say that would comfort you after the days of anxious waiting and the shock of parting with your Dear Mother. I am afraid what I might say will only make you feel the loss more keenly but I do not mean it that way.

You cannot know how deeply I felt when I received your telegram. It brought to me, like a flash, one letter I received from you which brought the news of my own Dear Mother's death. The place surroundings can never be forgotten. Those were terrible days for me. That was nearly a month after Mother's death and the shock left not grief but a dumb pain which could be overcome only by constant attention to duty and volunteering for all the dangerous work.

I sometimes think now that from then on I have changed a great deal. I know I learned to be terribly careless, in fact reckless. I have neglected a good many of the things I was taught to do at Sunday School and have followed pretty much my own way.

But here I am telling my own troubles when you have enough of your own.

You will miss your Mother very much May, but try to look on the brighter side. Your Father and Brothers and sisters need your smile and cheery word and you have them to cheer you. May God help and comfort you in the days to come.

Clara and I are here alone. Mr. and Mrs. Finlay Brownlee and Mr. and Mrs. Alex Sinclair motored down from Rocanville on Friday and got out to Johns yesterday at noon. I was coming in for the week end so they and John's all came in. We went to the Capitol last night and all stayed here. All went to church this morning and afternoon took a drive to City Park and out to John's for supper. Clara and I came in again for tomorrow is Civic Holiday here and I am taking the day off.

I am going to help John off with the harvest. We will be starting this week I expect as harvest is coming on early. I will likely be there until after threshing and can't say what I will do after that.

Good night Dear May and I will be looking for a letter soon although I don't expect you will find writing very easy.

Yours Lovingly,
Herb

Feb. 4: Fine. PT. squad and drill etc.

Feb. 5: Fine. Drill 4 hours a day. Battalion paraded to cinema at Chateau de la Haye. "Aladdin's Lamp."

Feb. 6: Fine. Went to the Chateau for bath and to show at Gouy Servins at night. 87th concert party.

Feb. 7: Rain. No parade. Wrote some letters.

125

France
[Petit Servins]
Feb. 7, 1918

My Dear Sister,

I suppose you have been looking for a letter every day and I should have written to you sooner but like you have been looking for one every day too. As yet none has arrived. There should be a Canadian mail soon now, if there has been no big storms. Well Clara, you have come through a great deal lately and I only wish I could have been there to have helped you, but since that was not to be, we must not complain. I can scarcely realize yet what has happened in so short a space of time. It seems that trouble has come in a double measure to us. I am wondering what you are doing now, if you have closed up the house and gone out with Jane. It will be a lonesome looking place now, with the house closed and nothing doing on the farm. I may get home to look after things but am not building any castles in the air. In the face of the food production problem, I think they should let me home for the summer months at least.

Dear parents, how often we annoyed and disobeyed them and still how they worked to give us the best.

We did not know how well off we were, that was the only trouble. Now we can look back on those days and see where we went astray. We are left to struggle on in the great race of life. May God give us strength to fight the good fight and run the straight race.

There is nothing to write about from here. The weather has been fine, but is raining this morning. We are out for a rest at present.

Hoping this finds you well and in good spirits.

Your loving Brother,

Herb

P.S. I hope to get a long letter from you soon.

JHG

Feb. 8: Rainy. Not much doing.

Feb. 9: Fair. Practised attack between Villiers and the ridge. Got back at 8:00 P.M. Tired.

Feb. 10: Fine. Marched to Columbia camp. Working party.

Feb. 11: Windy. Slept until 9:00 A.M. Working party to Cite de le Monte.

Feb. 12: Fine. Same as usual.

Feb. 13: Fine. Carry on.

Feb. 14: Fine. Sleeping in day time and working at night does not agree with me.

Feb. 15: Fine. Marched to Chateau de la Haie. Niagara camp.

Feb. 16: Cold. Payed. Some 38th boys came over to see us. Barrie and Armstrong.

Feb. 17: Cool. Church parade and bath.

Feb. 18: Fine. Inspection and short march. Pictures at night.

Feb. 19: Fine. Marched from Chateau to Camblain Chatelain. Full pack but road good.

Feb. 20: Rainy. A little PT. and drill in morning. Had next of kin changed. Wrote some letters. Cable from I.O.D.E.

126

France
[Camblain-Châtelain]
Feb. 20, 1918

Dear May,

It is some time since I have written so tonight I will try to make good. I received your paper and letters up to Jan. 12th so have a lot to answer for.

Days are very lonely and nights are long to me lately, but I am trying to keep a brave heart. I thank you for your words of sympathy. They are a great help to me.

We are out on rest once more, in the town where I joined the Battalion the second time, after a period of sixty-five days in the line.

It is good to get a nights sleep again and a few hours to oneself. Please accept this short note for now. Will write a long letter soon.

Sincerely,
Herb

Feb. 21: Fair. Marched to Houdain for rehearsal. Real tired tonight. Bonikoo Promanada.[10]

Feb. 22: Fair. 11th brigade reviewed by General Currie. Made a very bad impression.

Feb. 23: Warm. March to ranges at Pernes. Scored 35 out of 45.

Feb. 24: Fine. Church parade.

Feb. 25: Rainy. To gas school at Calonne Ricourt.

127

Somewhere in France
[Camblain-Châtelain]
Feb. 25, 1918

Dear May,

Something better than a Whizz Bang this time. They are, shall I say, perhaps very much to the point though, and are called after a certain small calibre German field gun which fires about a 3″ shell with the speed and accuracy, almost of a rifle bullet. Fritz often snipes with them to good effect. All you can hear is Whizz-bang, Whizz-bang, much quicker than I can write it. But the field card describes itself in the name. While actually in the trenches you are only supposed to use them or green envelopes, you see they do not need to be censored. The officer has not time to read letters there.

Plenty of storms eh. Well I hope March maybe a good month. The weather here is like April at home.

I too have been to some very good comedy shows, lots of good talent in the army, you know. And we sure enjoy them when we get the chance.

I hope you passed with honours in your exams. It must be pretty hard to work over those accounts all day and then study at night. I admire your pluck and wish you every success.

I had the pleasure of meeting some of my old chums in the _____ the other day and had a good long chat. I have not seen any of the boys in the 3rd since the first of December so cannot convey your message to Pte. Quakenbush. I'll drop him a line if I can find his number.

Now, May, I think this is all for this time, besides it is getting rather late so here's hoping this finds you in the best of spirits—not the kind that takes your senses though.

As ever,

Herb

Feb. 26: Fair. Went to dentist and had tooth filled.

Feb. 27: Fair. Went for a bath in A.M. Also battalion inspection in battle order.

Feb. 28: Fair. Parade in A.M. Got boots changed. Fired some on ranges.

Mar. 1: Cool. Marched to Houdain and were inspected by Sir Douglas Haig.

Mar. 2: Windy. To Pernes ranges in A.M. Payed in P.M. Had feed in evening.

Mar. 3: Misty. Marched to Hersin Coupigny huts.

Mar. 4: Rainy. Wiring in morning. Wrote some letters in evening.

Mar. 5: Rainy. Nothing doing all day. Concert at night. 14th R.G.A.'s.

Mar. 6: Fine. Bombing in morning.

Mar. 7: Fine. Battalion parade. Company in the attack. Cleaning for guard.

Mar. 8: Fine. On guard at battalion H.Q.

Mar. 9: Fine. Came off guard at 9:00 A.M. Slept until noon. Saw some 3rd battalion men. Went to concert in Hersin at night. 47th battalion concert party. Six letters.

Mar. 10: Fair. Church parade at 9:00 A.M.

Mar. 11: Fine. Left HQ at 3:00 P.M. Marched straight into Loviets Lane. Tired.

Mar. 12: Fine. Slept until 9:30 A.M. Working party at night carrying heavy trench mortar.

Mar. 13: Fine. Slept until noon and carrying light shells at night. A few shells going over all the time.

Mar. 14: Splendid weather. Got some mail today. Can't show out in day time. Relieved. Lievins.[11]

Mar. 15: Fine. Working party to supports at 7:00 A.M. Getting our share all right this trip. Home at 5:00 P.M. Rations.

Mar. 16: Fine. Working party at night but as Fritz opened up we did not do much. Home by 11:30.

128

Somewhere in France
[Liévin]
March 16, 1918

Dear May,

This is a beautiful morning, the grass is getting green and the birds are singing, the aeroplanes are humming and the shells are whistling. What a contrast between Peace and War, it is almost too great to realize.

I am sitting here facing the morning sun, with my back propped up against the wall of a shattered house in what once was a very nice town.

One of _____, so if you see a word like this you will know that another Peace messenger has gone over to Fritz.

Being in the middle of the month, we had a visit from the Pay Master this morning after which I went across to the Y and did a little shopping. We get 45 Francs per month but that does not last long, everything is getting so high.

I received your last letter about a week ago but have not got the paper yet. Canadian mail comes about every two weeks now. I saw Pte. Quakenbush a couple of times lately and I gave him the message that you sent. He looks quite the same as he did when we met him in D.C.[12]

Well I suppose by now you will be getting some thaws. By all accounts there is likely to be some floods there this spring. I bet this will be a good sugar year, always is when the snow is deep. I hope the rough winter is followed by a good summer and that the crops in Canada will be good.

Now May I have not got your last letter here so can't answer any questions and my stock of news (if you care to call it such) is exhausted so I'll say Goodbye for this time and will write as soon as we get out of the line again.

Yours sincerely,
Herb

Mar. 17: Fine. Went into front line.

Mar. 18: Fine. Slept awhile. Lines close here. Nothing falling close.

Mar. 19: Rain. Shelling in day so had to go to D company. Something doing on left.

Mar. 20: Fair. More bombardment by our guns. Fritz replied attack on the left at dawn.

Mar. 21: Fine. Big gas attack tonight. Reply with smoke[13] and shell (1500 projister shells on 11th brigade front).

Mar. 22: Fine. Going out tonight to Leivin for a few days. Everything O.K.

Mar. 23: Fine. Slept till noon. Got some reg. mail. Put in application for furlough. Wrote some letters.

129

Somewhere in France
[Liévin]
March 23, 1918

Dear May,

Here we are again in our cellar. In this town we sleep in the cellars for the bedrooms are too drafty owing to numerous windows of rather large and unshapely dimensions.[14] Am in the line again and glad to say going on not too badly.

We are having fine weather, just like May days in Canada. There is not much doing here out of the ordinary, so my stock of news is small. Say don't forget me at sugar time. I can almost smell taffy now.

Had a letter from Georgina the other day and sure got a surprise. She was speaking of J.R. I wonder if she thought I could or would tell her anything. She spoke of once, when she took a snap of Jack and I and wished those days back again. Perhaps she meant for my sake, but I am inclined to think for her own. She sent me a snap of Miss Phillips, Miss Gibson and herself which was taken at the school fair. It is good too and I am sure I see Jack Rae in it.

Well, so long May and I hope to hear from you soon again.

All the time,

Herb

P.S. Next week I'll be a "downstairs" Lance Jack, ha ha.[15]

Mar. 24: Beautiful day. Resting up.

Mar. 25: Warm. Reconnoitered position. Moved unexpectedly to Souchez Valley.

Mar. 26: Cool. Stand to at 3:00 A.M. Nothing happened. Parade at 1:30 for half hour. Communion in YMCA.

130

Militia and Defence
Ottawa, Ontario
March 26, 1918

Miss Clara Gibson
Balderson, Ont.

Dear Madam,

Re. 787167, Pte. J.H. Gibson, 130th BN. Inf. now 75th Batt. Inf.

I beg to inform you that instructions have been received from the above soldier through the Chief Paymaster overseas, transferring his assignment of $20. per month, to you, effective 1st April 1918. Payments will, therefore, be made accordingly.

Yours truly

for Director

S.A. and A.P.

Mar. 27: Cool. Parade at 9:00 A.M. BF and bombing lecture on new egg bomb. Marched to camp at Boyelffin. Odlum's composite brigade 47, 54, 72, 75, and 85th.

Mar. 28: Wind and rain. Motor lorries to Mt. St. Eloi. Into huts for night.

Mar. 29: Fair. Marched to Neuville St. Vaast for dinner. By Roclincourt to front line. Relieved 113th London reg. Oppy Wood.

Mar. 30: Fine. Nothing doing. Living in Funk holes. Holding block in Tommy Alley. C.T. Rain tonight.

Mar. 31: Fine. Advanced block 100 yards.

Apr. 1: Rainy. Advanced block another 100 yards. Some mail up.

Apr. 2: Fair. Posted 20 yards rear of block to use rifle grenades.

Apr. 3: Fair. Sleeping most of days. Pretty fair rations. Cpl. Brenand wounded. Left in charge of section. Relieved by 54th and went on left to relieve 43rd in out post.

Apr. 4: Rainy. No movement in day light. Three in small funk hole. Relieved by 87th and got lost coming out.

Apr. 5: Fair. Slept till noon. Funk holes in tired alley. Working party tonight.

131

France
[Funk hole in Tired Alley][16]
April 5/18

Dear May,

Your letter of March 10th received and as usual welcome as the flowers in May. This time I got it in the front line on a dark, wet, night and you can't imagine the pleasure it gave me just to see a note from you. Of course I did not get reading it until next morning but somehow its very presence was a shining star in the night.

It has been wet this few days and of course the trenches are in bad condition. However I am well and that means everything out here. Moved out to supports last night and believe me a wash and shave was most acceptable after over a week without either. We slept until noon, had dinner, cleaned up a bit and now it is just 3:40. I happened to have a couple of green envelopes and a few whizz bangs but this will be the amount of my correspondence for, well, hard to say, how long. This last ten days has been a rush and tumble. Going and coming, we know not where. Talk about the future and its mysteries but this is where you realize it to the fullest extent.

Well I hope your spring is turning there now and there will soon be no storms to stop you from getting home. I am glad you are getting along so nicely in your First Aid Course. It was misfortunate that you should lose your instructor.

I saw of Dr. Hanna's death in the Canadian Record. V.A.D. work is a great thing. You know I was in one of their hospitals. Lots of them dress patients as well as other work, of course under the supervision of the Sister in charge.

As you see this is the end of my paper.

Goodbye and best wishes.

Sincerely,

Herb

Apr. 6: Fair. But rainy and very dark at night. Major Bull took us on work got home early. 75th lost 2 men as prisoners scouting in no mans land.

Apr. 7: Working party.

Apr. 8: Rainy. Moved to dugouts on embankment. Rations.

Apr. 9: Fair. Working party in A.M. Making new dugouts. On ration parties.

Apr. 10: Fair. Working party in P.M. Relieved by 85th and moved out to Aubrey camp. Had good sleep.

Apr. 11: Fine. Payed in A.M. Bath in P.M. Saw E. Ferrier. Relieved 5th CMR Farbus.

Apr. 12: Fine. Slept most of day. A few heavies. Moved to Hayter C.T. Good dug out.

Apr. 13: Fine. Slept all day and all night. Parcel from May.

Apr. 14: Fair. Moved to Chaudiere line.

132

France
[Chaudière Line Dugout]
April 14, 1918

Dear May,

I take great pleasure in writing you today, to thank you for the parcel which I received last night. Everything was splendid and was in good condition, (so many parcels are broken up). The socks and tooth cleaning material were certainly good choices. You seem to know May, just what I need most. No one knows (except those here) how much a little parcel is appreciated in the line, and I don't suppose ever will. Letters of course come first, but parcels are luxuries.

This is Sunday, just 12 noon but you would never know it except that we moved today. Sunday seems to be our only day to move, in fact, we have moved every Sunday this last five weeks. I think I wrote you a short note about a week ago and said we were very unsettled. Well, have covered some ground since then and have been in some tight corners. Today finds us back to the scene of our operations of last New Year time. Pretty quiet now but no one knows how long the quiet will last.

No doubt you have been reading the papers and perhaps know more in general than I do. I have not seen a paper for over a month. I need not say more about the fighting, that's too common place.

I had the pleasure of meeting my old friend Ernie Ferrier[17] the other day, only for a few minutes though, sorry to say. We went for a bath at _____ and I stopped at a Y to get some eats and who should serve me but Ernie.[18] He got a surprise and so did I, although I had always been on the watch for him. "Oh!" says he "I thought you were in Canada." "Yes" says I "in Canada Trench." He looks fat and hearty. There was a huge line-up for eats and he was working and sweating to beat the band. I would have been glad to have a chat with him but we moved up the line the same night.

Did I tell you that my pal, Gorman, left the Batt. in February. I don't think I ever told you of he and I putting in for transfer to R.F.C.[19] before we left Blighty. We were just a week late, applications were stopped for a month and in the meantime we were sent to France, with the advice to apply here. Well Gorman did so, but owing to conditions at home and my applying for furlough, prevented me. He is now down at the base and will start training as soon as he is nineteen. He wishes I were with him. If I do not get home in the course of a couple of months, I shall apply again. Gorman is a good chap and I hope he succeeds. Imagine being two years and a half in the army before being of age, with ten months of that time in France. If all Canadians had the same spirit, there would be no need for conscription.

So since he left I am alone as far as boys from home are concerned. Most of the boys are from Toronto and only two of these were in the Company before I left. Our platoon Sergt. got wounded a couple of weeks ago. He was a 130th man and one of the best. He is now in Manchester Hospital and doing fine, and says he expects to make Canada. He had five shrapnel wounds. My section Cpl. got a slight wound and yours truly fell in for the responsibility. Glad to say we have got another Cpl. now, I'd sooner be a plain soldier.

Well, May, I said I was not going to talk of war, but here I have done so.

April, in Canada, sugar time, rills and rivers singing with pride the anthem of the free. Of course you will be having maple sugar and pancakes. Oh, I'll have to stop now or I shall be homesick.

Write soon.

Sincerely,

Herb

Apr. 15: Fair. Deep dugout. Working party to Toledo.

Apr. 16: Fine. Moved to Hayter CT. Got letter from Pte. Ward.

Apr. 17: Fine. Came out on advance party to cellar camp.

Apr. 18: Rainy. Working party at La Folie farm.

Apr. 19: Snowy. Bath. Saw M. Paul. Before C.O. regarding leave. Writing.

133

France
[Cellar Camp]
April 19, 1918

Dear May,

Hello! still debating eh! Well so am I, as to whether I should light another candle or save it for another time. Sometimes they are hard to get, the demand is so great. You know they are a soldiers only source of light. I have almost forgotten what a lamp looks like. Of course, I am sorry you did not win that debate. At present though, I will not give you my views on the subject, for I have learned to look on the tobacco habit in another light, this last few months. Like most other things of the kind, their use is abused, therefore causing injury.

Glad to hear that so many of our boys are getting home to Canada. I think that will keep up the spirits of those at home more than anything.

I saw Mel Paul today (an old Dalhousie chum). Had not seen him for a year and a half. Had an hour to talk but as he was going up the line could spare no more time. Also saw F. Adams last night. He looks fine. Was surprised to meet Cpl. Buffan of Lanark in the trenches this week. I thought he was in the Artillery. Am not sure but I think he is Eva's brother. And Archie Wrathall is gone. It seems every letter I get brings news of another death in our vicinity. So many have gone since I left. I wrote telling you of getting the parcel. Received it up in supports, "Atlantic," off where the sun goes down. Don't expect too much May, I'm not.

I'm sure Jennie and her Morton are happy. I have been intending to write a line to either her or the family to say that I had visited Hugh and Willie's graves. They are buried in a little cemetery on the top of Vimy Ridge.

All at present, looking forward to your letter.

I remain as ever,
Herb

Apr. 20: Fair. Nothing doing.

Apr. 21: Church service.

Apr. 22: Fine. Went to see the sights. Reminds one of the children at Regents Park. 4th division concert "Camouflage."

Apr. 23: Fine. Broke camp for front line. Vicinity of Quarry.

Apr. 24: Fine. Scouting this trip in. Like it fine. No patrols as yet. Rations.

Apr. 25: Fine. Very quiet. Received three letters from home.

Apr. 26: Rainy. Wrote two letters. Working on trench.

134

On Active Service
[Vicinity of Quarry]
April 26, 1918

Dear May,

Your last letter came a little quicker than a few former ones, but still 25 days seems a long time to cover the distance.

I remember quite well what I was doing on Easter Sunday. Was holding a block in a C.T.,[20] two hundred yards ahead of our front line, the location of which I cannot tell. I am afraid, May, that I cannot tell you those queries you want to know. The fact is I am not very well posted myself. I don't think the folks at home quite realize the vastness of the Western battle front. I compare your ideas of the front to those of an Englishman's of Canada. He thinks Ontario and Saskatchewan is only a stone's throw apart. For instance one "bloke" asked me if I knew a certain man in Canada. Says I, "Where does he live?" "Oh!" says he "he has a farm in Ontario." Here we know a little of what happens in

our own sector, but nothing more. If you want to know my views of
_____ they are simply this—we shall b_____ at his own game.

Am indeed sorry for Popplewell's in the loss of their only boy. It is
seldom one so young is taken away with that trouble. 'Tis but another
lesson to us to be prepared for we know not what hour the Son of
God cometh.

Quite a loss for Hughes' but they are only material and can be
replaced. I am glad they made use of my barns, they are not totally out
of business.[21]

Tell me May, if you will, do the people at home still think me a fool
for enlisting when I did. I know they have passed their opinions since
our home has been closed. If I could but get home for one month to
settle affairs I would be willing to come straight back again. I do hope to
realize these hopes sometime or other.

Hoping this finds you Hale and Hearty.

Yours sincerely,
Herb

Apr. 27: Fair. Working on trenches. Gas guard at night. Quiet.

Apr. 28: Fair.

Apr. 29: Raining. Relieved and came out to Embankment.

Apr. 30: Rain. Slept until noon and moved to better billets on Arras Rd.

May 1: Fine. Working party in Pictou. Rations. Some gas.

135

France
[Billets on Arras Road]
May 1, 1918

To Jane and Clara
My Dear Sisters,

Your letter of March 28 came along a couple of days ago and it
was one I was looking for, because I was anxious to hear how you got
home. Maggie wrote and said that Jane was sick at Powasson, so it was
a great relief to know that you had got home. I hope Jane soon recovers
and that you will be able to enjoy the use of the car. That will help you

both to forget, in a measure, the trouble that you both came through the last few months. Yes, Clara I know it must have been very hard for you to shut up the home and go away but it was the best thing you could do and I hope you will like living out there.[22]

Everyone writes me very nice letters, sympathizing with me, but do you know that even yet I cannot fully realize our loss. I can't seem to grasp it all. I miss Father's letters very much, the last one he wrote I keep in my breast pocket. It was written Dec. 6th almost five months ago. I also keep the last letter Mother sent, written by M.E. I often read them and try to understand but somehow I cannot. It will not be the home-coming that I had been looking forward to, but I know they are both happy in their last resting place and their dear souls have gone on to that place prepared for them. We must all strive to meet them there in the sweet bye and bye.

I would like to see you all now. All those nephews and nieces too, there will be such a change in them. Had a nice long letter from Janet last week. I did not know till then that Willie had bought Hugh's and the other house.[23] No one has told me yet of the sale. I have been wondering what you did with my papers, especially the Will. I believe I should make another one and have it sent to Ottawa, in case the old one was lost there would be no trouble.

Well I have been interrupted with my writing. I started this in the morning, but we have been out all day repairing the trenches, just got home and had supper. It is now 6 P.M. I have to go for rations tonight but that won't take long. Do you remember what happened on the 1st of May about 9 or ten years ago, the day I let the bloods run away?[24] It seems that at this time of year, all the memories of the past come back to me, like the leaves on the trees. T'was always a busy time of the year, making sugar, milking, cleaning grain etc., etc. but there is something charming about spring. The leaves are just coming out here, the grass is quite green. Has been cloudy most of the time for last ten days, with considerable rain falling, which has made the trenches somewhat muddy. However, we are lucky on this bit of quiet front, for as yet we have had none of the heavy fighting.

I am sorry to hear that Hugh has not improved in his ways any yet.[25] I just wonder if Ida ever got the letters I wrote to her, for she never answered. You might mention it to her sometime. Perhaps she has no time to write I know she has a bunch to look after. Ashcroft's don't write very often and I think Willie's might also write oftener. You and Maggie are my main stays now and I hope you write every week. Had a nice letter from Mrs. Bingley of Lanark and I must answer it soon. Also one from Jennie R. Did I tell you that Georgina wrote once, she promised to before I left but was a long time fulfilling the promise. You said you did not know if your letter was interesting, indeed it was. I wanted to hear about your trip out. Any letters, even a postcard, is interesting, don't worry about that. I guess I have not told you the outcome of my application for furlough yet. Well, I was called to see the Colonel about ten days ago and he said I would have to wait until leave opened up again. Leave stopped when the drive started and I don't suppose it will open until the worst is passed. My papers may come through from Ottawa before that, I hope they do for I would like to get home for at least a month to get affairs settled up.

Now this is getting to be a rather long letter, almost the full of a green envelope and I don't know what else I can write.

Give the friends out there my best regards and next time you write tell me where they all are living and all about anyone I knew. When I get back I mean to take a rest and will go out there for a few months.

I have been spared through eight and a half months in the line, but no telling what is before us. If the worst (as some call it) should happen, don't look at it in that light, but think of me as gone on to see my dear parents.

Now dear sisters don't grieve over much at our loss, it must be all for the best. God's will be done. Goodbye and be sure to write every week, be it ever so little. Love to all.

Your loving brother,
Herb

May 2: Fine. Working party. Regular home here.
May 3: Fine. Working party. Three Canadian letters.
May 4: Fine. No working party. Cleaned up and wrote letter.

136

France
[Billets on Arras Road]
May 4, 1918
10 A.M.

Dear May,

This is a most beautiful Saturday morning, clear and cool, just a slight breeze to wave the grass and rustle the quarter grown leaves.

At present my platoon is quartered by the side of a main road which runs between two well known towns. On either side, fields stretch, fields which once were the pride of some man's labours and by the look of the soil, I should judge, repaid him for his work perhaps sixty fold. The road itself is in comparatively good repair and is lined on each side with large trees, which resemble our Canadian elms (Horme in French). Many of them have been killed or shattered by shrapnel. It seems a pity to be spending our days thus occupied. I would just like to be plowing up these fields this morning. We have a regular home here. Not absolutely bombproof, but is boarded and floored inside with bunks and fireplace. I am sitting on one bunk with my paper on a box. There was not quite enough light so one chap tried to arrange two mirrors to reflect a ray onto my desk, but he got tired holding one in place so says "Oh, give her my respects." Another one says "tell her all about the weather, trees, etc. etc."

There was a Canadian mail last night, so was lucky to get three, yours, one from J. Spalding and one from my cousin in Muskoka. Canadian mail comes anywhere from 10 days to two weeks interval, so we almost know when to look for some.

I can always count on one from Perth and it is nearly always opened first. I really enjoy them very much.

Did I know Pte. Paul.[26] Well I should say so, and a great chap he was. Was surprised to hear that Capt. Hooper was back in England. I understand he was not wounded and that only wounded men could be exchanged. No I don't think I ever read "Mrs. Wiggs" but the name strikes me as being funny so the play must have been.

Now May, this is about all I have to say this time so will "halt" and go clean my rifle.

Au Revoir,
Herb

P.S. No use saying anything about events here for you will have them by press much quicker. The Canadians are not in the heavy fighting as yet.

JHG

May 5: Fine.

May 6: Rainy. Little working party. Lots of eats.

May 7: Rainy. Relieved by H.L.I. from the east, 6th battalion. Walked to Thelus Cr. May 8: Warm. Arrived by motor lorries in Cancourt at 5:30 A.M. Slept all day.

May 9: Warm. Cleaning all morning. PT and baseball in afternoon.

May 10: Cool. Musketry and bath. 124th played 75th baseball winning by 7-1.

May 11: Fine. Went to ranges in morning. Short route march in afternoon to Frevilliersbattle order. E. Ferrier running YMCA here.

137

France
[Cancourt]
May 11, 1918

Dear Sister,

Again I come for a little chat in the cool of the evening.

Your last letter came just a day or two after I had written so until now I did not bother writing for there is so little I can write about.

Rather a strange incident happened tonight. At present we are out for a little spell and the village we are billeted in had no **YMCA** until today. A load of supplies arrived this afternoon and they are just started to sell. Well you should have seen the rush when the news spread, for we were unable to procure any eats before unless from the French shops, where prices are sky high. Well as soon as I had a wash-up, I came along to get some chocolate (you see I am just as fond of that as ever) when who should I find to serve me but the chap who accompanied me on my last leave home—namely E. Ferrier. Needless to say we were both surprised and he invited me to sit inside and write my letter. As soon as the rush is past we will be able to have a chat. So I am perched on a biscuit box, with paper on a chocolate box, so am pretty well fixed.

Things are going pretty well now, nice warm weather etc. etc. I am with the Scouts now and find it rather a change from the usual.

1 P.M. Sunday May 12

Today I shall endeavour to finish this letter. In the morning we had church service and a short march after. It is cloudy and threatening rain, some change from yesterdays heat. You see we have as many changes in weather as in Canada.

Had a letter from my old pal O.R. Gorman. He is training for the Flying Corps at Hastings England. There should be a Canadian mail soon. Ernie and I had a great chat last night about old times. I am going up to see him this evening again.

I told you that Mel Paul had been killed a couple of weeks ago. I could hardly believe it for I saw him hale and hearty only three weeks ago. Such is the way in this uncertain world.

I have been in the Co. Scouts for some time and like it rather well, as it is a change from the usual.

This is Mother's Day for the boys in France, and everyone is reminded to write to the folks at home. Alas, I cannot write to dear Mother anymore so I remember you as being next in my thoughts.

This will be all for today and I trust you are all well. Remember me to all the friends.

Your loving brother,
Herb

P.S. I hope the boys have recovered from the measles.[27]

May 12: Fair. Church parade.

May 13: Rainy. Map reading in A.M. Marched to Villiers Chateau for gas in P.M.

May 14: Warm. Sketching. Battalion parade and route march in afternoon by Herpre.

May 15: Sketching. Route march in P.M. At least went to woods and had lecture.

May 16: Hot. Manoeuvres. Bethonsart, Villiers, Brulin and Savy, out of action first five ——.

May 17: Warm. Scouting. Route march and pay in afternoon. Baseball 75th vs. 102nd.

May 18: Hot. Tactical Manoeuvres. Captured the village of Bethonsart. Three letters from home.

May 19: Hot. Church parade and sports.

May 20: Hot. Work on reports. Bath at 10:00 A.M. Route march to Hermin in P.M.

May 21: Warm. Field manoeuvres in morning between Frevilliers and Bethonsart.

May 22: Hot. Sketching in morning. Baseball P.M. C beat A company 7–14. Battalion marched to Maisonal Bouche in evening to see final brigade match. 75th won 1-0.

May 23: Hot. Went sick with sore face. Stayed in all day.

138

France
[Cancourt]
May 23/18

Dear May,

Today I have two of your letters to answer in one. It is several days since I received the last one, but was waiting until there was something worthwhile to write about. It seems harder to find material for letters than it used to be. Do you see any difference in them? I think I told you of being out of the line, well we are still out and our daily routine runs something like this—Reveille 6 A.M. (really means 5 A.M. as we too are on the daylight saving plan) breakfast 7; P.T. 8 to 9, then being a Scout I take special training from 9 to 10. Afternoon we either have a route march or sports—the latter preferably. I like Scout work fine.[28] Last Sunday afternoon we had Battalion sports and of course there was keen competition between Companies. Our Co. took second place. There was all sorts of races and contests, the best being the obstacle race. Oh yes and we had Charlie Chaplin with us. You would have laughed to see the guy dressed up in an old civy suit, belonging to an ancient French generation, by the look of it.

Yesterday afternoon there was two baseball matches. C. Co. beat A. Co. by 7–14 runs and last night the Batt. marched to a nearby village[29] to root for our team in the final football match for Brigade championship. The old Six Bitts (75th) won. Score 1–0. So you see we think of other things than war.

It has been hot and dry since we came here, some days almost too hot for work but then the baths are close by. There is a small stream not far away and on it an old mill dam. Some of the lads go down and shower bath under the sluice but its rather cold yet. I got my face all sunburnt and has all broken out now so I have not shaved for three days, result is, I'm hardly fit to be seen, twixt whiskers, ointment and blisters, ha ha. It is a long time since I was on a Sick Report, this makes about half a dozen times in 26 months.

So much for this side now I'll answer some of your queries. How do you like the new time? Do folks get out to church in time now? I imagine it will be rather hard for the country people to get to morning service. You guessed that censored part correctly, but you need not worry, I think the same will not occur again.

Say! What is Ed. Watt doing? Is he still at war with the Huns or making speeches at Red Cross meetings? No hint at the Red Cross at all, they are doing great work.

What did the Colonel do in the great war, sifted ashes with his uniform, to save coal, eh. But I better stop now before I get nasty. Ernie Ferrier and I have had a good many things talked over since meeting here, those two among others.

Oh, no. I did not intend to convey the idea that I would be a Lance Corporal, simply that at the end of March, I would be entitled to a two years good conduct stripe. We call those wearing them, downstairs lance Jacks, because the stripe is a Lance Corporal's worn upside down at the cuff. Compre?

'Twas news to me of Russell being turned down, perhaps he will sign up now, what more than one lad has done.[30]

I think by the way Ernie talks that he thinks a good deal of Ethel A. I suppose you know all about that though. Georgina hasn't answered my last letter yet nor have I heard from Jack for sometime. I hope Roy's tooth it alright again, it's such a nasty thing.

Now I'll be looking for a letter soon and be sure to tell me of everything that comes off.

Give my best regards to anyone who asks and don't forget yourself.

Yours sincerely,
Herb

May 24: Rained. Most of day. No parades. Preparing to move. Bid Ernie good-bye.

May 25: Cooler. Marched to Camblain Chatelain. Same billets. Went out and had eggs and chips. M. Currie came to see me.

May 26: Cloudy. Stayed in all day. Face very sore.[31]

May 27: Fine. Inspection but did not go out. Details. Beat C company baseball 11-7.

May 28: Fine. Got M+D but Mr. Pike would not allow me to go on parade. Wrote three letters.

May 29: Fine. Some better today. Big air raid at night. Some bombs dropped close. Civilians have dugouts for cover.

May 30: Fine. Writing in morning. Wrote some letters.

139

France
[Camblain-Châtelain]
May 30, 1918

My Dear Sister,

Here we are again, this fine May morning, and I trust that you are all fine in Walhalla. Isn't it wonderful how the time flies? I can scarcely believe that there is only one more day in May. Just two years since we left Perth for camp and a very memorable morning it was too. I can see Mother yet as she watched us march by the day of the Presentation of Colours. Hers was the Good, Brave heart and I always thought that I would see her again but it was not to be. But they are better off were they are, don't you think so? How is Jane now and are Ida's boys better again? I suppose you will be learning to drive the car this summer and you will be able to take me for a spin when I get back. The farmers will have finished seeding I suppose. I expect by now you will have seen all the folks around Leroy. Who runs Hugh's store now? and is he still living in Cavalier. I had a letter from Wm. Ashcroft and he expects some of the Park boys over anytime, with the Americans. I have not seen any Americans out here yet, but we hear plenty about them. I am afraid they have yet to prove their fighting qualities which they blow up so much. Of course they will be good men and all that, but talk too much. I was just reading an article in the Sat. Evening Post about heroine in France or with the A.E.F.[32] The writer certainly has a great imagination for I am quite sure the real thing never happened. However good luck to them, we need 'em all. There is considerable fighting going on in the South, but I don't think the great offensive has started yet. We are still out resting up and are billeted in a fairly good town some miles behind the lines. Rations are pretty good and one can buy plenty of eggs, milk, potatoes and coffee, providing he has the price. At the present moment

I have 15 cents to my name, just enough to get two mess tins of milk. However Pay Day is not far off. Expect a Canadian Mail any day now and hope to get a few of the parcels which I am told are on the way. I think that our parcels are being held up somewhere.

I think this is all for today, hoping to get a letter soon.

Your loving brother,

Herb

P.S. Matt Currie called to see me last week. He looks fine.

JHG

May 31: Company went to Pernes Range. C company played battalion at baseball winning by 6-4.

June 1: Warm. Battalion went out for all day field manoeuvres. Feeling tough today. Got payed in the afternoon.

June 2: Fine. Church parade.

June 3: Fine. Battalion went to brigade sports at Dieval. 75th and 87th tied with 33 points. 75th won football 1-0.

June 4: Warm. All day march and manoeuvres at Frevilliers and Magnicourt. Pretty tired tonight.

June 5: Fine. Bath in A.M. and had remainder of day to rest up.

140

France
[Camblain-Châtelain]
June 5, 1918

Dear Sister,

Your letter of May 14th arrived today and I was indeed glad to hear from you. Glad to know that you are enjoying good health and that you like living in Walhalla. I am in pretty good health too but it is rather hot here at present and the roads are very dusty. Route marching through the dust and heat is no joke and I never could stand much heat anyway. When I'm trudging along with a pack and rifle I often think of home. I did not care about walking over to Harper or down to Balderson. That would be nothing now to me or any of the boys here. We just marched about twenty miles yesterday and nine the day before. On the 3rd of June we had Brigade Sports. The kitchens went with us and we had two meals out, just like a picnic, only instead of salads and pastry, we had stew and rice and jam. Had a good day though, all kinds of events. Our Battalion [75th] and another [87th] (I can't tell you which Battalion) tied for points but we won the football game after.

You say that you have only got two letters from me this year. Well it is quite evident that they have gone astray, for I have written at least twice a month this year. We have not got any Canadian mail since May 19th, yours being from the States it must have got through that way. There are a lot of parcels on the way also that I would like to get.

It is nice that you have met some Canadian people out there, but I suppose they too have become Americanized. Do you think you will go up to see Ashcrofts this summer? If you feel fit I think you should take a run up, it isn't far and you could go up to Antler and Reston. Use up some of that monthly allowance, you might as well have it.

The last letter I had from John, he had started work on the farm but they never mentioned having a car. They sure will run about some this summer, it will be fine for going over to the farm with anyhow.

I seldom hear from Roy at all now. I thought he had been marked B2 and would not be called up. I heard that O. MacLaren had gone up to Kingston to try to get a good job when he found out that he had to enlist. I'd just like to see some of those chaps now.

Do you ever have a line from Elsie at all? I wonder how she is getting along. Wonder who Jimmie gets to drive in the Ford now? Did I tell you of getting a letter from Georgina R. She wants to correspond now it seems. I wrote a letter to Margaret Pink the other day. I heard she wanted my address to write but I never got any letter so thinking it might have gone astray, I wrote anyhow. Really I don't know how she will take it, of course if she doesn't care to answer, I should worry.

This morning we had a fine bath and afternoon played ball.

Well I suppose you are reading all the war news. There is a big battle in progress just now.[33] We have been out for almost a month now. Don't worry too much about me. I'll be all right. I do hope that you get this letter alright, for I know how you look forward to getting them, although I have nothing of much interest to write.

Love to all,
Herb

June 6th.

Just received some Canadian mail today and expect some more tomorrow.

Goodbye,

JHG

June 6: Hot. Outpost work at Fusse de la Clarence. Ball game afternoon.
June 7: Fine. Marched to Magnicourt, manoeuvred all day and night on out post work.
June 8: Warm. Started home at 5:00 A.M. and arrived at 8:00 A.M. Had breakfast and went to bed for rest of day. Parcel from M.E. Also several letters and papers.
June 9: Fine. Brigade church service and presentation of medals.
June 10: Cooler. Scout training in A.M. Went to see E. Ferrier in evening.

141

France
[Camblain-Châtelain]
June 10, 1918

Dear May,

I must really answer this last letter of yours "tout de suite." T'was a "tres bonne lettre," so long and newsy.

We were a long while without any mail this time (from May 19th to June 6th) but we are lucky to get them even in that time. Got one box out of the half dozen that I have heard of which are on the way. It was from my sister and some maple sugar right from the woods, those dear Canadian woods.[34] Got a couple of papers this week and I see there is some improvements going around the old burg. I will not know the place when I get back. You will have to meet me at the station and escort me up town eh! Perhaps I better get off at Glen Tay and walk over-land.

So you are on the Ledgers now. Didn't I tell you that you would make good.

Are you buying any of those town lots? I believe I would invest in one if I were there. How about the car contest. I guess you would not care to bother with that sort of thing. They are not much good are they?

Well, May, we are still sticking it out here. Route marching is the principal part. Thirty Kilo's is a very good days march. Have done that a time or two. One day we went to sports and in the evening coming home we had some record breaker—covered about 5 kilo's in an hour and 5 minutes.

Yesterday there was a Brigade church service in the morning, after which there was a Presentation of Medals to men of the Brigade who have distinguished themselves in the past year. Our Battalion brought home two D.S.O.'s, two M.C.'s, one Croix de Guerre, and seventeen Military Medals. What do you think of that! First Friday is Divisional Sports day and Corp sports is to be sometime soon. I will write after they are over and tell you what prizes the Battalion won.

Au Revoir,

Herb

P.S. Ernie followed us to this town, am going down to see him tonight.

> *June 11:* Cool. All day manoeuvres at same place as before with tanks, artillery and aeroplanes.
>
> *June 12:* Fine. PT and instruction on digging in. Dismissed at 10:30. Received parcel from Mrs. Bingley. Lots of boys sick these days.
>
> *June 13:* Cool. PT and went to Ourton for bath. Box from Maggie. Writing.
>
> *June 14:* Fair. Shooting rifle grenades in A.M. Wrote some letters.
>
> *June 15:* Fine. All day at div. sports at Pernes. 11th brigade won highest place. On working party digging dugout at CCS from 12:00 P.M. to 8:00 A.M.
>
> *June 16:* Fine. Home for breakfast. Slept.
>
> *June 17:* Cool. Parcel from May. Bath and route march. Payed in evening.
>
> *June 18:* Fair. Gas drill and shooting rifle grenades. Slept most of afternoon. No mail today. Wrote letters.

142

France
[Camblain-Châtelain]
June 18, 1918

Dear May,

Don't know if I will get this finished in time for tonights mail or not, but must at least make a try for I see there are two of your's here still unanswered. It is a terror how the time flies when it comes to the matter of postponing letter writing. Since my last attempt, I have received your excellent parcel and wish to thank you very much for same. The cream candy was sure good, just finished it today. I have been very lucky lately, four parcels in a few days. Really my appetite is almost gone, from eating maple sugar. I think I will melt some of it down and have some syrup. Do you think I could manage that or burn my fingers. I'm sitting on my bed here in the attic, which we call our home and some home it is. The man of the house is a miner and the woman is a proper _____, shall I say D____l? the word is the nearest I can think of. They have seven kids, one boy a cripple. The oldest girl works at the mines cleaning lamps, and while at home is a regular crank. It is simply hair raising to listen to the Madam scolding the kids sometimes. I think I never saw such a poor housekeeper. We keep our part of the house much cleaner, even if I do say it myself. The little boy can't walk and has to crawl about in such a filthy state and for a wonder is very good natured.[35] But here I am writing a lot of stuff which is of no interest to you. A couple of the boys are into an argument, scarcely an hour passes without one. The question in debate is, Two parties travelling along a road in opposite directions. Do they meet or pass each other? Of course some fellows just argue for the sake of talking. Have had an easy day today. I was to go on a working party early in the morning, but when we fell in there were three men too many, so I was taken off. So we did an hours march with gas respirators on and then fired a few rifle grenades. After dinner I lay down to read but dropped off to sleep. It is now after supper, the end of another day at war.

Called on Ernie last night but as he was busy did not have much time to chat. He was telling me that I would be home for Lanark Fair, but I said "some hopes." Todays orders say that "no leave to Canada on compassionate grounds will be considered at present," so that puts the tin hat on my Furlough until winter at least. Can't be helped of course so will have to make the best of it. We expect to see some fighting soon now, for we have been out of the line since 7th May. It will be almost like going in for the first time if we don't go soon.

All we hear of the war is an occasional bombardment, an odd long range shell and a few bombs which fall from out the sky at night. Some days we get a paper and others we don't bother. Time enough when you get into it to find out, without reading of battles. Perhaps you think that an absurd statement, but really we are all fed up with the whole bloody affair. It would be such a change to have a nice table to eat your meals off and a bed to sleep in. If you could but see us dining, I am sure you would think it awful. However, we should worry.

Our Divisional Sports [at Pernes] are over and this Brigade carried off the spoils. Perhaps I never told you that I belong to the 11th Brigade, 4th Division. We had a splendid days outing. They were held in a rather nice town near here and we marched down in the morning, taking the field kitchens with us and had both dinner and supper on the grounds. There was everything from Lacrosse to Hand Ball. Worst part of it was, a bunch of us had to stay and go on a working party at 12 midnight. T'was rather cold hanging about until time to start work but considering the importance of the work, we did not mind. The task was digging dugouts for the staff and patients of a hospital. Tents and sheet iron afford no protection from heavy shells or bombs so one has to take to Mother earth for protection.[36]

I expect Corps Sports will be pulled off sometime in the near future. Will tell you how they came off.

Well, May, I think they might give you a few days off duty at least. I always think one works so much better after a little leisure. Pleased to hear of your success at exams.[37] Allow me to congratulate you. I'm sure if you cared to come across to England you could do so quite easily. They are conscripting women over there now, I believe. Of course I don't mean that as a hint, for you are doing fine work where you are. I merely mention that only in the light of the fine experience which you would gain by it. I say May, would you mind asking Mr. Smith for me if he knows how many Bankers, Lawyers etc. etc. have taken cover behind the false pretence of being farmers or land owners there by bringing down false evidence upon the real tillers of the soil. Does he know how many Canadians who have, during the past two years, left the city and purchased land, what for?—simply to save their hide. Is it then a greater disgrace for a man who has always been a farmer to seek to stick by his colours when food production is most essential or to be one of those usurpers from the circles of so called education. I hope I have made clear to you what I mean, my grammar never was good and my composing worse. I only wish I were near enough to give some of those fellows like Smith a piece of my mind.

But really here's the tenth page and I must stop before I get ruffled. Will be looking for your letter, telling of that play. Hope you get along good with your books and are always able to find your mistakes.

Reminds me of a little business of my own. The Pay Master took my Pay Book to balance it early in March and told me that I was $68.89 in debt. Naturally I made a complaint with the result that there was a big blunder to rectify. Instead of being $68 in debt, I have $110 credit. So even smart bookkeepers, like the army is supposed to have, make blunders.

Goodbye and good luck,

Herb

June 19: Warm. Gas drill. Route march to Cauchy la Tour in afternoon.
June 20: Fair. PT and grenade shooting. Got colours sewn on. Wrote some letters.
June 21: Fair. Town majors fatigue. Seven letters today. Four men wounded accidentally by Mills bomb.

142A

France
June 21

Dear May,

Here three days have gone and never got this letter away yet. Must see my Officer tonight and get it censored. In the meantime I have received yours of May 29th which was indeed very newsy. I am glad your play was a success and I wonder if the play gave a true conception of "Sunny France." Don't think me trying to criticize, but the word "sunny" doesn't seem to rhyme with the weather, _____ in France.[38]

Yes, I know Craigs quite well and many a good time Jack Baird and I had together in the good old days. Have not seen him for ages though and did not know he was in the army. So he is engaged eh!

No, May, I was not looking for my discharge at all, only wished to get back for a month or so to have business matters attended to but as I said before, it can't be done.

I am glad you think my letters worth while and I'll try to make them better. Just got five at noon today and two more now. Very sorry indeed to hear of Mr. Keays illness and hope he is recovering alright.

So long for tonight.

Sincerely,

Herb

Am registering this and enclosing French and German coin.

JHG

June 22: Fair. Another long march to training area.

June 23: Warm. Bath and church parade.

June 24: Fine. Bath at mines in morning. Scouting.

June 25: Fine. Practical scouting in Bois de Camblain Chatelain. Visited Brother Ferrier.

143

France
[Camblain-Châtelain]
June 25, 1918

Dear Sister,

Your welcome letter of 31st received, so I must answer today. I feel quite sure that you have not received all the letters I have sent.

Hope this finds you all well as it leaves me pretty good. The weather is not so hot now and we are not working so hard.

I am glad you like to live in the U.S.A. So you are working out. Well it is nice to be able to help anyone in a case of sickness, but Jane seems to need you there so I would not work out except in a case like that.

I have been getting a lot of mail lately, including several parcels. I wonder why the Americans won't let parcels come over? They must have as much means of transportation as we have. It will be alright though to send money for they have cut down our pay over here.

Since you say that you will stay with Jane, should I not be spared to return? I think I had better make another will, but it is hard to know just what to do.

Willie told me a few things in his last letter about the sale. I did not know until then that he had bought Hugh's place. He said that the proceeds were $1,100.00. Does that include the price of the lot? Why did you not tell me all about the business affairs? I feel as if there is some reason why I have been kept in the dark about the business and have had to write about it. I suppose it should not concern me greatly but I would like to have known what was sold and what it brought, also who got the proceeds.[39]

There has certainly been a great change out there also since I visited together. The friends are scattered so much since. I would like to have Willie Holwell's address.

The war news is very encouraging today. The Austrians are retreating and have lost heavily. Perhaps the war may end sooner than we expect and the sooner the better. We have sure had a good rest, __ weeks tonight since came out of the line.

Well, this letter seems short and uninteresting but really there is nothing much to write about unless the same old story of drilling and training. I think I'll take a walk down to see E. Ferrier tonight. He is in the Y. here.

I had a long letter from Annie May[40] this week—must answer it soon. Must close now with love to all.

Herb

P.S. You can tell Ida that I have never had a letter from her since leaving Canada, that I remember of.

June 26: Fair. Field day. These long marches are getting very tiresome. Don't see as they are of any benefit. Simply tramping down good crops.

June 27: Fine. Inoculated in A.M. Three letters from Canada. Moved to another billet in barn.

June 28: Warm. No duty. No mail today. Wrote several whizz bangs. Concert in YMCA.

June 29: Cool. Examination on scouting and practical work.

June 30: Hot. Brigade church service and Horse sports. Hon. Calder there.

July 1: Fine. Corps sports at Tincques. Duke of Connaught. Gen. Pershing, Sir. R. Borden, Sir. A. Currie, and several others there. 1st Division champions.

July 2: Hot. Reviewed by Hon. Bowel. Medals presented to C Company. B.B. team champions in battalion.

July 3: Fine. Battalion on manoeuvres. Scouts shoot on ranges. Artillery sports in P.M. Y Emmas at YMCA.

July 4: Fine. Bath at Ourton in morning. Went to YMCA but no show.

July 5: Fine. Inter platoon inspection. No. 9 platoon had picture taken in evening. Parcel from W. Institute.

July 6: Fine. Had final shoot of scout course. Made 82 pts. Went to Y Emmas in evening.

144

France
[Camblain-Châtelain]
July 6, 1918

Dear May,

It is several weeks since I have had a letter, so guess I'll drop a line anyway and tell you what we have been doing lately.

First of all the weather is fine and we are still in the same place as when I last wrote. They are not working us too hard at all, just drill in A.M., and have sports in P.M. Play a good deal of indoor baseball for Platoon Championships. I think there is more fun in it than outdoor ball. What do you think?

I spent the 1st of July at the Corps Sports and had a fine time. The weather was ideal and the different events keenly competed for. The crowd was large, as you may imagine, when every unit in the C.E.F.[41] was represented, as well as many men of the Imperial units. A guard of honour was mounted by the 2nd Batt. and certainly was a credit to the Canadian Corps, a finer body of men could scarcely be found in any army in the field today.

Among the Distinguished visitors were the Duke of Connaught (who inspected the guard), Premier Borden, Mr. Rowell and several other of Canada's foremost men, besides a number of French and Italian officers.

The 1st Div. carried off the Championships with 101 points. One of the most exciting events were some flying stunts, which were executed over the grounds by one of our aviators (Canadian I expect). He came swooping down so low, at a terrific speed, then shot upwards and turned so that the planes were almost vertical, then diving down again. I have seen some feats, but this one beats anything. The 1st Div. Concert Party put on their new play at night, but as I had to catch my lorrie at 7 P.M. could not stay for it. I met several of the old boys, but owing to the immense crowd, it was impossible to see them all. I should not liked to have missed this event, as it will be a day to remember. Sir R. Borden gave a speech at the opening of the concert but I did not hear it either. Ed. McKerracher was there and he looks just the same as when he left home. Say! did Mr. Quakenbush ever write? He is with the Machine Guns now, so is Tommy Booton and several more. I must be on the look out for Jim McVeity now that I know where he is.[42] I expect we will soon be getting some of the drafties to reinforce us. I believe there are over a million Americans over here now. Guess you can look for something big soon. Perhaps before you get this, we shall be into the thick of the fray.

Did you happen to see the speech, which Sir A. Currie made in London some few months ago, in the papers? I did not see it myself but heard of it. The Canucks are enjoying a well earned rest and I don't think there is a Corps in France who begrudges it to them.

Are you going to the Falls[43] on the 12th? I hear that is where they are celebrating this year. Haying will have started I suppose. How are they getting on for help, are the soldiers getting Furloughs?

Will be looking for a letter soon, May, and in the meantime best wishes.

Yours sincerely,

Herb

P.S. I hear that French leave is opening up. Will have something to tell you when I get mine. I intend going to Nice. Say! do you ever have any two per cent now? ha ha. Is the clothesline still in the same place? Ever go down by the Mississippi now?

JHG

July 7: Hot. Church parade at 11:00 A.M. Writing letters.

July 8: Hot. Scouting. Bath. Letters and parcel from Winnipeg.

July 9: Fine. Battalion sports today. Went to see Ernie in evening. Affiliated with battalion L.O.L.[44]

July 10: Fine. Marched to Dieval. Train to Mt. St. Eloi and to Anzin for night. (Marocuil).

July 11: Showery. Relieved 10th Scotch Rifles and 4th Gordans in front of Arras line. Quiet. Fair dugout.

July 12: Fair. Went on patrol at night. Fired on two parties of enemy.

July 13: Fine. Went to Y but did not see Ernie. Bigger patrol tonight but no luck. Wounded at 2:00 A.M. Carried out and to CCS. Lieut. Leonard scout officer killed. Also Etherington.

July 14: Went through operation.

July 15: Warm in bed. Doing fine.

145

42 C.C.S. BEF[45]
[Aubigny]
15-7-18

Dear Miss Gibson,

    I am so sorry to have to tell you that your brother has been wounded and at present in this hospital.

    He is wounded severely in the chest and abdomen and at present his condition is serious.

    Everything possible is being done for him and I will let you know again how he is progressing. Hoping to have good news for you soon.

Yours sincerely,
E. Robertson Sloan
Sister

145A (excerpt from the *Perth Courier*, July 19, 1918)

Mr. Wm. Gibson, Balderson, received word Thursday that his son, Pte. Herbert Gibson, infantry, was officially reported dangerously wounded and admitted to the 42nd casualty clearing station, July 14th. This is the second time he has been wounded, the first being last fall.

145B (excerpt from the *Perth Courier*, August 9, 1918)

Mr. John Gibson, Harper, received a letter from his brother, J. Herb Gibson this week stating that on July 14th, he had been out on a raid and received a bullet through his right side, going in below the shoulder blade, smashing a rib and coming out of his breast. With the help of a pal he managed to get back to the trenches where he was taken out on a stretcher to the dressing station. He also got a flesh wound in the thigh but luckily not very serious. He is somewhat weak yet but hopes to be in a fair way for recovery shortly. Mr. Gibson cabled to find out more about his brother and received the following answer on Wednesday.

"Canadian Red Cross Society reports, Private James Herbert Gibson at King George Hospital, Sanford Street, S.E. London. Gunshot wound chest, cheerful, able to sit up."

July 16: Warm. This is 42 C.C.S. at Aubigny.
July 17: Doing well. Fever down.
July 18: Examined.
July 19: Sample of blood taken from lungs.
July 20: Feeling effects of it.
July 21: Fine. Q.M.S. Baird called.

146

42 C.C.S.
France
July 21/18

Dear May,

Just a few lines today to say that I am lying in a cot here, propped up with pillows. I'm on my back again. Fritz has got me once more, a little harder than the last time but the worst is past now and I am doing fine. If I continue the same I think I should see old Blighty in a short time. Am hoping to at least.

I got a bullet through my right side about the 9th rib, which was pretty badly smashed, I think. Another in the thigh, but luckily it only went about a half inch deep.

Tea time now, will finish after. They only feed us five times a day here.

Funny, May, isn't it, how things come about. A few days before going into the line a bunch of us were talking about how the shell fire would act on us after two months out. Someone remarked "you'll see Scout Gibby finding the deepest dugout." "Oh," says I, "me for a Blighty this time" and sure enough second night in I got it.

Don't write to this address unless you wish for I shall be moved from here soon, dear knows where.

So long,
Herb

July 22: Visited by G.O.C. 1st army and D.M.S.

July 23: Fine. QMS Baird brought in chocolate.

July 24: Showery. Visited by several staff officers.

July 25: Showery. Base ticket ready. Bombing raid at night. Some Casualties.[46]

July 26: Cool. Left at 7:00 P.M. for base. Travelling all night. Arriving at Boulogne at 3:00 A.M.

July 27: Cool. Landed in 54th general hospital at Wimereaux. Very good place.

147

42 C.C.S.
B.E.F. France
July 27/18

Dear Miss Gibson,

I am very pleased to be able to tell you that your brother has improved very nicely and was able to be moved to the Base Hospital[47] yesterday the 26-7-18. Trusting you will soon be hearing from him with good news.[48]

Yours sincerely,
E. Robertson Sloan
Sister i/c

July 28: Fine. Outside in afternoon.

July 29: Warm. Marked for Blighty.

July 30: Left at 10:00 A.M. Sailed by Stad Antwerpan to Dover and to London.

July 31: King George Hospital. Ward E3. Stamford St. London.

Aug. 1: Very nice place. Canadian Red Cross visitor came to see me.

148

Ward E3 King George Hospital
Stamford Street
Waterloo Road
London S.E.
August 1, 1918

Dear May,

Hello! here we are again. Ha. Am in town too, now what do you think of that? Some town too, although I can't get out to see it, I know we are in the heart of London. Arrived here two days ago, after a journey of a good many stops and conveyances. It is just three weeks tonight since we went into the line, in front of Arras. Two nights after, I got this issue of lead, while on Patrol. It sure knocked the wind out of me, but after crawling a few yards I had to give up and take a rest. Luckily one of the other Scouts found me and helped me in. Owing to the very narrow trenches it was very difficult getting a stretcher through, so it was one and a half hours before they got me to the first dressing station. After that the going was easier, along a road on a wheeled stretcher about a mile to where the light Field Ambulance came and then to the Ambulance Station. After a dose of morphia and A.T.S., I slept all the way to the C.C.S.[49] Shortly after arriving here, they performed the operation. Some of my ribs were smashed so they had to remove several inches, sewed me up nicely—18 stitches and it is healed nicely. Only thing is that my lung is punctured. However that will heal up, I hope soon. I was glad to leave the C.C.S. for Fritz visited it quite frequently at night. He dropped bombs all around us—30 one night. The nearest was 50 yards and filled our ward with dust and smoke. One poor chap was killed and several wounded. Next move was by train to Boulonge, stopped there for a few days and then across. We struck a beautiful day and I enjoyed the sail. Funny it was the same Red Cross boat as I came home in the last time. There are 2000 beds in here, so you can imagine its size.

There are no other Canadians in this ward but the Canadian Red Cross visitor who called on me yesterday had all the names of those here. I only know one, Babcock, from near Lanark. Will see him soon as I can get up which I hope to do in a week at least. Now don't say you are sorry I am wounded again, May, for I consider myself to be real fortunate or lucky, as some put it. When one sees fellows minus limbs or eyes, I feel as though I were a whole man. It will be some time before I get any mail. Must send my address to the Record Office so they can forward it on. I wonder if you got the card and letter I sent you from the C.C.S.

What's the rush in Perth? Just the usual I suppose— The harvesting will be on now. How are the crops this year? Guess I would not be of any use to pitch sheaves even if I were there, ha. How are the farmers getting on for help at all? Are the soldiers getting furlough? Are food stuffs still as high as they were?

Well May, my side is getting rather sore sitting up so will close for today. I wish you were close enough to come and give me a visit. I feel rather lonely at times when other chaps people come in to see them and mine so far away, but still I know they don't forget me.

Trusting this finds you in the best of health and spirits.

I remain,

yours sincerely,

Herb

P.S. Be sure to put the number of my Batt. on the letters.

JHG

149

Canadian Red Cross Society
York Hotel, Berness St.
London
August 1, 1918

Near Relatives of Pte. J.H. Gibson No. 787167 75th Canadians who is at King Georges Hospital Stamford St. London, SE1 is suffering from wound in the chest. He was visited on 31st by our authorized representative, who reports he arrived at this hospital from France on the 30th. He was very ill in France but is now much improved, is able to sit up in bed and is quite bright and cheerful. You may be sure he is receiving every care and attention.

Yours truly,

Mrs. B. Masterton Smith

Aug. 2: Doing very well. But time goes slowly.

150

King George Hospital
Ward E3
Stamford St.
Waterloo Road
London S.E.
August 2, 1918

Dear Sisters,

Long before this reaches you, I know you will be looking for news and will be anxious to know how I am getting on. By the address you will see I am back in Blighty again. Arrived here on July 30th and find it a good place and the best of treatment. I knew soon as I got to the C.C.S. that I would get to England, but had to stay there almost two weeks before I was able to travel any further. Got quite a bad wound but being a bullet it was not torn much and there was nothing left in. Three ribs were smashed, so had to have an operation and they removed several inches. Wound is about the 9th rib, went in at the back and out at the front. Some splinters penetrated my lung and am still spitting blood. It took 18 stitches to sew up the cut they made. However, I have never gone back any, always improving, can sit up a little in bed and hope in a week at least to be able to be out and move around a bit. I soon tire of lying in bed.[50]

I wonder if you got any cable from Ottawa for I neglected to change your address when you went west. But John would surely get it anyway. I hope there are not so many rumours as was the last time, and that you will not think of the worst to happen. I sent a card from the C.C.S. you will soon be getting that as it is two weeks now since I sent it. There are no other Canadians in this ward, but there are several in the hospital. A Canadian Red Cross Visitor called on me yesterday and she had a list of names. I only know one, Babcock, from near Lanark. I never knew him at home but met him in France last winter with Mell Paul. Will call on him as soon as I can get up. Have an Australian next cot to me.

I am sending my address to the Batt. P.O. Clerk and also to the Record Office London, so should not be long before I get my mail back from France. The Red Cross lady is bringing me in some papers.

There are 2000 beds in this hospital and it is in the heart of the city. All serious cases here and of course the staff are of the very best obtainable.

Well how is everybody out there? Harvesting will be in full swing I expect. Is the crop good and how are they off for help? The Americans are certainly doing good work in France. I suppose your papers will be full of their deeds of valour. The tide is turned but I do not think Peace will come this year. I don't expect to see France myself again, if I can help it though. I think my fighting days are over.

Now I think this is all for today will write at least once a week. This letter will do the three of you. Paper is very scarce and dear over here now.

Love to all,
Herb

P.S. Be sure to put number of my Batt. on address.

151

London
August 2, 1918

Dear Brother and Sister,

I guess you will be looking your eyes out for a letter long before this gets there.[51] Well, I thought there was not much use writing until I got to Blighty and could send my address.

I got hit on the 14th July and got over here on the 30th. Was ten days at the Casualty Clearing Station[52] before I was able to travel any further. We were just two days in the line after our two months rest, when out on patrol one morning, I got this. It was a machine gun did the trick. I was lying on my side, one bullet got me in the back about the ninth rib and came out in front, another took the depth of itself out of my leg below the hip and a third went through the side of my boot just scratching my skin. Three of my ribs were so badly smashed they had to operate and I am minus several inches of staves. Some splinters penetrated my lung and I am still spitting blood. I required some stitches to sew me up where they cut but that is all healed up nicely now. Am able to sit up in bed a while. I soon got tired lying on my back or at

least sort of half sitting and lying, for if I lie down flat I should choke
right away. I thought I was hit in the stomach, I was so sick, but with
the aid of a pal I managed to get into the trenches and came out of
there on a stretcher. Now you don't need to worry for I am in a good
place and getting the best of treatment. This is a very large hospital,
2000 beds. I am about the fourth story, and can't hear the noise from
the street at all. There are a few Canadians here but none in this ward.
Our Canadian Red Cross visitor called on me yesterday and had a list
of names. Only one I know is Babcock from Lanark. I did not know
him back home, but met him in France last winter. He was in the 38th.
The Red Cross lady is bringing me some papers today. I do hope there
is no bad rumours this time like the last. I suppose you will be finishing
up haying and starting harvest. Guess I would not pitch much hay
these days. Just two years since I was to your place with Mother. Dear
me what changes in that time and how many people have gone from
around home. I sometimes think they are the better off too. It hurts
my side, so as this is two I have written this morning I will have to stop.
Remember me to all inquiring friends.

Love to all,
Your loving brother,
Herb

Aug. 3: Rainy. Some visitors but none for me. Wrote some letters.

Aug. 4: Fine. Remembrance Day.

Aug. 5: Fine. Everything as per usual.

Aug. 6: Fair. My Red Cross visitor called again with cigarettes and
Canadian papers.

152

August 6, 1918
Canadian Red Cross Society
12 Berners St. London

787167 Pte. J.H. Gibson 75th Battalion
King George Hospital Stamford St. Waterloo London.

Dear Madam or Sir,

Our visitor sends us the cheering report that Pte. Gibson is going
on quite nicely and is very bright and jolly, which always helps a lot. We

hope to have even better news for you next week. Meantime, write to him often.

Yours truly,
B. Masterton Smith

Aug. 7: Fair. Visiting day. But none for yours truly.

Aug. 8: Fair. Received some mail to day and cheque from pay office. Sent cable home. 75th took Le Quesnel. Capt. Cummins killed also Major Bull. Gray wounded. 8th of August Amiens drive started. 75th men killed at Amiens drive buried at Beaucourt and Le Quesnel.

Aug. 9: Fair. Very quiet today. Red Cross lady called with money for cheque.

Aug. 10: Warm. Australian and I had two visitors in afternoon.

Aug. 11: Warm.

153

King George Hospital
Stamford St.
Waterloo, London
Ward E3
Aug. 11, 1918

Dear Sister,

This is your Birthday and I have been thinking of you all day so now this evening I'll write a letter which will help to pass the time away, for it seems to hang rather heavily on one's hands, while lying here in bed. Of course I'm not complaining, for I am thankful to be here and I might be a good deal worse. I can sit up now, my cough and spitting blood has stopped, sleep well, eat well, so you see I have a lot to be thankful for. I think by next Sunday I'll be able to be up in the afternoon at least. I wrote to H. McNicol but have got no answer yet. Wish I had Willie McNicol's address.

Well I wonder what you are all doing out there. I expect you will be worrying your days about me after you got that telegram. No need to worry for I'm quite alright. Remember me to all the people and I send my love to you, Jane and Lester.

Au Revoir,
Herb

Aug. 12: Several local letters.

154

King George Hospital
Stamford St.
Waterloo, London
Aug. 12, 1918

Dear May,

Here I am again to trouble you with my tales of "weal or woe." I'm going to tell you of life as I find it in one of London's large hospitals. The building is six stories, with every modern convenience and contains 2000 beds. The roof is flat of course and there are shelters and seats up there for the patients who are out of bed to go for an airing. I have not been up yet, but I know there must be a fine view of the city. There are bus and automobile drives arranged too for those who can go out and they also get passes in the afternoon from 1 to 7, so when I get up I intend to see some more of London. My Australian friend who is in the next cot and I are going out. There are 28 beds in this ward and almost all occupied at the present time. The patients are all Imperials except we two Colonials. Shall I tell you of them? Two have lost their right legs, one has just come in with a new artificial one. Two others are paralized from the waist down. I feel sorry for them. Another has a very nasty wound in the head. I am told he has had half his brains removed but I scarcely credit it. Several more have wounds in the arms or legs and the rest of us in the chest. One poor chap across the floor from me, well I'm sorry for him, he's lost all his smiling powers if he ever had any. Not that he is any worse wounded than the others and he just sits there with a face as long as the Moral Law. Makes a chap feel lonely to watch him. Then we have a Jock,[53] he's a pill, just as much the reverse of the other fellow.

We have breakfast at 7 A.M. after which the beds are made and the sweeping and dusting done. Then the dressing of wounds. There are two day sisters and they seem to be kept busy too. Twelve noon is dinner and at two the doors are open to visitors. Of course, I have none but like to see other lads people come in. At four there is lunch and then we have a wash—in bed of course. Evening mail comes in and there is the usual discussion of events at the front. Seven P.M. is supper and at eight the night sister comes on. Nine o'clock all "up" patients must be in bed and lights out. The night is sometimes broken by spells of wakefulness,

either by your own troubles or someone elses. Six o'clock we are woken
for another wash and temperatures taken and it's breakfast time again.
Between times we fill in as best we can, reading or writing and with the
gramophone. So you have an idea how we spend day after day. Seems
hard for me even to be a month in bed, but fellows have been in this
hospital over a year.[54]

I expect to be up in the afternoons pretty soon now. Will have to go
easy for awhile as my side is very weak yet.

My old pal O.R. Gorman of the R.A.F. is coming to see me this
week. I shall be glad to see an old face. The Red Cross visitor brought
me a *Courier* to day, t'was like getting money from home. I expect some
mail back from France any day now. They will be old, but welcome
never the less. The Canadians are in the thick of the scrapping over
there again.[55] We trained for this stunt for one and a half months while
out of the line and here I missed it after all. Do you know, in a way, I
would liked to have been there. I have never been in an advance at all.
Lots of souvenirs you know, although I never was a hunter of them.
Had a few, but one was a Fritz dagger, was sorry to leave it behind. Well,
May, I hope I have not tired you with this scribble. Must stop now so
Good Night and Pleasant Dreams.

Sincerely,
Herb

Aug. 13: Slept most of day. Had a bath.

Aug. 14: Warm. O.R. Gorman called bringing chocolate and cigarettes. Four
letters from France.

155

Aug. 14, 1918

Dear Sir or Madam,

787167 Pte. J.H. Gibson 75th Battalion King George's Hospital
Stamford St. London was seen by our authorized Red Cross visitor
quite recently. She reports that the report is about the same, that he is
going on slowly but is quite cheerful and bright. A further report will be
sent next week regarding his condition.

Yours truly,
B. Masterton Smith

156

London
August 14, 1918

Dear May,

Hurrah! Guess how many letters I got today, yes, Canadian ones returned from France, and they are only six weeks old. Now you will be thinking I got a sack full, but only got four. Welcome as the flowers in May though and I expect more any day. Just wrote to you the other day, but must answer this fine long one and try to make up for that three weeks eh! Sorry May, if you missed them. I know how I have missed yours this last two months. I wonder how you get time to write, you seem to be the main spoke in the wheel around there. Well I shouldn't work too hard anyway, if I were you. Rome was not built in a day you know. No I don't know anything about an adding machine, have heard of such things, they must be a fine invention. Ten cents isn't a very great mistake, I'm sure. May, I think I would be as many dollars out, ha. So you never noticed any difference in the letters only those you didn't get, perhaps they were done in invisible ink. Sure thing, we talked often of home and people and things more especially where there were girls and eats. We never tired of talking about apple pie and cream puffs etc etc. Do you think Ethel will want an Airman? Ernie used to make me laugh—you know we were together a lot in June and July—the way he would talk of home and the war and when we get back what we'll do etc. Must write to him soon but will not say anything of what you told me.

Now come on and tell me that "funny thing someone said." I really can't wait for that indefinite time. Remember May, there is no censor between us now, so lets 'ave it. I think I told you all about the sports (I'm just writing this as I read your letter over so won't miss anything.) We had no thunder storms but it was hot enough for me. I am glad to hear that Mr. Keays is improving. Is Lorne doing all the work? He will be very busy if he is. I sent Elsie a Whiz Bang just for fun, about two months ago. I had a bundle of them and just addressed them to who ever I could think of and sent them off, about 15 at once.

It's really hard for me to believe that all those boys have gone. I don't see why they could not have been left at home until after harvest. I don't quite get this registration business. Do the girls have to register too? I'm sure I'd liked to have seen you V.A.D.'s march "Left Right Left, pick it up, there in the rear and Cover off"—is that it?[56]

G.G.'s Band up to Perth for a social. Well some class eh.[57]

I must tell you that I had a visitor today, my old pal O.R. Gorman called. You bet I was glad to see him. He looks real smart in his R.A.F. uniform, will soon be getting his stars. He has just finished one exam and is on leave before going to another school. Expect he will be up tomorrow again. He's away out to Regents Palace tonight.

Have another old hospital pal (Lamb by name, I think I told you of him before) coming next Sunday. He is a Sergt. in the Canadian Battalion now.

Say, May, if any of the boys are overseas will you try and send me their address. I might have a chance to see them.

Eight-twenty now, soon be lights out, so will ring off. Bon Soir, Pleasant dreams. I send you my love if I may take the liberty and trust you will accept a little bit anyway.

Sincerely,

Herb

Aug. 15: Feeling very good. Gorman spent afternoon with me.

Aug. 16: Got up for 1st time. Went up on roof. Got tired very quickly.

Aug. 17: Up afternoon. Sergt. Lamb called afternoon for a few moments.

Aug. 18: Two lady visitors. Also Mr. and Mrs. Parnwell called.

Aug. 19: Fine. Up afternoon.

Aug. 20: Warm. Pte. Lamb came up and spent the afternoon.

Aug. 21: Warm. Messers. Parnwell called. Up all day.

Aug. 22: Hot. Cpl. Moffat and I went out in afternoon for a stroll. No buses.

Aug. 23: Moffat, Pollard and I went to Madame Tussauds and picture Galleries and St. James Park.

Aug. 24: Visited Mr. Young's at West Norwood. Girls took us to Crystal Palace. Pleasant afternoon.

Aug. 25: Rainy. Hyde Park and naval pictures.

Aug. 26: Came to Ontario Hospital, Orpington.

157

Canadian Red Cross Society
12 Berners St. London
August 26, 1918

787167 Pte. J.H. Gibson 75th Battalion (1st Cent. Ont. Reg.)
King George's Stamford St. London

Dear Sir or Madam,

The latest report from our Red Cross visitor is very good. She tells us that Pte. Gibson is now up and able to go out.
With best wishes.

Yours truly,
B. Masterton Smith

Aug. 27: Cool. Writing. Went to concert in YMCA in afternoon.

158

No. 16 Canadian General Hosp.
Orpington, Kent England
August 27, 1918

Dear Sisters,

A short note today with my new address. I have not been here long enough to tell you how I will like the place but at least the air is fresher than in London. Came here yesterday and hard to tell how long I will stay or where I go from here. Have been up for the last ten days and although a little weak am gaining.

I hope soon to get a letter direct from you and then I promise to write a long one in answer. Hoping this finds you all well.

Love to all,
Herb

P.S. Address as above not forgetting to put Ward 36.

Aug. 28: Cool. Helped some in ward. Pictures and concert in afternoon. 75th moved to Arras.

Aug. 29: Warm. Took a walk to Orpington. Concert at night. 75th at Neuville-Vitasse.

Aug. 30: Cool. X-rayed in morning.

159

No. 16 Canadian General Hosp.
Orpington Kent
August 30, 1918

Dear Sister,

This is a nice warm morning, after a cool spell that we have had. It is just after eleven and I am just back from being X-rayed. The doctor gave me a look over yesterday and evidently found something wrong about my ribs so sent me down to have the electric "photo" taken. This is the first X-ray machine I have ever seen and it sure is some contrivance. My back and chest are quite painful yet at times and I am weak and short of breath. Doctor sent me to get weighed yesterday also, to see if I gain any in the weeks to come. He seems a very nice man and willing to do all he can for the men. Tomorrow I will see the "photo" and find out what is the matter. Don't worry though, I eat and sleep well. I do some light jobs about the ward for the sister. She is very nice. Is married and comes from Vancouver.

Went out for a walk yesterday afternoon, to the village of Orpington. It is about the size of Middleville, only has a railroad of course. Most of the boys in the ward are waiting to go home now, nice time to go back isn't it! Wouldn't mind if I were going too, however I don't expect ever to go back to France again.

Have not got any mail for awhile, surely I should get some direct soon.

There is moving pictures in the "Y" every afternoon and a concert every evening. Have some real good artists come down from London to entertain the troops. Westerham is only a short distance from here and perhaps I may take a trip over there some day. I think I will be able to travel some this fall but it can't be done without some money so I wish you would send me some. I may as well see all of this country I can while here, what do you think? Come to count up, I have only had five days leave (excepting sick Furlough) since I left home over two years ago so have not travelled much. We can get one pound a month in hospital, but everything is so expensive. I spend most my money in eatables, for a change from army grub, even in hospital it gets tasteless. So you might send me some of my wages, $20 will do and you better use money order and register the letter to make sure.

War news is good isn't it?

Trusting this finds you all well. Will say goodbye.

Love to you all,
Herb

Aug. 31: Cool. Medical inspection in morning by Major. Went to Green Street in afternoon.

160

No. 16 Canadian General Hosp.
Orpington Kent
August 31/18

Dear May,

I have started to ramble once more. "If you want to see the world," why, just join the army.

Came down here last Monday and this is only Saturday, perhaps next Saturday I'll be some where else. The Major comes around every Sat. morning on a tour of inspection so he had a look at "yours truly." Seemed well pleased, said I was doing well, recommended me to be sent to Kingswood Hospital as I was not fit for Convalescent yet. Such is life, however it takes a great deal of this to kill a chap, what do you think? I do nothing but eat and sleep and take a stroll daily for exercise. This is the first Canadian Hospital I have ever been in. It's quite a large place, all huts, and is very nicely situated near the village of Orpington which is only 15 miles from London. Cook's big poultry farm is here. Perhaps you have heard of it. Someday I mean to visit it. We get out in the afternoons every day and can get passes to London but as I just came from there have no inclination to go up. The YMCA provided us with entertainment. Pictures and Concert parties come down from the city to amuse the troops and some of them are hard to beat.

Something doing across "yonder" now. My Battalion has suffered quite heavily in Officers. My old Company Commander has been killed also my Platoon Officer.[58] The Canadians are still upholding their name and have given Fritz a couple of shocks. I think by this time next year that it will be all over. You may not see all the troops home then for it will take months to get us all home. Won't it be a happy day when the bands begin to play "It's a long long way to Tipperary." Have you heard that new song? Rather nice I think. Well, May, I suppose Perth is much the same as usual, any fun at all? Don't work too hard and have all the fun you can. By the way, I never hear who visits the cement block house[59] at all now, ha ha. 'Fess up now don't be shy.

Au Revoir,
Sincerely,
Herb

Sept. 1: Cool. Service at 10:30. Walk in P.M. 75th lost heavily. Dr. Hutcheson won Victoria Cross. Col. Harbottle wounded at Vis-en-Artois, Drocourt-Queant Line, Dury Mill.

Sept. 2: Cool. Went for walk to St. Mary Gray in afternoon.

Sept. 3: Fine. Helped to clean windows in morning. Letter from O.R. Gorman.

Sept. 4: Cool. Nothing new at all. Concert.

Sept. 5: Cool. Bunch of mail from home.

Sept. 6: Fine. Transferred to Massey-Harris home, Kingswood Dulwich London.

Sept. 7: Fine. Grand place. Went to city in P.M.

Sept. 8: Church service. Went to Footing Bec.

161

Massey-Harris Convalescent House
London S.E. 21
Sept. 8, 1918

My Dear May,

Have not had a letter from you for some time but never the less must drop a line.

Well here I am back in London after a ten day stay at the Canadian General Hospital at Orpington. I did not like that place, so the less I say about it the better, but this oh! Some place, some home! I'll not say anything about the house. You will be able to judge from the cards.[60] I may say though that the floors are polished, walls of panelled oak with deep borders of hand painting, windows coloured glass. The grounds, comprising some 30 acres, are simply grand. One of the cards shows you a glimpse of the gardens. There are bowling greens, tennis courts, in fact everything for the hearts desire. I only wish you could come and see it. We are five minutes from the famous Crystal Palace and a half hour by bus to the city. One would never know they were in London, plenty of fresh air, not a bit like smoky old King George at Waterloo. By the city I mean the Strand, Whitehall, Fleet St. etc. etc. We are allowed to go where we like between the hours of 2–9 P.M. so I went up to Westminster yesterday P.M. Yes and I must tell you about the board. You know that's what a soldier thinks of first, everything else take a second place. We get all we can put away. Not rich stuff, but real wholesome food. I thought three course dinners were a thing of the past but got a surprise of my life when we went to dinner here. The Major says I will be a long time in hospital yet so I am hoping to stay here for sometime—do you blame me? The Massey-Harris people have this property rented I believe and maintain it themselves. Now May, I expect a letter from you soon so will close this one as it is almost noon and I must not be late for dinner. Will enclose two cards, more later.

Trusting this finds you in the best of good spirits (no not McLaren's ha).[61]

Sincerely,

Herb

Card #1: The northside and part of the moat which you can just see. I think I sent you one of the lake. I have marked X at my room window.

Sept. 9: Invitation by Red Cross to new theatre play "The Chinese Puzzle."

Sept. 10: Fine. Went to Brixton to free show.

Sept. 11: Cool. Visited at Mr. and Mrs. Youngs in afternoon.

Sept. 12: Cool. Wrote some letters. Went to Empress theatre in evening at Brixton.

162

Sept. 12, 1918

Dear Sister,

I have not written for sometime, was waiting for a letter from you, but I've got tired waiting. Whenever I don't get mail I write some then usually in a few days get a bunch.

You will see by the above that I have changed my place of abode again and have struck a home this time. This is in the residential part of this wonderful city and is sure a lovely place, up on a hill. The house or mansion, rather, is in the middle of the grounds which are about 30 acres in extent. These cards will give you an idea of what it is like. There are about sixty here. We get all the good things to eat and plenty of it. Are allowed to go where we wish from 1–9 P.M. so I have been over good bit of the city. On Monday the Red Cross people invited us to the theatre and gave us the best seats. Tonight ten of us are to get to the Brixton Theatre and tomorrow there is a trip up the Thames River. We have been having very showery weather but I hope tomorrow is fine as we are to have tea on the deck. Guess I will put on some flesh here eh.

Just as I expected you would all get in a state when you got the cable. John had been cabling London after they saw the report in the paper. I do wish those Editors would not be so quick printing that sort of news. I suppose I was "dangerously wounded" but it never struck me in that light, perhaps that is the reason I recovered so quickly, I never worried over it.[62] My side and back is sore yet but in time I will be quite alright. Almost two months now since I got it.

I hope you are all fine out there. Suppose the threshing will be in full swing now. I must write to Maggie some of these days. Did you get up there yet?

I have been chumming with a chap from Morris. Moffat is his name. Well Clara this is all for today and I hope to hear from you soon.

Your loving brother,
Herb

Sept. 13: Fine. Boating trip down the Thames in P.M. Tea on board.

Sept. 14: Showery. Went to Strand to meet O.R. but missed him so went to picture palace. Supper at Eagle Hut.

Sept. 15: Fine. Visited K.G. Hospital.[63]

Sept. 16: Mountjoy and I went to the city P.M.

163

Massey-Harris Convalescent Home
Kingswood Dulwich London
Sept. 16, 1918

Dear May,

Now I have three of your letters which came in a bunch of thirty, so will answer them all in this one, beginning at the oldest one. In the first place I want to thank you May, for all the kind letters, they always brought a ray of sunshine into the deepest dugout or littlest funk-hole, but don't think for a moment that I will not prize them just as highly over here.

July 21st you had heard of that rather ominous telegram. And I see someone has been good enough to put my "phiz" in the papers again. I never wished notoriety and don't really deserve any for what have I done, only three months in the line, wounded, back to Blighty for almost nine, then eight and a half more and another Blighty. And still I have all my limbs and my eyesight and as for the chest, I hope that time will see it right as ever. So after all May, am I not very lucky? The fighting I spoke of has come off, but I did not stay to see it. More deeds of valour for the Canadian troops but sad to say many casualties. Most of my Battalion officers are gone, about eight more in the lists today.

I have had two letters from E. Ferrier lately. He was still O.K. and collecting souvenirs.

Not at all surprised to hear of Myles being married. Wonder what he is working at?

Last letter of August 18th was not so long on the way. You were going on your holidays then and I am sure you would enjoy those two weeks. Perhaps I will be home for your next holidays, but don't miss any for me ha. I might not arrive.

Oh, May! have you had to pay any postage on stampless letters from me? There were a few which I did not get the hospital stamp on. Be sure and tell me if you did. Will ring off now.

With best regards,
Herb

P.S. Most of the boys have gone to the theatre this A.M.

JHG

Sept. 17: Not feeling well so stayed in.

Sept. 18: Better today. Wrote some letters and went out after supper.

Sept. 19: River trip up Richmond way. Tea on board.

Sept. 20: Went up to Strand. Afternoon tea at Eagle Hut.

Sept. 21: Garden party given by Mr. J. Pearce. Spent a very enjoyable afternoon Thursly Rd.

Sept. 22: Cool. Visitors from Brighton.

Sept. 23: Fair. Went to Mme. Taussaud's and to Australian YMCA for tea.

Sept. 24: Fine. To Brixton picture palace. Tea at Herne Hill and called at Mr. Young's.

164

Massey-Harris Convalescent Home
London
Sept. 24, 1918

Dear Sister,

This is a lovely cool morning and I have just finished my little job for the morning. I clean up our ward, sweep and dust etc. Everybody has a little chore to do about the home after breakfast and then between tea and eleven we all go out in the gardens and help keep it in shape. There are only two gardeners left and they have to grow all the vegetables we use. I have been quite busy, do you know, going places. Had another trip up the Thames last week and then on Saturday we were all invited to a garden party at a Mr. Pearce's home. We had games a fine tea and then some singing and speeches. We certainly spent a very enjoyable afternoon. Yesterday, three of us went to the Wax Museum in the afternoon. I had been there twice before but the others wanted me to take them. You see I know something about London now. Intend going to the Tower of London this week. Then there are Theatre parties and another concert this week. So we are spending a very good time, are we not? I got thirty letters one day, have not got them all answered yet. Had one from Ida.[64] Tell her I will write to her next week. She says you don't go to see her very often. Now you must try and over look any little faults there may be. You know there is none of us perfect. I am glad you have got a nice girl friend to go out with. It will be some one to confide in and that is quite a deal.

My old chum O.R. Gorman has got his commission in the R.A.F. Say did you ever get the pictures he and I sent you last fall? Be sure and let me know if you did and if you sent the one to Mrs. Gorman. I am very sorry to hear that Jane had to go to hospital.[65] I do hope they could do something to help her. I am anxious to know how she got along. Write soon and let me know. Will write next week again so all for this morning.

Your loving brother,

Herb

Sept. 25: Fine. Went with YMCA party to the Palladium. Tea at Eagle Hut.

Sept. 26: Fine. At Brixton pavilion to see "The Splendid Coward" M. Streathern gave concert.

Sept. 27: Fine. Chum and I went to Leister Square to show. Tea at Beaver Hut. 75th took Bourlon Wood.

Sept. 28: Fine. Went to Clapham Com. in afternoon. Got home early tonight.

Sept. 29: Rained all day.

Sept. 30: Tea and entertainment given by Royal Colonial Institute at Savoy hotel.

Oct. 1: Fine. Went down to the Strand P.M. Home for tea. Pass changed to 8:00 P.M.

165

Kingswood, London
Oct. 1, 1918

Dear May,

Here's another three letters to be answered together, one of Aug. and two of Sept. I must say that you have certainly been a great correspondent and I am ashamed to send back my little letters. You see I have only myself to write about and that is not a nice thing to do is it?

Well! May, the time has been changed to the proper time again and as it is dark at 6:30 we have to be in at 8 P.M. instead of 9 P.M., small boys ha. What would I say if you came around to tuck me into bed? I'd repeat the chorus of that song "Goodnight Nurse." Have you heard it? It was sung to us at an entertainment yesterday given us by the Royal Colonial Institute at Hotel Savoy, London. Some class! eh. A special bus came for and brought us home. We had tea and then some of the best talent in London entertained us. About 400 men from the Colonies were there and a few Americans. You think I'll never come back to Canada if I get too familiar with London. Well, I am getting quite used to travelling about the city but I'd scarcely trade the white brick on the 8th for this.[66]

This is Wed. morning, got too sleepy to finish last night. Only sleep ten hours a night, hardly enough is it? Don't just know yet what I'll do today, perhaps go over to London Tower and see the sights. Have seen it before but could stand it again.

Glad to hear that the picnic turned out successful and you had a good time. I don't believe I could do a square dance now but May, I'll tell you what I could do, put away some pie or ice cream. Ha. Quite an idea selling little pigs, I'm sure. Do you have any flag days now. We have about two a week. I hope those snaps are good. I'd like one now please. Yes I have been up by the place you speak of. I don't expect to be here a great while longer now. Not many stay longer than six weeks. I'm here four on Friday.

So long,
All the time,
Herb

166

Kingswood, London
Oct. 1, 1918

Dear Sister,

Received yours of Sept. 5th this morning so I'll not delay but just answer tonight. Not a great while since I wrote so have not much news but will tell what little I have. You were well supplied with news about me I think. I never thought of the Sisters writing. I think it must have been the Scottish sister who wrote. They were all very nice but I never found out their names, guess I wasn't caring much what their names were, only Sister to me. John seems to have got all the cables, must have been three or four. The Red Cross people did pretty well for me, used to send up fruit twice a week but the visitor never had long to stay.

I wish you had told me what questions you wanted answered, I could perhaps have filled up this letter with them.

All you folks at home seem to think that I am trying to make light of my wounds but I can truthfully say that they are slight compared with some I see. A bullet through the chest is bad enough but lots are far worse. Then mine being a bullet is different from shrapnel.

I may not be in this place very long now as they do not keep men here much longer than a month. Will be here four weeks next Friday and have certainly gained flesh. The side is quite tender and weak yet but is coming along fine.

I am very sorry to hear that Jane is troubled with her leg again. Could they not do anything for her at the hospital? I am glad you like living there. You will be such company and help to her and Ida too. I think it an awful pity that any trouble ever was between any one of us. I hope that some day before it is too late that we will see the folly of it all.

I would not mind having a meal in the old caboose again either. Is Mary or Dorothy not married yet? Did John Nairn get married? Well I guess there are a few changes since I drove the sorrels on the tank.[67]

Have a great amount of writing to do these days. Only got fifty letters this last ten days. People who never wrote before and I suppose forgot there was such a person as I, until they saw a note in the Era. Pays to advertise eh. I'll just name a few and I bet you will be more surprised than I,—Lena Paul, Uisley; Mrs. R. Hart, Brandon; D. Fisher, Perth; L. Cavers, Harper; Janet McInnes, Smiths Falls; M.P. MacDonald, Ottawa and several more. If I visit all the places and stay as long as I have been invited to, I'll not need to work for about four years after I get home. But of course after the excitement dies down, they will forget. Well anyhow there is always the old "standbys." Oh! we were to a tea and entertainment yesterday afternoon given by the Royal Colonial Institute at the Savoy Hotel London. Some class, some tea, and the best stars of the stage on the program. There were about 300 overseas men.

Good night, sweet dreams,
Affectionately,
Herb

P.S. Will write to Ida next week.

Oct. 2: Rainy. Wrote some letters and to Clapham Jct. in afternoon. Pancakes for tea.

Oct. 3: Fine. Mountjoy and I went to Clapham concert by Miss Levey.

Oct. 4: Fine. Went downtown in P.M. Tea at Beaver Hut.

Oct. 5: Rainy. Mountjoy and I went to Brixton to show. Tea at Brixton and went to palace.

Oct. 6: Fine. Friend up from Horley.

Oct. 7: Fair. Downtown. War bond campaign on at Trafalgar Square. In mess now.

Oct. 8: Fair. Serving in the dining hall.

167

Kingswood, London
Oct. 8, 1918

Dear May,

Just a line today to say that I am still 'ir "swinging the lead." Been here a month now and not got kicked out yet, but I understand a Col. from Orpington is here today to look us over so watch for yours truly going down the hay road talking to himself ha.

Well anyhow I have spent a good time here and naturally hate to leave it but we can't always be in clover, besides I hear there is a war on. Went down to the city yesterday afternoon to see the sights. It was opening day of the new War Bond Offensive and the main attack was pulled off on the Trafalgar Square front. They fixed it up to represent a ruined French village behind the lines. This souvenir will explain and in some ways they made it very real indeed.[68] There was, of course, a great crowd, perhaps more than you would see at all our Fall Fairs combined, rich and poor alike. Isn't it interesting to watch a crowd of people and see the different types and expressions on their faces? Did you ever try it?

What think you of the War now May? Is it going to be over soon? We have made splendid gains but not without a cost. Our men claim to have cut the enemy down in heaps at Cambrai. On the other hand my Battalion came out of it with sixty-six men all told.[69] It is getting like winter again isn't it. I wear my great coat when I go out. All the fairs and everything will be over now and you will have a rest until Christmas entertainments start.

I am looking forward to spending Xmas and New Years in this country, last two in the trenches, this one in, well, a better place. Hope to get a letter from you soon now. Must close as it is almost noon and I help in the dining hall, thereby getting a pass until 10 P.M. instead of 8 P.M.

So long,
Herb

Enclosed also is program of concert given us by "Mummie."

Oct. 9: Rainy. Went over to Norwood but nobody home. Went to Brixton.

Oct. 10: Fair. Party went to Brixton Empress theatre.

Oct. 11: Rainy. Show at Brixton in evening.

Oct. 12: Rainy. To city in afternoon. West Norwood and Herne Hill in evening. Backshee pictures

Oct. 13: Met old friend of 1916.

Oct. 14: Fine. Bunch of us invited to see "The Female Hun" at Lyceum.

Oct. 15: Fine. Stayed in and had a sleep. To Crystal Palace in evening.

Oct. 16: Fine. Called on Col. Harbottle. Tea with Pte.'s Saunders and Armstrong.

Oct. 17: Stayed in until after tea. Out to Gypsy Hill.

168

Kingswood, London
Oct. 17, 1918

My Dear May,

First of all I must thank you for the nice parcel which I received today. I think I am the luckiest chap to have such friends as you. Also got one from my sister Mary E. today. I have eaten so much sweets that I'm afraid I won't be able to do justice to supper. Awful glad to be answering two of your letters today. You understand they come in "massed formation." Today something like twelve this attack, and now for the counter-attack! I hope I am able to reach my objective ha. Delighted to hear of all the doings, "especially after the garden parties" and the Show Fairs etc etc. Now you don't surely think I was trying to, er, "pull your leg," I merely asked those questions for something to say. I think I mentioned once before of being tired writing about myself. However if you look upon my silence as a bit suspicious perhaps I will tell you a little. I don't say that I have had absolutely nothing to do with the English girls (or Tarts). One can't walk about here in blue and not be noticed and out of the many I have met there are two, shall I say "specials." One I met two years ago while in London and the other while in hospital in 1917. They have both come to visit me, are very nice sensible girls, none of the "Flappers" sort for me. Perhaps it is wrong to be making pastime friendships but can you blame a fellow and besides so long as one keeps within the limits of respectability, there is no harm done.

Your letter of Sept. 9th spoke of something I sent you and May, like you, I hope to give with all my heart. It is rather a delicate subject to write upon and I feel that I can't say more today. I don't suppose that the barriers, which we once spoke of being between us, can be easily moved.[70] I don't think I have mentioned before, how I would love to see you again May. I imagine you will think this a very strange letter. My heart is too full to write.

Goodbye and best wishes,

Herb

168A ("Feed the Guns" postcard) 17-10-18

This is a view of Trafalgar Square made to represent a ruined French village, a scheme to promote the buying of the new War Bonds. It was not quite complete when this was taken. At night they shine war pictures on the canvas at the base of Nelson's monument which you can see on the right. More people at this place than at Perth Fair.

JHG

Oct. 18: Foggy. Went up to Crystal Palace in evening.

Oct. 19: London fog. Over to Mr. Young's in afternoon. To Brixton in evening. Met couple of very nice girls. Received letter from Jane.

Oct. 20: Raining. Visitor from Horley.

Oct. 21: Fair. Returned to Orpington. Met Sgt. Teasdale and Askew and Pte. Sykes.

Oct. 22: Cool. Mountjoy and I went to Bromley in P.M.

Oct. 23: Cool. Pictures in YMCA in P.M. Took walk to Orpington.

Oct. 24: Fair. Went to picture show at Bromley "Kaiser, Beast of Berlin."

Oct. 25: Fair. Stayed in. Concert in Y at night.

169

No. 16 Can. General Hospital
Orpington, Kent
Oct. 25, 1918

Dear May,

I must write to you again today for since my last have got some of
yours of July and early August. You mention getting the news that I had
been killed. Well, May, why should I have been spared when others are
called upon to make the great sacrifice. Yes, indeed I do remember that
summer evening when we drove and chatted together and it makes me
ask the question, Has absence made the heart grow fonder? and do you
really care so very much that I should return? You remember we did not
make any promises, and I think it was the very best way, don't you? You
have been my very best friend. Your letters always brought cheer into
billet, trench or dugout and I have seen you in my dreams and thought
of you when on outpost and patrol. I think my very first thoughts when
I was hit was "what will May think?" Had I not had someone to, as it
were reach out to me in "No Man's Land" that morning, I believe I
should have stayed there. There seems to be something in the air that
keeps a man from losing his senses in a fight, when hit, for I remember
almost fainting once with a cut finger. I also believe in the power of
prayer and when I get home I have a story to tell you of what I saw one
night. You have heard of the Comrade in White at Mons.[71]

You were wondering if I had got my German. Well I could hardly
prove it. It did not seem to be for me to do that part of it. Oh, I better
stop now, getting uninteresting.

Very quiet around here, so much so indeed, that my chum and I
have put in for a pass to go up to the "smoke"[72] tomorrow and got it
too, so 7 A.M. 26th will see us on the way to London town. Yesterday
we went over to a place called Bromley to the pictures. It was a new film
"Kaiser, Beast of Berlin," and was good indeed. This evening there is a
concert in the YMCA which I intend taking in.

We have some great arguments in the ward. They are about half
and half Imperials "Woodbines" we call them and Canadians. We kid
them about what we can do etc etc. Gee, they don't like it. I'll mention
one instance where we got ahead of the famous British soldiers. The 4th
Division were to take a certain part of the famous Hindenburg Line. An

Imperial Brigade was to help our 10th Brigade to get the first objective. Imperial Brigadier said "it is impossible, my men can't take it." "Very well," says Currie "we will take it ourselves" and did so. There is more discipline in the Canadian than British army. Sister has just been holding my hand. I feel fluttery in the region of the pumping station. Say we have some very ancient ones here and you should see the way they powder up. ha ha—trying to look young.

Well May here's hoping for a good day tomorrow and a letter from you soon.

Sincerely,
Herb

Oct. 26: Fine. Mountjoy and I went to London. Met two friends and had a good time. Went by bus. Home by train.

Oct. 27: Fair. Walked to Farnborough in evening.

Oct. 28: Fine. Stayed in to have board papers finished.

Oct. 29: Fine. Picture in YMCA. Did not go out.

Oct. 30: Fair. Pictures in P.M. To Green Street green for a stroll.

Oct. 31: Rainy. Down to Orpington for walk in evening.

Nov. 1: Very rainy weather so stayed at home am. Went to Biggin Hill aerodrome P.M.

Nov. 2: Fair. Bunch of us went to Bromley to show.

Nov. 3: Rainy. Church service. 75th took Estreux.

Nov. 4: Cold. Went to bed in afternoon.

Nov. 5: Fair. Mountjoy and I went to Bromley show "Out of Bounds."

Nov. 6: Fair. Pictures in afternoon. Walk to the village in evening.

Nov. 7: Fair. Letter writing. Concert by the Biggin Hill RAF.

Nov. 8: Rainy. Bunch leave for Canada. Also Imperials go on months leave.

170

No. 16 Canadian General Hosp.
Orpington, Kent
Nov. 8, 1918

Dear Sister,

Yours of Oct. 15th and glad to hear from you again. So you are home again from Tyner, $1.25 per day is pretty fair wages, more than I get.

We have a lot of sickness over here, too, have this "flu" all over the country. Several cases in this hospital but so far I have escaped it. I am helping in the ward now, getting meals for the bed patients. I do not know how long I will be here. They had my papers made out for a Canada Board last week but changed their mind so do not know where they will send me. About 90 left for home yesterday and a bunch going Monday. Nice to get home for Xmas eh! However, I think we shall all go home soon. Germany has until 11 A.M. tomorrow to say yes or no. Even if they do not accept our terms now, a very few months will settle them.

You do more motoring than in Ontario. I guess we will have to get one when I get home. Better decide what kind and also learn to drive so you can take me out for my outings.

Seem to be nice people you visited. Did you give them my address? The girls I mean!

Today is the Lord Mayors show in London. I had planned to go but owing to the Flu all passes are cancelled. There is always a fine procession.

Yes I hear from home quite often, especially from Maggie. She scarcely misses a week and sends me the Locals.

All for today. Remember me to the others.

Lovingly,
Herb

Nov. 9: Fair. Working in the ward kitchen.

Nov. 10: Rainy.

Nov. 11: Fine. Germans surrender. Armistice signed at 5:00 A.M. 75th Batt. in Anzin.[73]

Nov. 12: Went to London yesterday and today. A time to be remembered.

Nov. 13: Fine. Went to Farnborough and Orpington in evening.

171

Canadian Red Cross Society
12 Berners Street
London
Nov. 13, 1918

Dear Sir or Dear Madam,

The Red Cross visitor has seen Pte. Gibson several times and tells me he is now in the Orpington Hospital. He was moved there August 26th. The wound in the chest is steadily improving so that he is able to be up again and for the last month his general condition is continuing to improve in the most satisfactory way. We are glad to be able to send such a good account of Pte. Gibson.

Yours truly,
B. Masterton Smith

172

No. 16 Canadian General Hosp.
Orpington Kent
November 13, 1918

Dear May,

I scarcely know how to begin this letter or what to say when I get started. Are we all dreaming and will we wake up some of these days.

About noon on the 11th, yes the 11th of all days for me,[74] the news came through that the Germans had signed the Armistice and that the fighting had ceased. As the word passed from ward to ward, cheer after cheer, went up. The band was out together with a band from a nearby barracks, followed by a mob of wildly excited people of all sorts and ages. Soon as I could get away I started for the city (no Pass) and after waiting an hour for a bus, finally got away. We sang and shouted all the way there, although the rain poured down.

Such a mass of people I never beheld, everyone seemed to have gone mad. Flags everywhere, taxis, busses, lorries and all sorts of things crowded with soldiers and girls. Great processions on the street and you simply had to go with the crowd. I went up yesterday afternoon, too, and the crowd was larger than ever, it being a fine day. As quickly as possible the lamps were stripped of their "War Paint" and such a difference as the lights made.

We got home at 12 and no one said a word. There is to be one big night this week and I must take it in. I am too excited to write May, can't scarcely sleep this two nights.

·   More later.
Herb

Nov. 14: Fair. Drew kit for discharge to Bexhill.

Nov. 15: Fair. Left at 8:00 A.M. Travelled by London bridge arriving at 2:00 P.M. Went to Bexhill.

Nov. 16: Cool. Went to Hastings in afternoon. Very quiet. Sports in evening.

Nov. 17: Inoculation and medical inspection.

173

P.P.C.R.C. Hospital
Cooden Camp
Bexhill-on-Sea, Sussex
Nov. 17, 1918

Dear May,

What do you think of this for an address eh! You would think I were practising my A-B-C's. In words it means Princess Patricia's Canadian Red Cross Hospital, but then what is there in a name for to come to the point it is only a Convalescent Camp. I only came here on Friday and so far I don't care much for the place. You see this is where you start to do P.T. again and after so long doing nothing it sort of puts a fellow off his right temper. However, perhaps in a few weeks I shall be sent up to the demobilization camp, which is in Wales, to wait the boat for home. That is where all the overseas casualties are going now. At other times they would be sent to their "reserves" from here, to await a "draft" for France but the war being over and the reserves already full of "drafters" (I never call them conscripts) we need not return to the training camps.

It hardly seems right to hope to be home when the leaves come out again in the Land of the Maple, Hope and Freedom.

We are right on the coast here, not more than a quarter mile from the beach, too cold though for bathing.

I took a trip down to Hastings yesterday afternoon to see the old place. Looks much the same as it did one and a half years ago.

There is a rumour that leave is opening up again, hope it is true. I'd like a few more days now.

I'm going to do the post by putting this in with your Xmas card. Hope it does not get broken.[75]

Yours,
Herb

Nov. 18: Cool. Nothing doing.

Nov. 19: Cool. Classified chest and lung exercises 9:00 A.M. and 3:00 P.M.

Nov. 20: Fair. Duke of Connaught visited hospital. Col. Harbottle returned to Batt.

Nov. 21: Fair. Started on the exercises at gymnasium.

Nov. 22: Fair. Writing XMAS cards home. Concert in YMCA.

174

P.P.C.R.C. Hospital
Cooden Camp
Bexhill-on-Sea, Sussex
Nov. 22, 1918

Dear Sister,

I have not much to say today but will put in a line with this card. Have been busy all morning mailing Xmas cards home. I can't very well send you all presents so the cards will have to do. This will be another Xmas across the Atlantic. I expect to be on my Sick Furlough just about that time. Don't know if I'll go to Scotland or Ireland. Ashcroft's will be wanting me to go there I expect but am trying to get a special leave for that.

This is a Convalescent Camp with about 1200 men. I am doing chest and lung exercises in the gymnasium. It is a very quiet place but then I don't go out much anyway. Our old friend the "Y" keeps us entertained in the evenings with concerts etc.

Had some mail from home lately, plenty of "flu" down there, but none of our people had it then. I have a bad cold just now. I expect it was the change to sea air that gave it to me.

I have not heard anything definite about when we will go home but I expect they will send those in Hospital first. Anyhow, I hope to be home before spring. I don't know whether I will farm next summer or not, all depends on how this side of mine goes on. It has not improved much in the last two months, perhaps these exercises will help it.

I may take next summer for a holiday and visit to all the family at least I have been promising myself that.

Now I hope this finds you all O.K. Will be expecting a letter soon.

Lovingly,
Herb

Nov. 23: Fine. Went to Bexhill in afternoon with Beck 26 and Rennie 25. At cinema deluxe.
Nov. 24: Dull. To Bexhill.

175

P.P.C.R.C. Hospital
Cooden Camp
Bexhill-on-Sea
Nov. 24, 1918

Dear May,

Sunday evening and I am going to try and write you a kind of respectable letter. I have one of yours here which contains a mild "rep" for not writing for three weeks. Well that does seem a long time and I can't make any excuses either, for I was "not sick," as you had thought, nor was I "too busy up in the smoke" but if I did not write May, I at least did not forget you, for I think of you almost as much as of my own folk.

You said I had not told you how I was and want me to tell you particularly how I am. Now, May, I have not even told my sisters all, simply said I was gaining and still had pains in my chest. I'll tell you as near as I can, but there is one thing I wish you not to mention to anyone. When I was put in for a Canada Board, the chest and lung specialist had to look me over. It was a most thorough exam, I can assure you. After he got finished sounding etc., said to me quite of a sudden, "has your right shoulder always been dropped?" Well it sort of took the breath from me and took me about a minute to answer. Never was very square shouldered, but did not think one was lower than the other, did you? Anyhow it is lower now. I suppose owing to the absence of half a rib, stitching up of the wound and weakness of that side. My side is quite tender and I dare not wrestle with the boys as I used to. If I twist about it hurts like a knife stab. Then if I walk fast for a while I am all out of breath and ready to sit down. The X-ray showed the lungs clear but some glands enlarged, (they put on a long-handled name which I can't remember). Perhaps these exercises I am getting here will help—must try and pull this shoulder up. Now Dear, enough said.

Now what shall I talk about, lets see if there is any more questions to answer first.

Oh yes, you have been doing some nursing and working in the office too. Now you will be over-working yourself. It is a splendid work but you know the old "proverb"—one thing at a time.

You speak of your first night on duty. I too, will always remember my first night "guarding the Bull Dogs." I often thought of those nights when in the Front Line. No your hospital talk does not tire me, anything you are doing interests me and I shall try and be a good patient, only you will have to hold my hand in your dreams eh! Well I hope the worst of the "flu" is over now at home. It has sure gone on a world tour. I expect it is much the same as we had in France, at least <u>they</u> had for I escaped entirely.

Now I have your typed letter. You were speaking of Thanksgiving and what we have to be thankful for. Your wish came true before I got your letter. The Germans did surrender and on Monday or was it Tuesday, handed over the cream of their fleet. Isn't it grand, I don't pretend to be one of those "I told you so" sorts but always felt sure that we would win. A great proof that there is a Supreme Being working out some great blessing.

I took a stroll into Bexhill this afternoon (two miles) walked along the beach and watched the combers come in then had tea and walked home. There is a tram line out here but no cars on Sunday.

Heard some rumour today. It said the men in Cooden Camp are to be sent to Kingston, Ontario in the near future, too much to hope for though. Still, one never knows does one?

Now I must wind up. Thanks for Birthday Greetings. Shall I wind up with the key

Sincerely,
Herb

Nov. 25: Fair. Fine lecture on India by a Hindu professor.

Monday morning
Nov. 25, 1918

Just took a notion to write a couple more pages this morning. What shall I say. Oh! yes, I have just been to my P.T. class. I go at 9 A.M. and 3 P.M. for half an hour. We go to the gymnasium. It is more of a past time to me than anything else. It is quite an establishment all kinds of machines for arm and leg cases. I used to be on them at Epsom. Some look funny, like a bunch of overgrown kids playing with great toys such as bicycles, rowing, etc. Then there is the massage department, where you get "rubbed down."

About three hundred are going out of my Division next Friday. At that rate this place should soon be cleaned up.

Isn't it great to know that the great streams of wounded have stopped coming in. Of course the hospitals will be kept busy with the returned prisoners who will need treatment more or less. Isn't it cruel the way they are treating our men and theirs having all the comforts one could wish for as a prisoner of war.

One of our old 787 boys came in the other day and is in the cot next to me. I knew I had seen the face somewhere and then I heard his number. There are a few of our old boys here but none from Perth. I met one of my old Platoon mates (75th) who was hit the same night as me. He was not able to get in that morning and was out in No Man's Land for two days and three nights and finally managed to crawl in. Some experience, imagine, severely wounded and nothing to eat all that time. He got as big a surprise as I did on meeting, for each had heard the other was killed.[76]

Now May I'll say good morning and have a cup of tea, getting quite English ha.

JHG

Nov. 27: Fair. Hut orderly today so have no parade.
Nov. 28: Fair. Fisher and I went to Bexhill. Supper of eggs and potatoes.
Nov. 29: Fair. Reclassification. Fisher leaves on furlough. Over 300 went out.

176

P.P.C.R.C. Hospital
Cooden Camp
Bexhill-on-Sea, Sussex
Nov. 29, 1918

Dear May,

I don't know if I can collect my thoughts long enough to write a letter this afternoon or not but perhaps it will help to write to you. I just received a letter from a cousin, at noon, merely mentioning the death of my youngest sister, Ida.[77] There were no particulars at all, and I am in a state of suspense to know the truth. No doubt there are letters coming from home, this one arriving first. This brings back afresh all the anxious, lonely days of last year, waiting for more and better news. Patience is a virtue in all things and I possess very little of that. Oh,

May, I wonder if it is not a mistake. Still the letter said that someone
had a letter from John's wife telling them, so it must be true. This is
a very foggy and cheerless day. It is only just after 3 P.M. and I can
scarcely see to write. Just now the lights have come on making it a little
more cheerful.

You want my opinion about going to train for a nurse. I really do
not know what to say May, indeed. The work is the most noble a girl
can undertake and as far as you being able to make good, there is not
the slightest doubt. Your banking experience will be helpful to you
but above all you have the courage and determination to overcome
hard problems. Besides when you have the natural liking for that kind
of work it should come easy to you. Yes, I have seen a good deal of
hospitals and nurses and find that there are what one might call "born
nurses." Some have the work instilled in their very nature while others
will never make what I would call a good nurse for they have not the
"knack" or interest perhaps in the work. To some the art of dressing
and making one comfortable seems to be a second nature while others,
well they have missed their calling. The only fault I find with your plan
is the Military part of it. I would much rather see you in civil hospital.
You know one does not always get a square deal from the military
authorities. I infer from your letter that it is massage work only, which
this training offers. I think you would find that hard work with very little
variations. I know you would make a good nurse. You have the right
disposition but I can hardly say that I would like to influence you one
way or another. If I were talking to you I could explain myself better
and perhaps you and I could understand each other better. What ever
you undertake you have my best wishes.

Now, May, I think I have said enough and hope I have made myself
quite plain. I wrote you a few days ago telling about myself. Did you get
it? We go before the M.O. once a week, that is on Fridays. Today when
I went in our doctor (a jolly fat old spectacled chap) says "oh a rib gone
eh." "Yes" says I, "when are you going to put in my false one?" Anyway,
I got "Carry on" and expect I shall be doing that for an indefinite
period. I hear they are going to ship the casualties home at the rate of
20,000 per month. We have had 152,000 casualties, about one half of
which are home, so I figure to get home by March or April.

Au Revoir,
Herb

You were just starting to celebrate. How did Perth behave?

JHG

Nov. 30: Cold. Rennie and I went to Hastings afternoon. Quiet. Went to picture show.

Dec. 1: Rain. Church service.
Dec. 2: Foggy. Lecture at night on Switzerland.
Dec. 3: Rainy. Concert in YMCA by Gordon Party.
Dec. 4: Fair. Went downtown for supper and to cinema deluxe.
Dec. 5: Foggy. PT as per usual. Concert in Y in evening. Two letters today.
Dec. 6: Downtown in evening. Met a couple of tarts.
Dec. 7: Fine. Bexhill in afternoon. Went to St. Georges cinema. Came home early.
Dec. 8: Church service.
Dec. 9: Rainy. Downtown for supper and to cinema.
Dec. 10: Fair. Went to Hastings in the evening. 75th at St. Symphorien.
Dec. 11: Fair. Stayed in all day. Wrote some letters.
Dec. 12: Rain. To Bexhill for supper and to show.
Dec. 13: Fair. To Hastings.
Dec. 14: Rainy. Cinema at Bexhill and to Hastings in evening. Marked for discharge.
Dec. 15: Rain. Bexhill with some friends.
Dec. 16: Fair. Parade to hospital representative. To Hastings.
Dec. 17: Fine. To kit store. Got Khaki out to repair. Hastings. 75th at Ramilies.
Dec. 18: Fair. Down to Bexhill to meet friend.

177

Cooden Beach
Dec. 18, 1918

Dear May,

Yours of Dec. 1st was not so long getting across as some late ones. I am glad too as it gives me an opportunity of answering it before going on my Leave. Yes, May, some leave at last. You see I got fed up with waiting for Boards etc. so last time before the MO. I said I felt good, so got marked out. I leave here on Friday morning and so will have both

Christmas and New Years to myself and expect to report back to the
12th Reserve Witley. I expect you will be surprised to hear of me being
AIII again and I am too myself. In fact at times I do feel as well as ever
I did and then there are other times not so good. Anyhow, as far as
getting home soon is concerned, I think the chances are equally as good
from the Reserves as from here.

After a great deal of weighing and planning I resolved to take my
Leave ticket to Aberdeen, Scotland. I did really intend to see Ireland
while over here but to tell the plain truth, I got cold feet when I thought
of the passage of that choppy little Irish Sea. I am a very poor sailor,
you know. So I am going to Aberdeen and then to Glasgow and Dundee
and a few more places. I'll drop you a line from some of the places
and you can answer to my old address 75th Canadian, 12th Reserve
Battalion Witley Surrey England.

Say if you were only here to go with me wouldn't it be fine. We
would make a regular tour of the Isle. We are calling this our Victory
Leave and I mean to make the best of it, only hope the weather keeps
good. So long for today and Cheerio.

All the time,
Herb

Dec. 19: Fair. Busy getting ready to go on leave.

Dec. 20: Fair. Left at 8:30 A.M. London 12. Met friend and went to Gaiety.

Dec. 21: Fair. Went to Wyndham Theatre and to Chapman after. Stayed in
Salvation Army club.

Dec. 22: Rain. Left for Scotland 10:15 P.M.

Dec. 23: Cold. Arrived Dundee at noon. Stopped at YMCA.

Dec. 24: Fair. Went to Glasgow. Arrived at 4:30 P.M. Stopped at
Armstrong Hotel.

Dec. 25: Fair. Breakfast at 10:00 A.M. To zoo in afternoon and tea party at
Mrs. McThieson, 2 Morris Place, Glasgow.

Dec. 26: Rain. Trip to Loch Lomond. Train to Tarbet and steamer down
Lomond. Dinner at Ross's Hotel.

Dec. 27: Rainy. Went to Paisley museum, Coats Church and Abbey. Party
in evening.

Dec. 28: Fair. Visited City Hall, Fire Station, museum and art gallery. Called
at 9 Blythswood Road in evening.

Dec. 29: Rain. Cathedral in A.M. Tent Hall in P.M.

Dec. 30: Wet. To Edinburgh via Lanark. Dined with parson.

178

Glasgow, Scotland
Dec. 30, 1918

Dear May,

Just a line this A.M. to say that I am still in the pink. This is my fourth day in the city and am enjoying my stay very well indeed, considering the sort of weather we are having. Almost continuous rain ever since I struck Scotland. Spent Xmas very quietly. I was surprised to find that the Scots do not celebrate Xmas to any great extent. New Year's is their day and worse luck I have to go back on the 30th. They only gave us ten days. Had a free Xmas dinner in the Club here and went to a private house for tea and spent a most enjoyable time. Thursday I went to Loch Lomond and although the rain came down in sheets would not have missed the trip. Will tell you all about it bye and bye. Yesterday I visited the old city of Paisley and now (Sat.) A.M. just waiting for a party to go to the Municipal Buildings. Tonight have an invitation to supper at a private home. Gee! but the time does fly. Have wired for an extension but received no reply yet.

Well, must say

Au Revoir,
Herb

Dec. 31: Fair. Called on Mr. Thompson. Visited Forth Bridge. Saw the year out at the Tron Church.

Notes

1 A "funk hole" was a small hole each soldier dug for himself into the wall of the trench.
2 This letter was sent in an "Active Service" envelope, a letter sent from the front line with a signed affirmation by the sender that it contained only personal or family information. Nonetheless, such letters were still subject to censorship.
3 He is feeling very blue in this letter and seems to have a premonition of bad news.
4 The "Maple Leafs" were the concert party of the 4th Division. "Aladin France" was the title of a pantomime (as well as a play on words) of a lad in France.
5 An explosion at a munitions plant in Trenton, Ontario, in 1917 killed several from Perth. One of those killed was a seventeen-year-old whose nineteen-year-old brother was killed in France.
6 Herb carried this letter with him throughout the rest of the war.

7   This was the first letter Herb received telling him of his mother's death. He received it while on post at the front line the night of January 29, 1918. It was a clear, moonlit night, so he read his letters from home. How lonely he must have felt. He carried this letter in his wallet for the duration of the war.

8   On the outside of the letter was written "Received while on post in front line (Hill 70) on night of 29th of January 1918. Clear moon-light so read letter from home."

9   Although this letter was written in 1921, we have placed it in here because it reveals more about Herb's thoughts and feelings than his other letters written in 1918.

10 Beaucoup Promenade, perhaps?

11 A suburb to the northwest of Lens.

12 D.C. = Drummond Centre.

13 The smoke was to provide cover.

14 "Windows" refers to shell holes and bomb damage to the house.

15 See letter 138 explaining the "Lance Jack" military honour: a ribbon ("stripe") for two years' good conduct.

16 "Tired alley" may refer to a reserve trench.

17 Ferrier was wounded on March 1. Initially, Herb heard that he had lost a leg.

18 He had a bath and went to the Y at Aubrey Camp on April 11. See diary entry for April 11, 1918.

19 R.F.C. = Royal Flying Corps.

20 "Holding a block in a C.T." = watching an area.

21 The Hugheses, who were neighbours on the Eighth Line, had lost their barn in a fire.

22 Herb's sisters Jane and Clara were now in North Dakota.

23 "Hugh's and the other house" may refer to Hugh Gibson's farm, and the original old stone house opposite it and just down the road from Lammermoor.

24 "The day I let the bloods run away": Herb had once let the team of well-bred young horses run free. This was probably when he lost his front teeth!

25 Hugh Harper, Ida's husband, was a very difficult man. Ida was probably very unhappy and thus did not write to Herb. She died on November 4, 1918, aged 32 years, leaving three small boys, John (6), Russell (4), and Wallace (3).

26 Mel Paul was killed in action. See letters 133 and 137.

27 The boys would be Lester Gibson, and John, Wallace, and Russell Harper.

28 Russell Morris did not enlist. His wife's parents (the Whites) later bought Herb's farm for $5,000.

29 Maisonal Bouche, according to Herb's diary.

30 Herb's diary says he was "sketching"; this is likely related to the scouting course he was taking.

31 His face was sunburned; see letter 138.

32 A.E.F. refers to the American Expeditionary Force. See letters 38 and 55.

33 The big battle that Herb refers to here would be the great offensive retaking the
    Amiens Line. He was out of the line for a month preparing for his battalion's
    drive, which began on July 11.
34 Mary Ellen sent him the maple sugar.
35 Could this be the home of Louis Lanfant? That name and Camblain-Châtelain
    are written in the back of Herb's 1918 diary. There is also a home mentioned in
    letter 114. It could be the same one, but this is purely speculation on our part.
36 Herb describes being on a work party digging dugouts at a hospital. The
    Germans often bombarded field hospitals.
37 May would have written her St. John Ambulance exams.
38 The play would have been put on by the Red Cross to raise money. May said
    she joined everything "in those days"—including, for example, Daughters of
    the Empire.
39 Herb's brothers, John and Willie, sold the stock and some furniture from the farm
    and disposed of the proceeds as though Herb was not coming back from the
    war. Hugh's place was the farm opposite the stone house at Lammermoor, and
    Hugh Gibson had left there for Walhalla. Hugh was the brother of Grandfather
    (William R. Gibson). Herb did take some furniture west with him in 1919.
40 Annie May is Mrs. Colin McNichol.
41 C.E.F. = Canadian Expeditionary Force.
42 He mentions Hubert Quackenbush and Jim McVeety. Both were killed short-
    ly after.
43 "Falls" refers to Smith's Falls, for the July 12 parade of the Orange Lodge.
44 L.O.L. = Loyal Orange Lodge.
45 C.C.S. = Casualty Clearing Station. BEF = British Expeditionary Force.
46 See letter 148.
47 The base hospital at Wimereaux, on the French side of the English Channel
    west of Calais.
48 Herb's Uncle John received a similar telegram sent to Balderson, but did not
    keep it.
49 Herb was in the front line north of Arras when he was wounded. Herb's July 10
    diary entry says he marched to Dieval, took the train to Mt. St. Eloi, and then to
    Anzin for the night, so he would have joined the front line near there. (Also see
    Herb's diary of June 15 and letter 142.)
        May said he told her that he was losing a lot of blood from the wound in his
    hip, and coughing blood too. There were seven of them and he was the lead
    man. They had crawled out to a listening post in no man's land when a noise
    alerted the Germans, who raked the field with a machine gun. One soldier
    wanted to go for a stretcher, but Herb said no, he would go back with them or
    else he would not be found. The soldiers who helped him back to the trench
    truly saved his life; Herb said he was losing consciousness, and would never have
    been found in time had he been left there. A soldier threw a greatcoat over him
    on the stretcher; later Herb found among his possessions a matchbox cover that
    was not his own and must have been in the coat pocket. He remembered only

going around corners or being jarred in the tunnels. The light field ambulance was horse-drawn. The operation was performed at the hospital at Aubigny.

50   When Iris was about 5 years old, she suffered a broken nose. That evening the family went downtown, and on the way home she told her parents she was going to be sick to her stomach. They got out of the car and there, at the side of the road under a streetlight, she brought up blood. Herb told May that it gave him an awful shock, and took him right back to France. After twenty-three years, this event triggered a "flashback" to France and his experiences there.

51   This letter to Mary Ellen, who lived at Poland, Ontario, appeared in the *Perth Courier*, September 6, 2018.

52   The letter says "Canadian Clearing Station," but should have read "Casualty Clearing Station."

53   "Jock" was a common English expression for Scots, sometimes pejorative, sometimes not.

54   In comparing his condition to those of others, Herb made light of his wound— however, it was very serious and changed his life. He had to sell the farm he loved and had longed for.

55   The Battle of Amiens began on August 8. The 75th and 87th battalions sustained heavy losses.

56   V.A.D. = the Volunteer Aid Detachment, a branch of the St. John Ambulance. May was a V.A.D. in Perth. Some were nurses, who could afford to pay their own way to England to work.

57   G.G.'s Band = Governor General's Band.

58   Herb's diary entry for August 8 says Maj. Bull and Capt. Cummins were killed when the 75th took Le Quesnel and the drive for Amiens began.

59   The "cement block house" was May's house on the Eighth Line.

60   There were only two cards enclosed. One showed the Massey-Harris convalescent home, a large Victorian mansion in Dulwich, in south London, England, used as a hospital for injured Canadian soldiers. Massey-Harris was a large Canadian agricultural equipment manufacturer based in Brantford, Ontario.

61   McLaren's was the local distillery. Herb had a good sense of humour and it shows in many of his letters, such as letters 93 and 94. Note also his comments in letters 152 and 155.

62   May did hear that Herb had died of wounds, but the following day the paper published lists of the "dangerously wounded."

63   The King George Hospital.

64   He mentions—at last—a letter from Ida.

65   Jane had asthma and an ulcerated leg.

66   By the "white brick on the 8th" he means his farm, which was called "Elmshade."

67   The "caboose" was a local place near where May was staying, and "sorrels on the tank" refers to a team of horses. We believe the places and names he mentions in this paragraph were all in North Dakota; Herb had visited there in 1908.

68   Three enclosures accompanied this letter. Two were show programs and the third is a souvenir of the "Feed the Guns" war fundraising campaign.

69 See Herb's diary notes for August, September, and October regarding the 75th Battalion in action.

70 The "barriers" of which Herb speaks may have been religious in origin, and might have related to dancing, card playing, etc.—but Mother says they were "nothing serious." Religious differences were taken more seriously then. They also held different political views: the Gibsons were Liberals while the Keayses were Conservatives.

71 At Mons, the British forces were badly outnumbered. Had the Germans attacked then, the war might have been over. When asked later why they had not attacked, the Germans said that when they looked out they saw legions of soldiers in white along the British positions, and feared that they themselves were outnumbered. The British soldiers felt that these were their guardian angels.

   However, we do not know whether the story of the "Comrade in White at Mons" refers to this or some other phenomenon, and are not certain that Herb ever did share it with May after he returned to Canada. Whatever the case, Herb's beliefs likely sustained him through the war.

72 Going to the "smoke" meant going to London.

73 The flu epidemic was worldwide. May was working nights in the Haggart home where flu cases were being nursed, and she would go into the bank at about 3:00 p.m. to be marked present. This lasted about two weeks, until the epidemic slowed down. She nursed a young girl who died. The girl's parents gave May a round ivory mirror as a gift and in appreciation of her nursing care.

74 The armistice happened on Herb's twenty-ninth birthday! May said she went straight to the church in Perth when peace was declared. It was a Thanksgiving service, and all the bells were ringing. There were also parades.

75 May did not remember what he sent.

76 We do not know the name of this platoon mate.

   One day many years later, however, Herb was getting off a streetcar in Winnipeg and met a man who said to him, "the last time I saw you, you were lying on a stretcher and I thought you were dead" (although we have no knowledge of who this man was).

   The name J.L. Johnston (of Hamilton, Ontario) appears in Herb's 1919 diary. When visiting Hamilton in about 1965 or 1966, Herb began talking about his pal John Johnston, and wondered if he might still be in Hamilton. Iris got out the phone book and found a listing for a John Johnston, so she called. She told the lady that answered who she was and why she had called, and asked if her husband had been in France with the 75th Battalion. Imagine the surprise when she said yes! Eric (Iris's husband) took May and Herb to Hamilton that evening. May said that Mr. Johnston called Dad "Gibby" and they had a chat. She was sorry that they did not bring a camera or call the *Hamilton Spectator* to record the reunion of these two First World War veterans forty-eight years after they had been together in France. See letters 112 and 114.

77 Ida died of flu in Walhalla. Jane took Wallace and John, and Russell came to Lanark to live with their father's relatives. Ida was 32 years old when she died.

1919

Jan. 1: Fair. J. Machan and I went sightseeing in Edinburgh, Castle, Knox home, Holly Rood. Spent evening with the ladies.

Jan. 2: Fair. Left for south at 10:00 A.M. Changed at Grantham for Peterboro and for Ripton. Got drive to Mr. Ashcrofts' arriving at 8:30 P.M.

Jan. 3: Fine. Slept until 9:00 A.M. Went shooting rabbits in P.M. To Abbotts Ripton in evening.

Jan. 4: Fine and cool. Went to Huntingdon in morning and shot rabbits in afternoon. Mr. Ashcroft got 3 and I got 2. Called at Mrs. Danes.

179

Abbots Ripton
January 4, 1919

Dear Sisters,

By the heading you will see that I am having a holiday. Started off on leave on Dec. 20th and visited London, Dundee, Glasgow, and Edinburgh having a good visit in each place. I also managed to see Loch Lomond and Lanark, my two greatest ambitions. The weather has not been the best, so much wet weather. This is like home here though, these people are so kind. Have been just eating and sleeping and hunting rabbits with Mr. Ashcroft. Some of the girls are coming to see me tomorrow. Will have to be going back to camp on Monday though. I hate going back but will have to get there to see about getting home. I think they are sending the farmers home first.

I expect there will be some mail for me when I go back and am hoping for some parcels too. Well I wonder how you are all getting on now. Is the weather very cold out there?

You can address your next letters to 75th Canadian 12th Reserve Battalion Witley Camp, Surrey England. Will write more when I get there.

Love to you all.
Herb

Jan. 5: Rainy. Mrs. Ashcroft and I went to Church.

Jan. 6: Fair. Left for London. Went to Hippodrome at night.

Jan. 7: Fair. Left London by 11:10 A.M. from Waterloo arriving in Witley Camp Surrey at 2:00 P.M.

Jan. 8: Fair. On fatigue in ration stores. Machan, Sommerville and Gardners came over.

Jan. 9: Rainy. Orderly room. Eight days RW, sixteen days no. 2.[1]

Jan. 10: Rainy. On guard. Back to soldiering once more.

Jan. 11: Fair. Came off guard and turned in equipment. Went to concert at 6th Res. in evening. Met military from the "Hill."

180

Witley, Surrey
Jan. 11, 1919

Dear Sister,

Received your registered letter when I came back off leave. Thanks very much. That will come in handy for I won't be able to draw any money for a couple of weeks. You see I stayed almost eight days over my leave and got a few days C.B. for it and the eight days pay stopped. However, luckily, I did not come back to camp penniless.

It is very quiet here but have met quite a few that I know. Some old 130th boys and some who only came over this year. Saw E. Ferrier, E. McKerracher, R. Scott, the two Gardiner boys and two Somervilles. I think I told you in my last letter of meeting J. Machan in Glasgow. I told you where I had been on leave so there is not much more I can tell you about that. Hope to see you all in the course of two or three months.

You and Jane seem to have quite a full house or do those people only have their meals with you. You were wanting to know what I was intending to do next summer. Well I'll tell you. I had planned to stop around home for a couple of months and straighten things up and then go out to Dakota and Manitoba for awhile. Now since John is on the farm I think I will just let him stay on it a summer and I'll take a rest. In that time he would be able to look about and get a place to suit him. You could come back too perhaps and then we could go out to Jane's together eh! I could cable to you when I sail and that would give you plenty of time to get ready and be back before me. Say if you need money you are quite at liberty to use my wages, that is what I signed that over to you for. Now do.

Well J. Machan has come in to see me so will ring off.

Love to yourself, Jane and Lester,[2]
Herb

Jan. 12: Fair. Church service in morning.

Jan. 13: Foggy. Fatigue at Milford station in morning.

181

No. 2 Coy. 12th Res. Batt.
Witley Camps
Surrey, England
Jan. 13, 1919

Dear May,

I had hoped that the next time I wrote to you that I could tell you that I was leaving for home but that day seems a few suns away yet. A large draft left here yesterday morning for Canada, at least they go to a camp near Liverpool and wait there for a boat. I hope to be on the next draft but hard to say when it will leave. However some day I shall surprise you all, just walk in when you are not expecting me.

Ernie Ferrier is here and I see him quite often.[3] He is a funny chap says he is not in a hurry to go home for a few months as he is afraid he loses some of this "blood money," we call it. It goes by the length of service, I think. Camp life is terrible slow here—no town near just a few army cinemas. We do some P.T. to keep fit and the Draftees are going to the Khaki College. I met the Gardiner boys here and a few more from around that part.

I am looking for a letter from you any day. Hope one comes soon. I will tell you all about my trip to Scotland when I get back so will sign off for this time.

As B4,
Herb

P.S. Say May, don't stop writing just because I may be started home. It will be fun getting them returned.

JHG

181A (excerpt from the Perth Courier, March 7, 1919)[4]

Pte. E. Ferrier went overseas with the 130th Batt. He was 22 months in France. He was in the engineering corps at Vimy Ridge and went over the top at Avion. In Sept. of 1917 he did forward work with the YMCA and was gassed. He reached England in Oct. 1918 and was in hospital for some time. He reached home last Fri.

182 (telegram)

2 Paid
Halifax N.S.
2-6-19

Miss C. Gibson
Walhalla N.D.

Arrived Safely.
Herb Gibson

Jan. 14: Rain. On draft for Canada. Drew equipment. Went to 6th Res. to see J. Machan.

Jan. 15: Rain. Left at 9:30 A.M. for RHYL N.W. arriving at 9:00 P.M. Had supper and went to bed.

Jan. 16: Showery. Registration and Dental Parades. Went to pictures in evening.

Jan. 17: Cool. Nothing doing in morning. Had Medical Board. Met some old chums in evening.

Jan. 18: Fair. Did nothing all day. Barrie, James and I went to Garrison Theatre in evening, "Comedy's Half an Hour" and "Seven Women."

Jan. 19: Fine. Out walking in evening with James and Barrie.

Jan. 20: Fair. Signed last pay sheet and moved to dispatch company.

Jan. 21: Fair. Received R parcel from MBK. On inlying picket. Only moved to another hut to sleep.

Jan. 22: Fair. Went to P.O. and got money order. Went to movies and met E. Ferrier.

Jan. 23: Cool. Went for a short route march. Ferrier, Barrie, James and I went to Rhyl in evening.

Jan. 24: Dull. Route march just to pass the time. Went to Abergiles.

Jan. 25: Fair. James, Barrie and I visited St. Asaph in afternoon. Smallest town in the world possessing a Cathedral. Built A.D. 500, destroyed by Edward the First's army in 13th century. Rebuilt 1752. 130 steps to tower.

Jan. 26: Fine. Church service in Y.

Jan. 27: Snowy. Went to Garrison Theatre. "Freedom of the Seas."

Jan. 28: Fair. Pictures in A.M. Medical inspection in afternoon. Expect to leave in morning.

Jan. 29: Fair. Left camp at 11:00 A.M. Marched to Abergele and train to Liverpool. Embarked and set sail at 8:30 P.M. Feeling tough.

Jan. 30: Fine. Passed sight of Irish coast in the forenoon. Not feeling any better.

Jan. 31: Strong fair wind. Steamed 408 miles. Lay on deck all day.

Feb. 1: Cold and windy. Worse, so stayed below all day. Sea a little rougher but not to say stormy.

Feb. 2: Fair. Went to hospital.

Feb. 3: Cold. Feeling better. Calm.

Feb. 4: Cold with some snow. Got up for a while in A.M. but back to bed.

Feb. 5: Lovely and clear. Got up and discharged from hospital. Sighted land about 2:00 P.M. Anchored in Halifax Harbour about 8:30 P.M.

Feb. 6: Disembarked at 9:00 A.M. Pulled out for Quebec at 10:30. Stopped at Truro and several places.

Feb. 7: Fine. Passed Campbellton at 2:00 A.M. Riviere Du Loup at 11, Levis at 4:00 P.M. Landed at the Emigration Buildings at 7:00 P.M. concert and eats by the IODE.

Feb. 8: Fine. Getting papers etc. Two trains left for Toronto at 4 and 6 P.M. Held over for transfer. Went to bed at 9.

Feb. 9: Fine. Left for Montreal at 1:30 P.M. Arrived at 6:00 P.M. and had supper. Left for Perth at 10:00 P.M. Arrived in Perth at 2:00 A.M. and went to Hicks house.

Feb. 10: John came in. Home at noon. Reception at night. Brothers and sisters gave me a clock.

Feb. 11: Fine. All the friends gone but Joe's. Andersons came.

Feb. 12: Fine. Joe left for home. Watts came in afternoon. Roy Keays and I went to town in evening. Lecture in Town Hall.

Feb. 13: Fine. John's took me to Lanark and Willie met me at J. Gunns for supper. Feb. 14: Stormy. Called on Aunt Mary. Franks came over in the evening.

Feb. 15: Stormy. Willie and I went to Wm. Borrowman's funeral. Nairn's for dinner and Mather's for supper. Got home at midnight.

183

Lammermoor, Ont.
Feb. 15, 1919

Dear Sister,

It is almost a week since I got home and I have never got a line written to you. I expect you got the telegram I sent you from Halifax.

We left Liverpool on the 29th Jan. and had a fine trip over. Got to Quebec on the 7th Feb., and left there on the 9th at 1:30 P.M. getting into Perth at 2 o'clock on Monday morning. Ed McKerracher and I were together and we slipped in with out anyone knowing. We went to bed at the Hicks house and phoned out home next morning. John came in for me, got home just at noon. Well they had great preparations underway. Somehow they knew I was in Perth before I was out of bed and had phoned to the friends. There were Joe's and Willie's, Sandy and Maggie, Uncle John's, Nairn's, Mather's, Affleck's, Colin's, Johnny McNicol's and all the neighbours, that is the old people and Mr. and Mrs. Greig. I was surprised to see so many and we had a nice social evening. John's and Willie's and Mary Ellen's gave me a handsome clock. The weather was fine so most of the people from this side stayed until the next day. I missed you though, if you Jane and Maggie could only have been there.[5]

I hardly know how to say how much I missed Father and Mother. It seemed just like visiting John's as I used to before we went there to live, only there is a vast change on the children. Elma is like a young woman now, very quiet and so are the others. Jean is a cute little thing. Willie's children are nice too. Herb is a stout little chap. You see I came up here last Thursday and will be here a week. I go back up to Kingston for my Discharge on the 25th. Then I will be finished with soldiering. Won't be sorry either. After that I am taking a month to visit and then about the middle of May perhaps will go out to Jane's. I am wondering if you are not on your way back. Perhaps it would be just as well if you did not come as it would leave Jane very lonely. I am anxious to see you both too but will hardly get out before the time I mention.

I have been up to the graveyard and the boys have put up a nice stone to Father and Mother. We are talking of getting one for Gracie and Archie too. I called to see Aunt Mary. She is greatly failed and is in bed all the time. I will be going over to Paul's tomorrow. Mary Ellen can hardly wait until I get there.

William's were over yesterday to see me and Frank's came last night. I must go over and see Nellie. I scarcely knew Olive, she has grown so much.

The old place looks much the same, just a few new fences, that's all. The verandah on Willie's house makes a great difference.

Well I think this is about all I have got to say this time.

Old Mr. Borrowman is to be buried today. He died very suddenly. Lena Nairn is home I hear.

Write soon.

Love to all,
Herb

184A (excerpt from the
Perth Courier, February 28, 1919)

On Monday evening a presentation took place at the house of Mr. and Mrs. John Gibson, Balderson, when Pte. J. Herb Gibson was the recipient of a handsome gold watch, donated by the Harper Red Cross Society. Miss Keays, Secretary, read the address, and Mr. G. Cunningham made the presentation to which Herb responded

May Keays.

in a fitting manner. Pte. Gibson arrived home on February 10th and at that time there was a welcome awaiting him he did not expect, when we received a mantle clock.[6] About eighty-five friends attended. He left on Tuesday for Kingston where he expects to get his discharge.

184A (invitation sent to Herb, reprinted as an announcement in the *Perth Courier*, March 7, 1919)

An invitation from the Perth-Upon-Tay Chapter I.O.D.E. for Pte. J.H. Gibson and Friend[7] to attend an "At Home" on Friday March 14th 1919 at the Town Hall, Perth to give "a social expression of welcome and appreciation of service to all members of the Canadian Expeditionary Force from Perth and vicinity."

Feb. 16: Cold. Went over to Joe's.

Feb. 17: Fine. All went up to Mr. Paul's. Also called at J.A. Pauls.

Feb. 18: Fine. Helped Joe draw some hay. S. McDougall and Mrs. F. Harvey came in evening.

Feb. 19: Fair. Joe took me to Wm. Mc for dinner and Eastons for tea. Gunns, Andersons and McNicols at Willies in evening.

Feb. 20: Fine. Willie brought me home and Olive came with us. Called at Erskines.

Feb. 21: Snowy. Willie bought horse from Bells and went home. Red Cross gathering here at night and presented me with Gold watch.

Feb. 22: Fine. Went to Alex Keays for tea.

Feb. 23: At Church. Took May to town at night.

Feb. 24: Fine. Over to Harper in morning. Went to bed early.

Feb. 25: Cold. Left at 9:30 and took 12:45 train for Kingston arriving at Barriefield Huts at 4:00 P.M. Met Barrie and Boniface.

Feb. 26: Fair. Up for Board but papers not here. Dental inspection and sent up town to have plate repaired. Met J. Saunders and went to show.

Feb. 27: Fine. No papers so nothing doing. Went up town for plate. Met E. Ferrier getting home.

Feb. 28: Fair. Paraded to O.C. per discharge. Barrie and I went up town in evening.

Mar. 1: Fair. Papers at last so had Medical Board. Marked C.1. Up town in afternoon. Met T.L. Simpson. Went to Grand Theatre Play, "A Night in Honolulu."[8]

Mar. 2: Fair. Service in YMCA.

Mar. 3: Fine. Came home on six days leave. At J. Pennitts in evening.

Mar. 4: Stormy. Took Elma and Arthur to school and went for them. John at saw.

Mar. 5: Fine. Maggie and I made new arrangements upstairs. At Andersons's at night.

Mar. 6: Clear and cold. John at saw at J. Hughes. Went over and stayed for tea. Got telegram to return.

Mar. 7: Cool. John brought me to town and took 12:45 train. Went to show in evening.

Mar. 8: Fine. Nothing doing. Met R. Norris[9] uptown for supper and then to movies.

Mar. 9: Snowy. Church service.

Mar. 10: Fine. Passed U. Officer. Transferred to Dispatch Co. Uptown with W. Trail.

Mar. 11: Fine. On Q.M.S. fatigue in A.M. Helped put in new mattresses in P.M. Show in evening.

Mar. 12: Fair. Short job in morning. Just lying around all day.

Mar. 13: Cold wind. Took on job as night fireman. Movies in YMCA.

Mar. 14: Cool. Went to bed at 4:00 A.M. and slept till 9:00. Everything jake. Concert in Y and movies.

Mar. 15: Fine. Slept most of the day. Received cheques. Movies at night. Very good pictures.

Mar. 16: Rained all day.

Mar. 17: Cloudy. Received some mail today. Movies in the YMCA.

Mar. 18: Fair. Overslept this morning. Uptown for supper and went to movies.

Mar. 19: Fine. Slept most of the day. Concert in Y tonight. Programme, eats and dancing.

Mar. 20: Fair. Concert by St. Georges Chapter IODE. Splendid.

Mar. 21: Fair. Expecting some mail. None came. Progressive euchre for a change. Seven wins.

Mar. 22: Fine. Slept till noon. Movies in YMCA in evening. R. Norris kept me company to 1:30 A.M.

Mar. 23: Fine. Did not get up for Church. R. Norris and I walked to Kingston in evening.

Mar. 24: Fine. Two letters. Concert in YMCA.

Mar. 25: Fine. Wrote to Maggie and Clara. Pictures at night. Fine weather here.

185

Kingston
March 25, 1919

Dear Sister,

Have I answered your letter of March 2nd yet? Don't believe I have. Maggie forwarded it on to me.

I have not much news to write but can at least say that I am leaving the army next week for good. This will be the best home coming of all, for I will be my own boss then. I am anxious to get home too for I had a letter from Janet yesterday saying that Aunt Mary had taken a stroke and was very low. I only called to see her for a few minutes when I was up there and maybe I will not see her again. William Keays is very poorly again too. Elsie and Leo are home I think. It is too bad I never got up to see him when at home. There seemed to be so many places to go and I wanted just to stay right at home for awhile.

What was that you said about getting me a chain. Well if you intend on doing that I want you to make the choice yourselves. You see if I bought it, it would not be quite the same, would it? I must hunt up my other one when I go home.

Yes I will let you know when I am coming. Will most likely come by St. Paul, as I want to see that part.

Won't we have a grand time eh. I hope to be out by the 1st of June. There are so many places I want to go here and then I want to help John fence some.

I hope the boys have got over the flu and no more of you got it.

Goodbye,
Love to all,
Herb

Mar. 26: Fine. Got several letters and parcel at Express office. To show up town with Norris. Finished firing.

Mar. 27: Rained most of day. Had bath and change. Movies tonight. Snowing and getting cold.

Mar. 28: Stormy all day. Uptown to see 45th Batt. come in. Concert in Y. Mr. O'Hara there.

Mar. 29: Still stormy. Movies cancelled owing to break down of electric wires. Three years' service in C.E.F. finished tonight. Went to bed early.

Mar. 30: Fair. On kitchen fatigue.

Mar. 31: Cold. Discharged from the army. Norris and I at Marks play.[10]

April 1: Fine. Norris and I start for home at 11:00 A.M. Out home at 7:00 P.M.

186

Balderson R.R. #1
April 3, 1919

Dear Sisters,

Here I am back home once more for good. Got my discharge on the last day of March and got home April 1st. Gee! but it is great to be home and know that you do not need to take anybody's orders.

J.H. Gibson — a life well lived.

John's are all well. We were to town yesterday afternoon and I got a new suit. It is dark blue serge. Clothing is an awful price. You can't get a decent suit under $40. John got one yesterday also. I have to get a rain coat yet but I have not got enough funds on hand so I want you to send me $50.00. The army does not pay all at once. I have $70 per month for the next five months coming in. We have been having very bad weather lately, snow, rain and cold but it is milder this morning. It was very fine for a while and some people made some syrup but I am afraid this frost will spoil their trees. John is talking about getting a few trees somewhere to make a little but we have not decided yet. Bob Anderson is making in Hailey's bush. Wm. Keays is very low. I was up there yesterday morning to ask for him. The family are all home. Howard just arrived from Vancouver Tuesday night and Rob and Elsie have been home a couple of weeks. Elsie looks fine and seemed pleased to see me. Mrs. Paul and Mrs. Smith are there also. Poor Aunt Mary passed away before I got home. They sent a telegram to Kingston but I did not get it. I am very sorry I did not go over again when I was up there. I expect Franks are feeling bad over it but can't be helped now. Mr. McIntyre down the 8th line is very low too and being an old man is hardly likely to recover. I hope you people have all recovered from your sickness. Surely the flu must soon be over now.

Well I guess this is all for today. John has gone to the sawing at Fergusons. Was into Andersons a few minutes yesterday and had some new syrup. Why don't you write to Mrs. Anderson. Lloyd McKerracher got home last week.

Goodbye. Write soon,
Herb

187

January 5, 1969[11]
The Lanark Era
Lanark, Ontario

Dear Leonard,

As the year 1968 was drawing to a close on New Years Eve my mind travelled back 50 years to New Years Eve in the city of Edinburgh, Scotland. I was stationed in England with the Sixth Canadian Reserve which reinforced four Battalions on active service in France, which were the 38th, 2nd, 21st and P.P.C.L.I. and was located at Seaford, Sussex. The Reserve was moved to Witley Camp just before the Armistice was signed Nov. 11. While there I went to Brandshott Hospital with the mumps and when released from there I returned to Witley Camp. As we had been quarantined with mumps I had never been given leave to Scotland. So the day after Xmas I started on 8 days leave to Glasgow and Edinburgh. The other boys in camp had their leave earlier so I was alone when I arrived in Glasgow. The first day I met Thos. and Harold Bulloch from Hopetown who also were on leave. We went to Loch Lomond and the Ship Yards on the Clyde. Their leave was just over and mine was just starting and I was lucky enough to meet with Herb Gibson from Lammermoor who had got hospital leave after convalescing from France. Herb was alone also and we were both real pleased to have someone from home. We spent some time in Glasgow and stopped in Lanark for a day on our way to Edinburgh. We called on a cousin of Thom. Davidson in Edinburgh and New Years Eve went to a Carnival and then made our way to the Old Tron Church on Princes St. to bring in the New Year. When the clock came to 12 o'clock we were really mobbed by very friendly Scottish lassies who helped us to bring in the New Year in real fashion. We were obliged to see them to their home and the next day they showed us around the sights of Edinburgh.

My leave was coming to an end so we left Edinburgh for London. Herb stopped off in England to visit with his brother-in-laws friends in England, the Ashcrofts. A few days later he arrived in camp where later on he was sent home to Canada. Mr. Herb Gibson passed away a year ago and also Thos. and Harold Bulloch a few years ago.

I hope this preamble may be of interest to some of the people who remember the end of the "War to End all Wars" but proved to be not true as 25 years later the world was again in the midst of World War Two.

As the New Year of 1969 begins it really makes one wonder what is in store for the rising generation. With all the strikes for more wages and the university student unrest, there is not much prospects for Peace on Earth for all Men.

With best wishes for a happy New Year.

Sincerely,
James Machan

Notes

1   See letter 180: a few days' C.B. and eight days' pay stopped.

2   Lester was Jane's (Herb's sister's) son. He was 12 years old at this time.

3   Ernie Ferrier came from the Scotch Line, near Balderson, Ontario. He was in the army with Herb from the beginning (see letter 14). Ferrier was wounded (letter 50) and after that worked in the YMCA huts.

4   The *Perth Courier* also published four excellent letters home from Ferrier dated November 17, 1916; June 22, 1917 ("from a dug-out"); August 24, 1917 ("over the top"); and October 19, 1917. A further article also stated that a letter had been received from Ferrier in which he said he "saw Pte. Tom Butler just a few days before he was killed and also Pte. Herb Gibson just before he was wounded."

5   Pearl Burnham (Herb's cousin) went to the bank and told May that Herb was home, so she left the bank to go meet him. Herb went first to his farm home at Balderson, where John and his family were again living. On February 13, he went to Lanark and Lammermoore, and on February 22, he had tea at May's home. She recalled that many people said his colour was poor and he did not look strong.

6   May said Herb chose to be married on February 10, 1931, because it was the anniversary of his return home.

7   May and Herb were both there.

8   "C.1" refers to health status. According to the British Army's medical categories, a status of C meant "free from serious organic diseases, able to stand service in garrisons at home," while C1 meant "able to march 5 miles, see to shoot with glasses, and hear well" (http://www.epsomandewellhistoryexplorer.org .uk/MedicalCategories.html). See also letters 56 (n. 43) and 140.

9   Richie Norris, an army friend from Althorpe (Christie Lake).

10   A play by the Marks Brothers group of Christie Lake, Ontario.

11   James Machan was a friend of Herb's.

AFTERWORD

James Herbert Gibson and May Bell Keays were married in St. Mark's Anglican Church, in St. Vital, Manitoba, on February 10, 1931, twelve years after he returned home. His wounds had forced him to sell his farm and he sought a new lifestyle. In the meantime, Grandmother Keays died in 1921 and May left the bank to assume her mother's role. It was 1928 before she felt free to leave. Herb, being of the old school, did not want to marry before he had a home for his bride. That little home was 26 Oakleigh Place, St. Vital (later a neighbourhood in Winnipeg), and although those were very hard depression years, they were happy there. They had two daughters: Evelyn Alena, born December 25, 1931, and Laura Iris, born January 17, 1935. They left Winnipeg in June 1939 and moved to Trenton, Ontario. Herb worked first at Batawa and then at the #6 Repair Depot, RCAF Station Trenton. Although the war likely left lasting impressions on him, he did not typically discuss his experiences. Instead, he found his own peace over time, including a period during which he was able to "live by a clear calm lake" and with his family. He retired in 1955 and enjoyed twelve years of retirement before his death on October 17, 1967. He is buried in Elmwood Cemetery, Perth, Ontario.

L. Iris Newbold

LIST OF PERSONS ASSOCIATED WITH THE LETTERS

ADAMS, Fred: A soldier friend, son of the Perth photographer who took a lovely picture of May. He returned home.

AFFLECK, Lance: A soldier friend from Lanark.

ANDERSON, Bob: A neighbour farmer.

ANDISON, Willie: A soldier friend from Carleton Place and brother of May's friend Leita.

ARMSTRONG, Ethel: A friend of May's who worked with Stella Paul at the Merchant's Bank in Perth. She often wrote to E. Ferrier.

ARMSTRONG, Fred: A soldier friend from Perth.

ARTHUR, Mrs. Dena: Sister of Ray Paul, who moved to Vancouver.

ASHBY, Bill: Soldier from Fallbrook. He lost an eye during the war and returned home in 1917.

ASHCROFT, Towers and Maggie: Herb's sister and brother-in-law. They lived in Manitoba with their children Effie, Emily, and Willie.

ASHCROFT, William: The brother of Tow Ashcroft, who lived in Abbots Ripton, Cambridgeshire, England.

Bairds: Neighbours and distant relatives.

BLAIR: A soldier friend in France.

BLOCK, Leo: Married Elsie Keays, May's cousin.

BOOTEN, Tommy: A soldier chum who came home.

BRIGGS, Oscar: A neighbour of Herb's who owned a car.

BROWNLEE, George: The brother of Maggie Gibson, John's wife. He enlisted and survived the war.

BRUNTON, Nellie, Effie, Bella, Grace, and Johnny: Herb's first cousins. Johnny did not enlist.

BRUNTON, Uncle Richard: Father of Johnny, Effie, Bella, Nellie, and Grace. Mrs. Brunton was Helen Nairn and a sister of Herb's mother. The Bruntons were from Prospect.

BUFFAN, Eva: A friend of May's who worked with her in the Bank of Nova Scotia in Perth. Her brother Archie was in France. They were from Lanark.

BURNHAM, Pearl: Herb's cousin. Daughter of Colin and Annie May McNichol. She and her husband Elmer lived in Trenton in the 1940s.

BUTLER, Thomas Earl: A soldier friend of Herb's who came from the Sixth Line Bathurst. His father was a farmer. May knew him well. Herb and Tom were at Valcartier together, but got separated in England. They saw each other only once or twice before the night of March 1, 1917, when they met before going "over the top" before dawn. Tom was killed that morning.

BYGROVE: A soldier friend in France who returned home.

CALDWELL, Tom: A soldier friend from Lanark. His family owned the woolen mills there. He came home from France. Herb saw him at West Sandling.

CAMPBELL, Lindsay: A friend from Balderson who did not enlist.

CAVERS, Lawrence and Jim: Friends from Balderson. Lawrence moved to the United States to avoid enlisting. They went to school with May.

CLOSSES, Johny: A friend of Herb's family from Lammermoor.

CRAIGS: Neighbours and distant relatives.

CURRIE, Sir Arthur: The commander of the Canadian Corps. He was regarded as a skilful strategist, perhaps partly due to the fact that he was not a professional soldier, which allowed him to be more innovative. He was largely responsible for the success of the Vimy Ridge battle.

CURRIE, Matt: Neighbour who went west about 1905, and a soldier in France.

DACK, A.: A soldier, possibly from Carleton Place.

DAROU, Mae and Myrtle: Sisters from Harper who went to school with May and wrote and sent parcels to Herb.

DING: A mentally challenged Perth resident and "character." See letter 79.

DRYSDALE, Effie: A daughter of Tow and Maggie Ashcroft. She lived in Lanark.

EARL, T.: Tom Butler.

EDWARDS, Harold: A soldier from Lanark who came home from France. He was a brother of Marguerite Newman who lived in Trenton during the 1940s. May was related to Marguerite and Harold as their mother was Dorothy Keays (Richard Keays was Dorothy's father).

ETHERINGTON, Pte. Clement: Killed in action during raid of July 13, 1918, aged 23. No known grave, but he is remembered on the Canadian National Vimy Memorial.

FERGUSON, Mr.: A minister at a Methodist Church, maybe the one in Playfairville.

FERGUSON, Bob: Farmer at Balderson.

FERGUSON, Jim: Soldier whose unit cut wood in Scotland during the war. He married Violet Gibson.

FERRIER, Ernie: A soldier friend from the Scotch Line in Perth. He was wounded in the leg and then worked in the YMCA huts. Herb met him a number of times in France.

FLETT, Miss: Possibly a Red Cross visitor.

GIBSON, Euphemia Nairn: Herb's mother.

GIBSON, Hugh: Brother of William R. Gibson, Herb's father. He sold his property to Uncle Willie and moved to Dakota.

GIBSON, Jane: Father's sister. Jane had married James Gibson in Walhalla, North Dakota. Her son was Lester.

GIBSON, Janet Gunn: Willie Gibson's wife. Margaret, Irene, and Herbert were their children.

GIBSON, Maggie Brownlee: John Gibson's wife. Iva, Elma, Jean, and Arthur were their children.

GIBSON, Violet: A second cousin to Herb and the sister of Frank Gibson. She married Jim Ferguson, who survived the war.

GIBSON, William Russell: Herb's father.

GORMAN, Orville: A good soldier friend of Herb's. Part way through the war, he transferred to the air force. He lived in Smith's Falls after the war, and Herb regretted not seeing more of him.

GREER, Craig: A soldier from Maberly. The night Herb was wounded, he was taken prisoner. Iris met him once and he said, "I hope you know what a fine man your father is."

GREIG, Mr. and Mrs.: The Presbyterian minister and his wife.

HAIG, Sir Douglas: The Commander of the Imperial Forces.

HARPER, Ida (née Gibson): Herb's youngest sister, who lived in Walhalla. She died of flu in 1918, at age 32. She was the mother of John, Wallace, and Russell. Her husband was Hugh Harper, originally from Lanark.

HOLWELL, Willie: An American friend.

HUGHES, Ligh (Eligh): A neighbour farmer.

HUGHES, Myles: A neighbour farmer who moved west.

HUGHES, Sir Sam: The Canadian minister of militia. He was described as being bigmouthed and incompetent. Thanks to him, the Canadian troops were poorly equipped, poorly trained, and armed with the useless Ross rifle. Sir Sam's Inn in Haliburton was his home.

JACKSON, Wilbur: A schoolmate of May's who enlisted.

JANES, G.: A bomb carrier from Appleton who was badly wounded the morning of March 1, 1917. Herb dressed his wound. He visited him in hospital on November 10, 1917.

JORDAN, George: Conscripted and sent to England in 1918, but did not see action in France. He married May's sister Lottie in 1924.

KEAYS, Alex and Lena: May's father and mother.

KEAYS, Bill (William): May's uncle, who farmed across the road from Grandpa's place. His children were Elsie, Robert, Howard, and Lorne.

KEAYS, Elsie: May's cousin, who married Leo Block and lived in North Bay.

KEAYS, Fred: A second cousin of May's. He married Jennie Wilson. They lived in California and mother went there with them in 1929.

KEAYS, Laura and Neva: Mother's sisters. Neva was secretary of the Harper Red Cross Society. Laura Iris Newbold was named after Laura, and Evelyn Walters after Neva (her middle name was Evelyn).

KEAYS, May: May.

KEAYS, Roy: May's brother. He tried to enlist, but was turned down.

KNOWLES, Hugh and Willie: Brothers from Balderson who were killed. Herb went to see them in the "next town to Bajus," and also visited their graves.

KNOWLES, Jennie: Hugh and Willie's sister. She married Morton Publow, and he and his brother were both killed near the end of the war, with word of their deaths arriving after the armistice.

LAMB, Pte.: A soldier chum from Hespeler. They met in hospital in England.

LEIGHTON, Dick: A soldier from Harper who returned home.

LEONARD, Lt. John, MC: Killed in action during raid of July 13, 1918, aged 21. No known grave, but he is remembered on the Canadian National Vimy Memorial.

LIGARY, W.: A soldier from Lanark.

LOWRY, Mr.: Probably a Presbyterian minister.

MACDONALD, Alex: Brother of Margaret MacDonald.

MACDONALD, Henry: Father of Alex and Margaret MacDonald.

MACDONALD, Margaret Pink: Herb's first girlfriend, possibly from 1908–12. She was a teacher at Lammermoor and then a nurse. She married one of the members of the Dumbells group.

MACGREGOR, Mrs.: Sister of Mrs. McQue. See notes on Mrs. McQue.

MACHAN, James: A soldier chum and a relative of Glen Machan of Waterloo.

MATHER, Harold and Scott: Neighbours. Harold went to France and came home. Scott stayed on the farm, but died of a heart attack at a very young age.

MATHER, Johnnie: Relative in Middleville. He did not enlist.

McCALLUM, Lett: Wounded at the same time as Herb. Returned to Smith's Falls in 1917.

McINTYRE, Lena: A church friend of Herb's from Balderson.

McKERRACHER, Edgar: A soldier friend. He survived the war, though he may have been wounded. He arrived back in Perth with Herb.

McNAUGHTON, Jim: A farmer from Balderson.

McNICOL, Colin and Annie May: Parents of Pearl.

McNICOL, H. and Willie: Relatives.

McNICOL, Mary Nairn (Aunt Mary): A sister of Herb's mother, and the mother of Arthur and Keith McNichol.

McNICOL, Pearl: Herb's first cousin.

McQUE, Mrs.: Related to the Keays. Her father was John Miller.

McTAVISH, Mrs.: A friend of Clara's from the Eighth Line.

McVEETY, James (Jim): A friend in the 130th at Barriefield and Valcartier. He was very young (17) and a band member who did not expect to see action. May stayed with his mother and aunt in Perth for a while. Jim was killed in action on August 26, 1918.

MILLER, Hugh: Brother of Lett. He was also a soldier and married a war bride.

MILLER, Lett: A second cousin of May's. His father was the younger brother (Sam) of May's grandmother on the Keays side. He was a soldier in France. He came home to live on the Scotch Line.

MOFFAT: A soldier chum from Morris, Manitoba. They met in London in September 1918.

MONK, E.: A soldier friend from Franktown.

MOORE, T.: A soldier.

MORRIS, Russell: Did not enlist. He was a neighbour farmer whose wife's parents (the Whites) bought Herb's farm for $5,000.

NAIRN, Bob (Rob) and Lena: Cousins of Herb's from Middleville. Bob married Allie. Lena married a Paul.

NAIRN, Mary, Dorothy, and John: Probably friends or relatives living around Walhalla.

NAIRN, Aunty Phemie: Mother of Rob and Lena. Iris remembers visiting Aunty Phemie in Middleville.

NESBIT, Tom: He was not from Perth, but he worked in the bank for a while. He joined the air force.

NOONAN, Orville: A soldier from Christie Lake.

NORRIS, Ritchie: Army friend from Althorpe (Christie Lake).

NORTON, R.: A soldier.

PARK, Alex: A neighbour farmer.

PAUL, Bob: A relative of the Nairns. He was a prisoner of war. See letter 12.

PAUL, Charlotte Keays: May's aunt, and the mother of Stella Paul. May lived with her in Perth while working in the bank. Her husband Alex Paul died young. He was Ray Paul's uncle and also related to Rob Nairn.

PAUL, Jim: Ray Paul's father and brother to Aunt Phemie Nairn and Alex Paul.

PAUL, Mary Ellen and Joe: Herb's sister and her husband. They lived in Poland, Ontario.

PAUL, Melville: A soldier friend from Lanark. Killed in action.

PAUL, Ray: A neighbour farmer and cousin at Lammermoor. He did not enlist. He was married to M. Pretty and their son is Brian Paul, who has a large maple syrup business.

PAUL, Stella: May's cousin. Married Jimmy Lunn.

PENNY, Pte.: A soldier chum.

PENMAN, Clara G.: A relative who lived in Lanark.

PHILLIPS, Jack, Charlie, and Mary: Charlie was the Anglican minister at Balderson. Jack also became a minister. Mary married Dr. Cameron. Mary Cameron attended St. Matthew's Church, in Burlington, and Iris Newbold took May to visit her. Jack enlisted, but did not get overseas.

PUBLOW, Morton and Orville: Killed in action. See entry on Jennie Knowles. Orville was killed in action on September 2, 1918.

QUACKENBUSH, Hubert: A soldier friend who was killed in France in 1918. May met him at a dance at Drummond Centre and he gave her his pass, which had been used by several soldiers that evening. It is in her scrapbook.

RICHARDSON, Georgina: From Balderson. She taught school and was a friend of John Spalding's, but she did not marry him.

RIGG, Pte. Thomas: A soldier who once wrote to Aunt Clara looking for a reply and, with luck, a friend.

ROBERTSONS: Sisters from Pilot Mound, Manitoba, who read my father's letters in the *Lanark Era* and wrote to him. Their brother had been killed in France.

SCOTT, Jack: Served in France. He was taken as a prisoner of war.

SCOTT, Ronald: A soldier friend in France.

SIMPSON, Lett: From Lanark. He was in the 130th.

SINCLAIR, Annie: A neighbour of May's.

SMITH, Mr.: A "grumpy" bank accountant who did not stay in Perth long.

SMITH, Sgt. Maj. Bob: May's cousin from Barrie. Bonnie Roberts is his great-niece. He served in the Boer War. He lived in Balderson and then went back to France.

SMITH, Mrs. Deborah: Mother's great-aunt (her grandfather's sister). She had no family and lived in a stone house on Gore Street beside Knox Church, in Perth.

SMITH, Sara Keays: May's aunt and sister to Alex Keays. Mother of Bob and great-grandmother of Bonnie Surrey Roberts. She lived in Barrie and had a large family.

SPALDING, Jack (John): Herb's friend, who tried to enlist but was turned down. He kept the store at Harper, which he bought from Uncle John. Uncle John moved back to the farm on the Eighth Line after Iris's Grandparents died. J. Spalding wrote to Herb.

STEWART, Jack: Soldier chum of Herb's. It is unknown whether he survived the war.

STEWART, Lloyd: From Perth.

STEWART, Milton: From Saskatchewan. Killed in action.

STRANG: A soldier friend in France.

TRAIL, Jim: A soldier friend from Lanark who was wounded on March 1, 1917, and later killed in action on September 2, 1918.

TUFTS, Arthur: A soldier friend from Lanark who was killed in action. Herb mentions Arthur's father writing to him to enquire about his son in letter 59.

WALTERS, J.: Killed in action. May didn't know him, but he was likely from Lanark.

WATT, Col. Ed: Colonel of the 130th. See letter 86.

WATT, John: Father of Ethel and Mabel. Lived at Balderson next to the Presbyterian Church. Distantly related to Herb.

WILSON, Earl: From Saskatchewan. He was killed in France.

WILSON, Jennie: A friend of May's who married Fred Keays (a second cousin to May). May went to California with them in 1929. Her brother was Earl Wilson.

WILSON, Roy: From Perth. He was among the first of the 130th boys to be killed (on March 1, 1917).

INDEX

Bold page numbers indicate photos